SMALL AND MEDIUM ENTERPRISES IN DISTRESS

Since the outbreak of the East Asian crisis in 1997, world attention has focused on the debt restructuring and corporate reform of financial institutions and large enterprises in the affected economies. Although the SME sector has been more severely hit than big firms and responsible for the rapid rise of unemployment, it has been completely neglected both by local governments and international donors. There are signs of economic recovery since late 1999, but it is far from sustainable and the vast majority of SMEs continue to be left aside. This book is the first to deal with SME distress throughout the crisis and beyond. It challenges the negative effects of structural adjustment policies adopted in Thailand and elsewhere in the region. It provides suggestions and case studies for promoting local SMEs domestically and possibly internationally. Important reading for specialists in business economics, entrepreneurship and small firms, and Asian-Pacific development economics.

Small and Medium Enterprises in Distress
Thailand, the East Asian crisis and beyond

PHILIPPE RÉGNIER
Director, Modern Asia Research Centre
University of Geneva, Switzerland

LONDON AND NEW YORK

First published 2000 by Gower Publishing

Reissued 2018 by Routledge
2 Park Square, Milton Park, Abingdon, Oxon OX14 4RN
711 Third Avenue, New York, NY 10017, USA

Routledge is an imprint of the Taylor & Francis Group, an informa business

Copyright © Philippe Régnier 2000

All rights reserved. No part of this book may be reprinted or reproduced or utilised in any form or by any electronic, mechanical, or other means, now known or hereafter invented, including photocopying and recording, or in any information storage or retrieval system, without permission in writing from the publishers.

Notice:
Product or corporate names may be trademarks or registered trademarks, and are used only for identification and explanation without intent to infringe.

Publisher's Note
The publisher has gone to great lengths to ensure the quality of this reprint but points out that some imperfections in the original copies may be apparent.

Disclaimer
The publisher has made every effort to trace copyright holders and welcomes correspondence from those they have been unable to contact.

A Library of Congress record exists under LC control number: 00132844

ISBN 13: 978-1-138-72910-0 (hbk)
ISBN 13: 978-1-138-72905-6 (pbk)
ISBN 13: 978-1-315-19012-9 (ebk)

Contents

List of Tables	ix
Preface	x
Acknowledgements	xiii
List of Abbreviations	xv

INTRODUCTORY CHAPTER: DEVELOPMENT OF SMEs IN INTERNATIONAL THEORY AND PRACTICE   1

SMEs through the Crisis in Thailand: A Brief Overview (1997-1999)   1
Classical and More Recent Paradigms of SME Development in Developing Countries and Emerging Economies   3
East Asian SMEs in Distress: The Coverage of the Debate and its Relevance for Thailand   7

PART I
SMALL ENTERPRISE DEVELOPMENT IN THAILAND AND THE IMPACT OF THE EAST ASIAN CRISIS

CHAPTER 1: THAILAND, AN ENVIRONMENT CONDUCIVE TO ENTREPRENEURSHIP?   13

Economic History and Profile of Local Entrepreneurship   14
Small Entrepreneurship and Development of SMEs   17
The Contribution of Thai SMEs before the East Asian Crisis   21

CHAPTER 2: ABSENCE OF SME LEGISLATION AND LOOSE CLASSIFICATION OF SMEs   27

Lack of SME Legal Definition until 2000   27
Towards a National Definition under the New SME Bill   29
Registration and Taxation of SMEs: Red Tape and Malpractices   31
Drafting an SME Master Plan (1999-2004) without Proper Data   35
Exploring Alternative Sources of Information   37

CHAPTER 3: THE EFFECTS OF THE EAST ASIAN CRISIS ON THAI SMEs (1997-1999)   39

Collapse of Demand Preceding Credit Crunch   39
Domestic Demand in Disarray   40
SMEs Facing Credit and other Financial Difficulties   41
SMEs Coping with Supply Constraints and Rising Input Costs   43
SMEs in Distress: A Comparison with Large Enterprises (LEs)   44

CHAPTER 4: SMEs FACING SURVIVAL AND COMPETITION CHALLENGES   49

The Need to Create an SME Vulnerability/Resilience Index   49
Competitiveness Recovery of the Thai Economy and the Possible Contribution of Thai SMEs   52

PART II
STRUCTURAL ADJUSTMENT UNDER THE INTERNATIONAL MONETARY FUND AND SME GOVERNMENT POLICY

CHAPTER 5: THAI SMEs: THE ROLE OF THE PRIVATE AND PUBLIC SECTORS BEFORE THE CRISIS   61

The Need for an SME Policy: An Open Debate   61
The Role of the State during the Pre-Industrialization Period   62
Dual Industrial Policy and Positive Discrimination of SMEs   64
Big Business, SMEs and Politics   66

CHAPTER 6: THAI SMEs AND STRUCTURAL ADJUSTMENT POLICY (1997-1999)   69

SMEs in Distress but Absent from the Emergency Rescue Agenda (1997-1998)   69
The Rationale and Implementation of a New SME Policy   71
A Critical Assessment of the New SME Policy (1999-2004)   73

CHAPTER 7: THE CREDIBILITY OF THE NEW SME POLICY — 88

Beyond Political Rhetoric — 88
Bureaucratic Hazards — 90
SMEs and the Real Economy: Facing the Limits of a Fragile Recovery (1999-2000) — 92
SME Policy Credibility among the Small Business Community — 96

PART III
THE RESILIENCE OF SMEs LINKED TO FOREIGN FIRMS

CHAPTER 8: LINKING LOCAL SMEs AND FOREIGN FIRMS OPERATING IN EAST ASIA — 103

The Current Debate — 104
Background of the 1999 Survey — 105
Current State of SME National Data — 107
Results of the Three Country Surveys — 108
Tentative Conclusions — 112

CHAPTER 9: THE POTENTIAL RESILIENCE OF THAI SUBCONTRACTORS LINKED TO FOREIGN FIRMS: SME CASE STUDIES — 116

First Case Study: O.E.I. Parts Co., Ltd. (Automotive Sector) — 116
Second Case Study: Sathien Plastic & Fiber Co., Ltd. (Plastic Sector) — 121
Third Case Study: A & V Plastic Group Co., Ltd. (Plastic Molding Sector) — 124
Fourth Case Study: MIS Thailand Co., Ltd. (Electrical Sector) — 129

CHAPTER 10: THE POTENTIAL RESILIENCE OF FINAL GOODS PRODUCERS LINKED TO FOREIGN FIRMS: SME CASE STUDIES — 133

First Case Study: CRP Jewellery (Thailand) Co., Ltd (Jewelry Manufacturing Sector) — 133

Second Case Study: Lom Thai Co., Ltd. (Textile Apparel Sector) 137
Third Case Study: Hesco Food Industry Co., Ltd. (Agro-Food
    Sector) 140
Fourth Case Study: Husan Industrial Co., Ltd (Electrical Sector) 144

CONCLUSIVE CHAPTER: SME POLICY ALTERNATIVES   149

SMEs Looking After Themselves 150
Building Networks between the Private and Public Sectors 154
Development of Intra-private Sector Collaborations and Linkages 157
Prospects 162

Bibliography   *167*
Index   *180*

List of Tables

Table 1.1	Economic Performance of the Top 100 Firms in Thailand, Classified According to Capital Ownership and Nationality: 1979 and 1984	15
Table 1.2	The Contribution of Manufacturing SMEs in Thailand: 1963, 1970 and 1996	19
Table 1.3	Working Experience and Education Background of SME Entrepreneurs	22
Table 1.4	Number and Percentage of SMEs in Total Manufacturing by Size of SMEs	22
Table 1.5	Contribution of SMEs to Manufacturing Employment in Thailand (1997)	23
Table 1.6	Size of Firms by Sector of Production (in per cent)	23
Table 1.7	SMEs by Regions and Sectors (1997)	24
Table 1.8	Average Value of Gross Output and Value-Added per Size of Enterprise	25
Table 1.9	SMEs' Sources of Capital	25
Table 2.1	Thai SMEs Classified According to Total Assets and Number of Employees	28
Table 2.2	Definitions of SMEs in Various Foreign Countries	29
Table 2.3	Classification of SMEs According to Fixed Assets	30
Table 2.4	Classification of Enterprises According to Both the Number of Persons Engaged and Registered Capital	31
Table 2.5	Average Amount of Registered Capital per Employee of SMEs in Thailand (Capital-Labour Ratio)	32
Table 2.6	Format of SME Registration by Regions (in per cent)	33
Table 4.1	Perceived Causes of Current Output Decline (SMEs and Large Enterprises) According to World Bank, Thailand Country Report 1999	50
Table 6.1	Lending to SMEs by State Financial Institutions (1999)	76

Preface

Since 1998 we have observed a worldwide inflation of diagnosis, studies and theories attempting to explain, justify or criticize the recent East Asian economic crisis and its treatment. In the most affected emerging economies themselves, various studies have been conducted or are still currently being performed on the impact of the crisis on the major economic and financial sectors. However, almost no studies have been done to examine the effects of the crisis and structural adjustment policies on small and medium-sized enterprises (SMEs). This shows how far this category of firms has been neglected and this has been even more surprising in the case of Thailand, whose government has initiated since early 1999 an ambitious project to draft a first SME Promotion Law and to implement an SME Master Plan until 2004.

The idea for this book emerged toward the end of 1997, when the first effects of the crisis became clear. It also referred back to previous and more minor financial crises quite long ago such as in 1979 (fall of a major finance company and collapse of the Thai stock exchange) or in 1983-1984 (failures of 15 financial institutions in Bangkok and rescue by the Ministry of Finance of 32 others).

The 1997-1998 crisis seemed originally of a purely financial nature, affecting the conglomerates and other big corporations of East Asia. Therefore, it can be understood why very little was initially said on its possible spillover effects on the real economy and manufacturing in particular. No concern was immediately expressed about the possible collapse of a number of local SMEs. This is rather surprising considering that the large majority of SMEs, and not only in emerging economies, are generally perceived as fragile and vulnerable to sharp market fluctuations. But everyone knows that SMEs rarely constitute a strong lobbying pressure group.

From early 1998 unemployment figures started to rise rapidly in all the affected economies of the region, and Thailand was no exception. On the one hand, large enterprises were not as yet engaged in significant corporate restructuring and were not responsible for massive cuts in jobs except in the financial sector (a number of financial companies were closed down). On the other hand, both registered SMEs and micro-enterprises of the informal sector were a major source of unemployment, especially among unskilled and seasonal workers. Furthermore, the crisis led to a credit crunch which badly hit the SME sector. In addition to the collapse of domestic/regional demand, it was directly responsible for the multiplication in SME bankruptcies.

It was only more than one year after the beginning of the crisis and during the last quarter of 1998 that East Asian governments and international donor agencies started to look more deeply into the key structural factors behind the crisis. Bad loan management and other financial malpractices were denounced and a number of other fundamental economic weaknesses were also gradually addressed despite early warnings by a few leading economists such as Paul Krugman.

The relative loss of competitiveness and export decline among East Asia's most affected economies even before mid-1997 was underlined. Thailand was right there in the front line, as illustrated by two regional industrial surveys conducted by the World Bank in 1997 and 1998. Even more interestingly, the productivity problem was not exclusively detected among big scale manufacturers and exporters, but also among the so-called supporting industries (medium-sized enterprises) and local SMEs at large. The structural weakness of the 'missing middle' was pointed out in terms of an important shortage of middle-sized and growth-oriented SMEs acting as leading subcontractors and venture firms in their own right. This problem also referred to the low density of industrial linkages between local SMEs and large outsourcing firms, both foreign and national.

By the time this research project was started during the spring of 1999, big corporate restructuring and SME promotion had apparently become a priority issue. This was particularly true in the case of Thailand, where the Cabinet started to address the SME problem together with Japanese assistance in late 1998. Unlike other East Asian economies, problems of SMEs have stood quite high on the 1999-2000 political agenda in Thailand. In the context of forthcoming legislative elections, the SME issue is expected to remain present in the political discourse and the media after the adoption of the first SME Promotion Bill in January 2000. This could constitute a rather drastic turn in industrial policy compared to previous neglect. During several decades of rapid growth since the 1960s and until the 1997 crisis, the development strategy was exclusively based on big scale industrialization and high concentration of domestic and foreign investment in manufacturing and services.

There is little doubt that this book has been conceived during a very timely period. Research, which started at the SASIN Graduate Institute of Business Administration in Bangkok in May 1999, attracted the interest of the Industry Minister himself. In the opposition, the young and raising Thai

Rak Thai party has also devoted much attention to the destiny of SMEs. The SME issue has become an important segment of the wider debate related to the economic recovery since late 1999 and to the future directions of the Thai economy at the crossroads of the 21st century.

This book covers the debate in five distinct ways. The Introductory Chapter presents an overview of the SME international experience both in OECD and developing economies. Part I looks at the economic and social contribution of SMEs in Thailand before and after the crisis of 1997-1998. Part II reviews government policy and especially the various SME promotion initiatives adopted since late 1998. Part III explores the assumption that local SMEs linked to large firms and foreign ones in particular operating in Thailand have been more resilient to the crisis than other categories of SMEs. The Conclusive Chapter suggests a range of SME development policies which have not yet been tested in Thailand but are derived from interesting experiences elsewhere in our global world.

Dr. Philippe Régnier
Director
Modern Asia Research Centre
University of Geneva
Rue de Lausanne, 63
1202 Geneva, SWITZERLAND

Acknowledgements

**To my Family and
All our Beloved Friends in Thailand**

This book could neither have been conceived during the first impact of the East Asian crisis in 1998 nor finalized in 1999-2000 without substantial field research work in Thailand. Having been granted the privilege to take scientific leave from my academic home in Geneva, Switzerland, I was able to spend eight full months in Thailand between July 1999 and February 2000 together with my family.

Without the support of my colleagues at both the Graduate Institute of Development Studies and at the Graduate Institute of International Studies, University of Geneva, this research experience would not have coincided with the drafting period of the first small and medium enterprise legislation ever envisaged in Thai modern economic history. I would like to express my deep thanks to all of them, and to Dr. Heiner Hanggi in particular, who agreed to replace me as Director of our Geneva-based Modern Asia Research Centre during my absence. After 12 years of intensive dedication to my various assignments in Geneva, it has been a unique opportunity to live and work again in Southeast Asia for the second time in my life.

Similarly, without the support of local scientific partners and the full cooperation of the Royal Thai Government, the book would never have been completed. The whole research project that resulted in this publication was based in Bangkok at the SASIN Graduate Institute of Business Administration, Chulalongkorn University. My most sincere appreciation goes to Professor Toemsakdi Krishnamra, Founding Director of SASIN and to my local research partners: Professor Adith Cheosakul (SASIN), Professor Naoki Kuriyama (Faculty of Business Administration, Soka University, Tokyo), Mr. Bancha Chumchaivate (M.A. Eco. Chulalongkorn University, SASIN MBA) Senior Research Assistant, and Mr. Chatrchalerm Khosoongnern (M.A. Eco. Chulalongkorn University) Junior Research Assistant. The collaboration of Prof. A. Cheosakul and Mr. B. Chumchaivate with the elaboration of most of the SME case studies used in Chapters 9 and 10 was especially appreciated. Prof. N. Kuriyama helped with the revision of the first draft during his visit in Bangkok in January-February 2000. Both research assistants have also been very supportive regarding various organizational and translation matters. Last but not least, the editing assistance of Rochelle Powtong and Karen Chavanich (SASIN Centre for Business Communication in English) has been extremely valuable.

During the formal inauguration of the research project at SASIN on May 19th, 1999, the Thai Minister of Industry and the Swiss Ambassador, in addition to all the members of the project scientific advisory committee were present. Their support was particularly heartening. The project received full collaboration and support from the Thai authorities, the Swiss Embassy and the Swiss-Thai Chamber of Commerce whose President, Mr. Paul Somm, met the author of this book nearly once a week for the duration of the project, until the beginning of the year 2000. Special thanks are also addressed to Mr. Damri Sukhotanang, Director General, Department of Industrial Promotion (Ministry of Industry), to Swiss Ambassador Bernard Freymond and his Deputy Mr. Heinrich Schellenberg, and to Professor Suthiphand Chirathivat, Director of the European Studies Centre and newly appointed Dean of the Faculty of Economics at Chulalongkorn University.

I cannot name here all the personalities approached or interviewed during the project. An indicative list is provided together with the bibliographical references at the end of the book. I wish to emphasize how kindly our research team was received by all of them, including the SME entrepreneurs, both those whose stories are included as final case studies in Chapters 9 and 10, and those whose were not.

My main objective was to publish the first book ever written in English on Thai SMEs in order to put the spotlight on this neglected category of enterprises and to initiate a debate on its future trajectory. Of course, I take full personal responsibility for any critical and perhaps too foreign views, errors, misunderstandings or misinterpretations contained in this book. I hope that the reader will forgive a number of them, which are due to various research constraints and rather short writing delays in the last days before the end of my scientific leave.

A final but very special word goes to my wife and our two little children, who have shared the life and experience with me in the so-called 'amazing' and 'smiling' Kingdom of Thailand between mid-July 1999 and mid-March 2000. Their affectionate support has been of tremendous help all along. In many ways this book is also a symbolic contribution to our little Thai daughter. While writing, I was inspired by the same loving spirit that guided my wife and myself to meet her in Bangkok for the first time in October 1998. Just like her, Thailand stands deep in our hearts forever.

Philippe Régnier
Bangkok, February 20th, 2000

List of Abbreviations

ADB	Asian Development Bank
AFTA	ASEAN Free Trade Area
ASEAN	Association of South East Asian Nations
BHT	Baht (Thai currency): US$1 = BHT 37 (1999)
BMR	Bangkok Metropolitan Region
BOI	Board of Investment
DIP	Department of Industrial Promotion
FDI	Foreign Direct Investment
FTIP	Foundation of Thailand Productivity Institute
IFCT	Industrial Financial Corporation of Thailand
ILO	International Labour Organization
IMF	International Monetary Fund
IRP	Industrial Restructuring Plan
ISMED	Institute for SME Development
JICA	Japanese International Cooperation Agency
MITI	Ministry of International Trade and Industry (Japan)
MLSW	Ministry of Labour and Social Welfare
MNCs	Multinational Corporations
MoI	Ministry of Industry
NESDB	National Economic and Social Development Board
NGOs	Non Governmental Organizations
NIEs	Newly Industrialized Economies
NPLs	Non-Performing Loans
NSO	National Statistics Office
OECD	Organization for Economic Cooperation and Development
OECF	Overseas Economic and Cooperation Fund
PIOs	Provincial Industrial Offices
RIPCs	Regional Industrial Promotion Centres
SET	Stock Exchange of Thailand
SFAC	SME Financial Advisory Centre
SICGC	Small Industry Credit Guarantee Corporation
SIFC	Small Industry Finance Corporation
SMEs	Small and Medium-sized Enterprises
TBA	Thai Bankers' Association
TCC	Thai Chamber of Commerce
TFB	Thai Farmers Bank

TFI	Thai Federation of Industry
TMB	Thai Military Bank
TNCs	Transnational Corporations
TQM	Total Quality Management
UNCTAD	United Nations Conference on Trade and Development
UNDP	United Nations Development Program
VAT	Value-added Tax
VT	Vocational Training

Introductory Chapter
Development of SMEs in International Theory and Practice:
Do They Matter for Crisis Management and Recovery in Thailand?

SMEs through the Crisis in Thailand: A Brief Overview (1997-1999)

In July 1997, a combined domestic and external financial crisis started to hit Thailand rather dramatically. The crisis was mainly private-driven and strongly linked to the overall mismanagement of the big financial institutions and related business groups active in both manufacturing and services. While spreading to other emerging economies in Northeast and Southeast Asia, the intensity of the crisis also deepened in Thailand and reached most sectors of the real economy during the last quarter of 1997 and the first quarter of 1998.

When the crisis peaked, SMEs were particularly affected, but most of the domestic and external attention continued to concentrate on the fate of the conglomerates and financial institutions. However, more than two million workers in the formal sector, and employed primarily in urban SMEs, lost their jobs, and it is estimated that the number of SME bankruptcies doubled in 1998 compared to the pre-crisis figures of 1996 (International Labour Organization, 1998, 1999; Jomo, 1998; Siamwalla and Sopchokchai, 1998).

The economic and psychological impact of the shock has gone deep into most levels of society, especially the middle class, but has come as little surprise from an analytical point of view. It must be recalled that both the Thai government and big corporate associations failed prior to the crisis to attribute any significant role to small entrepreneurship and local SMEs in macro-economic and industrial policies. Through decades of rapid economic growth and impressive capital gains, the contribution of SMEs was largely ignored in economic terms as well as in social and political ones. At the same time, small entrepreneurship was not dynamic enough at the grassroots level to impose itself as a significant lobbyist, as it is in Taiwan and Korea for example (Regnier, 1998, pp. 206-28 and 1996, 225-32), and in most OECD economies (OECD, 1997; Loveman and Piore, 1992; Piore and Sabel, 1984; Sengenberger and Porter, 1998), except possibly Japan (Whitaker, 1997).

Furthermore, the problems and prospects of micro and small firms in the process of East Asian rapid economic and financial liberalization during the 1990s was largely ignored (Salazar, 1996). In harsh words, they had to survive, catch up or die, and their strategic importance to meet the new globalization requirements was considered as not fully demonstrated (Howard, 1995; Jennings, 1997; Karagozolu and Lindell, 1998).

In the immediate aftermath of the crisis, the structural adjustment policies supported by the International Monetary Fund focused on debt restructuring and financial reform of the large firms exclusively, and this priority has remained very high on the pre-election agenda of the Thai Cabinet as of 1999-2000.

A campaign to help local SMEs in distress has nevertheless gained momentum since the second half of 1998, partly inspired domestically by local political lobbying, and also externally by major bilateral and multilateral donor agencies, Japanese economic aid in particular. Some tentative governmental measures have been gradually announced since December 1998, and both the Office of the Prime Minister and the Ministry of Industry have been pushing for the rapid adoption of a first-ever SME Promotion Bill and an SME Master Plan before the end of 1999. Together with the support of the World Bank, the Asian Development Bank, and the Japanese OECF, various public and private financial institutions are supposed to take the lead in extending preferential loans and venture capital to existing and newly established SMEs in the period of 1999-2004.

This book does not necessarily challenge the supposed wisdom of concentrating reform efforts in the private and public large-scale enterprises in Thailand and elsewhere in the region. The debate is still raging as to what extent the taxpayer should be burdened to pay for the various mistakes of the big economic operators, and the following pages do not attempt to repeat this discussion.

Our intention is to explore the real situation of the SME sector in 1997-1999, because it has tended to remain in the shadows of the East Asian crisis.

To Thailand's credit, it is among the very few emerging economies of the region which has officially opened the SME debate and started to plan targeted action in addition to the mainstream policies focusing on so-called more urgent issues, especially in the field of reforming the large-scale financial and corporate sectors.

An analysis of the current SME situation in Thailand, from both theoretical and practical angles, should concentrate on the demand-side and supply-side of the recent crisis.[1] At least three factors have been affecting the health of SMEs and their potential for sustainable recovery. On the demand-side, domestic demand for their products has collapsed and remained weak due to the decline in purchasing power of individuals (for consumer goods) and corporations (for intermediate goods). On the supply-side, two factors have played negatively, the rising costs of production inputs (especially imported inputs), and the overall scarcity of credit from the institutional financial sector combined with the large proportion of non-performing loans and the increase in lending rates.

The internal difficulties of SMEs to cope with the downturn stems from their lean organizational structure, their limited resources and their lack of core competencies. Theories indicate that strategic options for the improvement of the internal corporate organization in terms of resources, capabilities and competencies have to be explored when the external business environment is averse.[2]

Two phases of SME turnaround responses have to be addressed in order to figure out the so-called 'rightsizing' strategies during and after the crisis. A first retrenchment phase consists of a combination of cost cutting and asset reducing activities in order to reach a second recovery phase with the appropriate responses to regain the pre-crisis level of business performance. The central issue here is that most SMEs tend to downsize only partly and are not able to meet their initial goals of reducing expenses, while at the same time increasing productivity and competitive advantage.[3] The related issues of whether, when, and how to downsize are extremely important. Various authors have discussed prescriptions of best practices for downsizing.[4]

They will be further discussed in Part I of this book. As long as these problems are not properly tackled, not only recovery but also a more competitive role for SMEs in the Thai economy will remain an open question.

Classical and More Recent Paradigms of SME Development in Developing Countries and Emerging Economies

The need for industrial development to serve growth, full employment, socio-economic equity and regional development cannot be overemphasized. It is well known that the primary and tertiary sectors by themselves are not in a position alone to achieve these objectives satisfactorily. When the industrialization process stems from an agricultural base (such as in Thailand), agriculture-industry linkages obviously take on special significance. In the context of inadequate and lethargic development of domestic industrial capital, many developing countries placed an overriding reliance on large-scale industrialization primarily in order to attract foreign direct investment and to promote a few public or private domestic corporations in some key strategic sectors. However it was later realized that a broad-based industrial development drive would also have to place a great emphasis on small- and medium-scale ventures.[5]

The rather sudden government interest to promote small enterprises tends to be derived from newly perceived weaknesses in the industrial development policies conducted for several decades (Arghiros, 1997;

Muscat, 1996; Parnwell, 1996; Tambunletchai, 1999). The Thai Cabinet, and the Ministry of Industry in particular, are also attracted by the entrepreneurial experiences in a number of developed countries and newly industrialized economies where large and small were married in a rather coherent strategy of production growth and equity distribution.

First, the argument that small enterprises can promote productive employment more effectively than large firms has become more and more widely accepted based on the following facts:[6]

- that they are more labour intensive, without necessarily being too costly or unprofitable, thereby making investment costs per job generated in small enterprises comparatively low;
- that requirements in terms of initial capital, management and other scarce resources are low and therefore with little assistance, various segments of the working or under-employed or unemployed population can be encouraged to set up a business of their own in a drive to promote self-employment and new enterprises;
- that small enterprises create more jobs for the unskilled than for the skilled, and therefore are worth promoting in any developing environment where the unskilled form the predominant part of the labour force; and
- that small firms are more likely to generate indirect employment opportunities than large ones since the former usually produce and subcontract locally, whereas the latter have a much higher propensity to import raw materials and capital goods to produce for both the domestic and export markets.

Secondly, it has been recognized that the societal profile of most developing countries is characterized by the scarcity, among other resources, of entrepreneurial and managerial talent. The low levels of local capital accumulation and the under-developed bourgeoisie make that the existing or potential entrepreneurial class is of small size: most enriched small and medium farmers, local traders and transporters, small industrialists are yet struggling to come up the economic and social ladder. State capital was expected in the past to intervene and fill the gaps created by inadequate development of domestic private capital, but the more recent neo-liberal orientations of economic thinking tend to keep more and more state capital out of direct production activities. However a successful accumulation process driven by private entrepreneurship under so-called free or deregulated market policies can only materialize if a sizeable and diversified class of numerous small entrepreneurs at grassroots level, and possibly medium and larger ones at the top end, is stimulated by local and external environments to build up a vibrant production base, and widen and deepen it over time. The very existence of such an entrepreneurial class is seen as a fundamental condition if a free operating market is to produce the promised result of rapid and diversified growth.[7]

Thirdly, there is also strong evidence that the existence of a large base of SMEs is desirable if some kind of balanced two-leg industrialization has to be both domestically and externally market driven by SMEs and larger firms.[8]

Domestically, given the low concentration of income and wealth at the bottom of society, mass low-priced consumer articles offer opportunities for local producers without being hampered by lack of scale economies. Small entrepreneurs can gradually emerge, whereas mercantile capital accumulated by the local trading and financial elite tends to concentrate either in non-manufacturing sectors or in manufacturing ventures with foreign partners.

Externally, foreign direct investment is not attracted to any significant extent into sectors producing exclusively for the domestic market (except possibly in very large countries, but even there domestic demand for mass consumption goods tends to be low), leaving a window of opportunity for local entrepreneurs. But in addition, any strong FDI-oriented development strategy requires a diversified local entrepreneurial class. The last few decades have shown that foreign investors, from both transnational corporations and smaller firms, tend to rely on local partners for their production operations. Joint ventures but also various types of outsourcing and subcontracting (upstream and downstream from the production line) have a multiplying effect on the dynamism of local supporting industries and SMEs, including the creation of new ones.

The development of SMEs is perceived as a necessity if Thailand is to advance from its current status of an emerging economy to the stage of a newly industrialized economy, and then to join the ranks of the industrial nations. In this endeavour, the absence or existence of a dense group of suppliers of components, parts and intermediate goods is perceived as rather crucial to strengthen domestic industrial capacity and also attract foreign investors.

Fourthly, as already suggested by the history of industrialization and post-industrialization in most OECD countries, there is some kind of continuum between small-, medium- and large-scale firms over time (Acs, 1999). In addition to what SMEs can achieve in the fields of development of entrepreneurial abilities, employment creation, and greater regional and local balance of production patterns, SMEs can play a complementary role to large firms.

In the process of capital concentration, it is well documented that small enterprises do not go out of existence. In fact, after a transitory period of relative decline of SMEs from pre-industrialization until industrial taylorism, the trend reversed and SMEs once again continue to play a vital role in present day developed economies.

In the light of this historical experience, it can be expected that small firms will also play a fundamental role at the various higher stages of developmental process in various parts of the world. In certain areas, they are expected to perform some productive activities in different types of direct or indirect partnership with large firms.

In other areas, they are expected to be highly specialized and autonomously competitive (Jennings and Beaver, 1997; Storey, 1987). Yet it will remain possible to identify various fields in manufacturing and services where smaller scale would be more efficient than larger scale. Therefore, there is an interesting element of production linkage, cooperation and complementarity between SMEs and large firms in the midst of business competitiveness and socio-economic conflict.

Since the mid-1980s, coinciding with the aftermath of two major oil shocks and other types of industrial restructuring primarily in the developed countries of the first generation, the significant contribution of SMEs to overall economic development in both industrialized and emerging nations has become a new focus of intense empirical evidence, further research work and policy makers' attention.

Some of the basic reasons can be summarized as follows:

- in most OECD economies and in the most flourishing emerging economies as well (such as Taiwan for example), the SME sector does represent one of the strongest pillars of the economy. In historical terms, the density of SMEs was quite high during the pre-industrialization period, then it declined during the first phase of industrialization before rising again in the following phases; looking today at the United States as the most dynamic OECD economy, local SMEs are the prevailing source of all new jobs created in the USA, a trend which started in the 1970s (Brusco, 1995; Storey, 1994; Bridge, O'Neill, and Cromie, 1998);
- the situation is not radically different in the developing countries, here SMEs both in the formal and especially so-called informal sectors do represent the bulk of local socio-economic life;
- SMEs are internationally recognized in terms of their strong capacity for mobility, flexible production and specialization both in times of rapid expansion and sharp market fluctuations as well. The so-called 'Japanese miracle' has been largely attributed during the second half of the 20th century to the exceptional density and flexibility of the SME sector. This was well demonstrated after the two oil shocks of 1973 and 1979;
- as we enter the 21st century, SMEs are perceived as being particularly strong when they produce innovative diversified and flexible clusters and networks of competence in order to match a more and more sophisticated demand for highly differentiated and specialized products

and services (Bukley, 1997; Schmitz and Nadvi, 1994; Sengenberger and Pyke, 1991). In the age of E-commerce and other new IT communication technologies across borders, SMEs are perceived as rapid and creative responders to new market opportunities.[9] The smaller the size and the more specialized a new potential market is, the more difficult it will become for large firms to enter these niche markets. In other words, SMEs have an important role to play in market creation and technology innovation.

East Asian SMEs in Distress: The Coverage of the Debate and its Relevance for Thailand

The treatment of the recent crisis in East Asia, though not focusing much on the SME issue, has at least indirectly prolonged and reinforced the debate mentioned above. It is likely that the SME issue will become more important over time when the medium and possibly long-term consequences of the crisis will be more deeply addressed and evaluated.

Since early 1999, bilateral donors and international agencies have started to identify a number of key structural industrial factors behind the 1997-1998 crisis in addition to the already well-documented financial mismanagement before and during the crisis.[10]

Among the factors underlined, three of them particularly apply to the case of Thailand:

- the rapid industrialization pattern of Thailand has put an overemphasis on conglomerates and large enterprises to the neglect of SMEs;
- the lack or weakness of sector linkages between high tech production and local supporting industries (including local SMEs) can partly explain the relative decline of Thai industrial competitiveness during the 1990s even before the outbreak of the crisis in mid-1997;
- due to the recent crisis having induced drastic reduction in domestic demand, the role of both independent SMEs and SME-type supporting industries vis-a-vis larger firms should contribute, directly and indirectly, to the necessary development of exports and the reduction of costly imports (mainly of components and parts used in final products to be exported). However, this does not mean that such a SME boosting export drive should replace the fundamental role of SMEs on the domestic market front. Actually, both approaches are complementary in many ways.

These two interesting arguments widen and deepen the more traditional arguments in use in Thailand, and also elsewhere, by the advocates of a stronger role for SMEs. These arguments are generally of an economic and social nature:

- economically, the contribution of SMEs in Thailand is significant. According to existing estimations and available statistics, they are supposed to represent 98 per cent of total existing establishments, 62 per cent of total employment, over 60 per cent of total manufacturing output, 47 per cent of total value-added and about 55 per cent of total exports. In the future, SMEs may be expected to absorb labour surpluses from agriculture, to contribute to flexible specialization in manufacturing, and to more and more capital intensive production as innovative firms or together with large ones;
- in social terms, and especially throughout the 1997-1999 crisis, the contribution of SMEs is perceived as the main source of employment (formal and informal) and of cheap basic consumer products. It is also envisaged as an instrument of socio-economic development and equity distribution among not only many segments of the population but also among regions outside the Bangkok Metropolitan Region (BMR), which accounted for over 57 per cent of total manufacturing output in the year 1996 before the crisis (against only 10 per cent for the Northern, Northeastern and Southern regions together). The development of SMEs can potentially contribute to the reduction of the widening social gaps which emerged during the last decades and to the deepening regional disparities in per capita income between the richest region (BHT 225,743 or US$ 6,270 for BMR) and the poorest one (BHT 27,000 or US$ 750 for the Northeast).

In addition to economic and social arguments, there is also a political dimension to this debate. Though it is not much argued in the specific context of Thai politics so far, the history of the industrial revolution shows that a dynamic small entrepreneurial culture and the existence of a dense and diversified class of small and medium-sized entrepreneurs are intimately related to the sustainable performance of pluralistic regimes (I would say democratic regimes, but the concept might sound too Western-influenced). Small entrepreneurs tend to belong to and cooperate with the middle class, and they can pressure local and central authorities to adopt and implement good governance practices (Girling, 1996; Hewison, 1997). For instance, they can lobby and negotiate for the improvement of both hard and soft infrastructure in favour of local industry and community. In other words, the concept of good governance can be associated with regimes able to promote a sound environment for nurturing entrepreneurial and self-employment capacities among various segments of the population. Such argument can be illustrated by the modern industrial history of various Asian and European countries well known for their very dynamic small entrepreneurial culture such as Italy in Western Europe or Taiwan in East Asia.[11]

At the crossroads between two centuries, Thailand seems in 2000 to be recovering gradually from the crisis and to continue on its path forward to further democratization. In this connection, there is little wonder why some leading academics, politicians and other lobbyists are pushing the SME issue in open public debate. It is the first time that small entrepreneurship might become a political and societal issue, as it has been for different but also similar reasons in South Korea since 1992 and especially since the election of President Kim Dae-jung in December 1997.

Notes

[1] Dierman (1998); Tambunan, T. (1999), *The Importance of SSIs and the Impact of the Monetary Crisis on the Industries, The Case of Indonesia*, Paper presented at the International Conference on SMEs at New Crossroads, University Sains Malaysia, Penang, 28-30 September.

[2] Hill, C.W.L. and Jones, G.R. (1995), *Strategic Management Theory, An Integrated Approach*, Houghton, Mifflin Publishers, Boston.

[3] Hofer, C. W. (1980), 'Turnaround Strategies', *Journal of Business Strategy*, vol. 1, no. 1, pp. 19-23. Pearce, J. A. and Robbins, D.K. (1993), 'Toward Improved Theory and Research on Business Turnaround', *Journal of Management*, vol. 19, no. 3, pp. 613-36.

[4] Cameron, K. S. (1994), 'Strategy for Successful Organizational Downsizing', *Human Resources Management*, Summer 13(2), pp. 189-212; Baron, J.N. and Kreps, D. M. (1999), *Strategic Human Resources, Frameworks for General Managers*, John Wiley and Sons, New York.

[5] Lakshman, W. D.; Regnier, P. and Senanayake, S.M.P. (1994), *Small and Medium Industry in an Intermediate City*, Faculty of Graduate Studies, University of Colombo, Karunaratne & Sons Publishers, Colombo.

[6] Birch, D. L. (1982), *The Job Generation Process*, The MIT Press, Boston; Haltiwanger, D. and Schub, S. (1996), *Job Creation and Destruction*, The MIT Press, Boston. See also Penrose (1980).

[7] Caird, S. (1988), *A Review of Methods of Measuring Enterprising Attributes*, University Business School, Durham. Chaubey, N. P. and Sinha, D. (1974), 'Risk-Taking and Economic Development', *International Review of Applied Psychology*, vol. 23, no 1, pp. 55-60. See also Gough (1969); Mc Vey (1992); Sahlman and Stevenson (1992).

[8] Dijk and Marcussen (1990), Grunsven (1998). See also OECD (1996); Piore and Sabel (1984); and Porter, M. E. (1998), *Competing Across Locations*, Harvard Business School Press, Boston.

[9] Dieter (1998); Schmitz (1998). See also Porter, M. E. (1998), 'Clusters and the New Economics of Competition', *Harvard Business Review*, November-December; Dijk, M.P. (1994), *Technological Dynamism in Industrial Districts, An Alternative Approach to Industrialization in Developing Countries*, UNCTAD, Geneva; Humphrey, J. and Schmitz, H. (1996), 'The Triple C Approach to Local Industrial Policy', *World Development*, vol. 24, no. 12, pp. 1859-77.

[10] OECD (1999), *Industrial Restructuring in the Asian Economies*, A Report by Dr Zhang Gang (Stockholm School of Economics) to the Industry Committee, Paris.

[11] Goodman, E. and Bamford, J. (eds) (1989), *Small Firms and Industrial Districts in Italy*, Routledge, London.

PART I

SMALL ENTERPRISE DEVELOPMENT IN THAILAND AND THE IMPACT OF THE EAST ASIAN CRISIS

1 Thailand, an Environment Conducive to Entrepreneurship?

The study of private entrepreneurship in general, and small entrepreneurs in particular, has been neglected in Thailand. The attention of both Thai and foreign researchers has not been devoted to the study of domestic capitalist groups, probably because of the relative absence of big brand names known beyond the borders of the domestic market. Most attention has focused on foreign direct investors and the internal/external operations of transnational corporations, especially Japanese ones. In the field of SME studies, recent books like the one published in 1998 by Roy Tomizawa are extremely rare, and even this one concentrates on small foreign entrepreneurs established in Thailand, not on pure Thai small entrepreneurs (Tomizawa, 1998).

Regarding the extensive analysis of the 1997-1998 crisis in Thailand and elsewhere in the region, it is surprising that the numerous books and studies published on the subject make little mention of the SME sector. This is hardly understandable, considering that it represents, together with large firms and public corporations, one of the three pillars of the economies badly hit by the recession!

The boom and bust of the East Asian economies, and more particularly of Thailand, has been of interest to local and foreign observers over the last 2-3 years. However, 'the analytical framework provided by existing theories on the development and role of entrepreneurship may prove to be inadequate to account for the specificities of certain situations' (Pongsapich, 1994, p. 1).

Not only has the overall pattern of Thailand's intermediary products and growth been rather unusual, even compared to the other emerging economies in the region. The profile of local entrepreneurship has also been rather specific, and the role or non-role of small entrepreneurs has to be investigated in this context.

Different from most other emerging economies, and despite the economic weight of a prosperous agriculture, modern industrial development in Thailand is not based on agrarian capitalism like in some old industrialized countries such as Japan or France. Local rice millers and rice exporters have never become interested in manufacturing but only in finance and real estate. The emergence of a strong class of small and medium entrepreneurs was thwarted by governmental policy focusing exclusively on the promotion of big scale groups. There was a role only for a merchant class, made up especially of Sino-Thai importers seeking business alliances with the Board of Foreign Trade and foreign partners.

Economic History and Profile of Local Entrepreneurship

Thailand's industrialization has relied on a tri-polar structure of dominant capitalists: foreign capital and state apparatus have been the driving forces, whereas pure indigenous private entrepreneurs have never played a major role. Capitalist development has principally relied on three types of groups.[1]

First, state and public enterprises, including military and bureaucracy-related firms, were initiated during a period of state-led industrialization between the late 1930s and the early 1950s. Most of them have continued their operations and represent about one third of total output up to the present day in sectors such as energy, transportation, tobacco, glass and sugar.

Second, transnational corporations (TNCs) have gained control of another third of the economy and have been involved in most sectors: resource-based industry (oil refining, gas, tin), import-substitution industry (auto-assembly, synthetic textile fiber (chemicals), export-oriented industry (electronics, etc...), consumer goods (cosmetics, medicines, soft drinks, etc...), and trading.

The remaining big third of total business transactions are managed by Thai private firms, most of whose owners are of Chinese ethnic background, which have expanded over the last three decades. Most of these firms belong to a small number of highly concentrated family business groups having oligopolistic market control in three major sectors: finance (including commercial banking), manufacturing (cement, sugar, agro-food,...), and export activities.[2]

Historically, the tri-polar structure of Thai capitalism has been established since the end of the 19th century. The three promoters have been the Royal Privy Purse Bureau,[3] European capitalists (involved in trading and in rice milling, saw milling, shipping and banking), and overseas or locally-born Chinese businessmen. This last category has been divided into three groups: royal tax collectors expanding into their own trading activities and rice industry, compradores serving the European trading houses and commercial banks expanding into Siam, and merchants based in East Asian seaports and moving into the Siamese rice industry.[4]

On the one hand, there was no marked development of any native group of capitalists. Most of the Thai people were alienated from not only capitalist activity but also wage labour in the growing industries, and they formed the lower classes mostly engaged in paddy farming linked to the expansion of rice trade.

On the other hand, the Chinese, played an insignificant role in developing the modern manufacturing industries of Thailand. There are

Table 1.1 Economic Performance of the Top 100 Firms in Thailand, Classified According to Capital Ownership and Nationality: 1979 and 1984

(Unit: million BHT, %) US $ 1 = BHT 37 (1999)

Type of Firm	1979		1984	
	Annual Sales[a]	Total Assets	Annual Sales[b]	Total Assets
State-owner & Public Enterprises	[19][b] 54,271 (22.8)	[19] 206,617 (36.3)	[19] 177,888 (33.3)	[23] 540,771 (38.3)
Thai Private Firms	[44] 75,979 (31.9)	[52] 304,279 (53.6)	[51] 213,453 (40.0)	[56] 793,602 (56.2)
Foreign-owned Firms [c]	[37] 107,652 (45.3)	[29] 57,261 (10.1)	[30] 142,209 (26.7)	[21] 76,843 (5.5)
Total	[100] 237,902 (100.0)	[100] 568,457 (100.0)	[100] 533,550 (100.0)	[100] 1,411,216 (100.0)

Source: Suehiro (1989), p. 275.
[a] Annual sales amount of a financial institution is calculated by its gross revenue
[b] Figures in brackets indicate the number of firms
[c] Foreign-owned firms indicates a firm in which foreigners own 30 per cent or more of the shares

four possible reasons for this attitude: Thailand had the lowest import duties in Asia and lacked control of its own customs until 1927; European industrialists dominated the infant industries; the state did not give incentives to the Chinese even if they had the intention and capital to invest in manufacturing; and local Chinese would save their earnings and send large-scale money remittances to China, Hong Kong, Singapore, or Malaysia.

Before and especially after WW II until today, the Chinese involved in Sino-Thai capitalist groups have not been only merchant oriented but also politically patronized. They have always remained highly influential but in the shadow of the ruling bureaucracy and military elite. Four key families have constructed giant conglomerates active in manufacturing and trading, but also dominating commercial banking and other domestic financial institutions. These conglomerates have been mainly engaged in marketing development, while foreign partners (TNCs) have brought in industrial technology and know how.

Therefore, it can be argued that just a few Chinese capitalist groups have been responsible for the Thai industrial take-off and later industrialization in the 1970s and 1980s. Due to the absence of large indigenous or smaller private industrialists, these capitalist groups had to face various constraints in their own industrial development.

First, there has been a clear limitation in the scope of their economic power. Although they played an oligopolistic role in selected sectors, they had to operate in a very limited domestic market and could not expand much at the international level. Most of these groups would have collapsed, if both the bureaucracy and foreign partners had not provided appropriate support over time.

Second, they have opted for a high concentration in finance and agro-industry. But even in these sectors, the room for manoeuvre has remained limited compared to the prevailing intervention role of the bureaucracy and state agencies on the one hand, and the predominant role of transnational corporations on the other hand.

Third, no industrial capital and know-how have been developed within these groups, which are primarily import-substitution or export oriented. The capital accumulation pattern has remained merchant- and market-oriented, but has not evolved from industrial capital into finance capital like in the OECD economies. According to Suehiro (1989, pp. 284-85):

> One important factor is the historical conditions of the country, namely the establishment of a colonial division of labour in prewar times and the presence of the multinational enterprises in the postwar period. These two phenomena are new economic conditions that capitalist groups in the industrialized countries have never experienced. Another significant factor is the fact that the majority of domestic industrial groups emerged from a class of manufactured goods importers. Unlike in Japan or other industrialized countries, Thai technical experts and factory owners seldom developed their businesses into big business groups. In addition, manufacturing industries, into which mainly importers advanced under industrial promotion, were concentrated on the production of finished consumer goods for the domestic market. These types of industries did not require constant innovation of production technology. Moreover, foreign partners constantly provided necessary technology. Crucial for domestic industrial groups were innovation in the distribution system and the development of a marketing strategy in these industries. Merchant-

or market-oriented activity, in this sense, was a rational alternative under the given circumstances.

Fourth and last, family-type ownership has also been a limitation. It seemed to work favourably for the growth of domestic capitalists in earlier times, but less in the 1980s and 1990s. Today, they have to face a new stage in their capitalist development, and are meeting new regional and global competitive challenges. The traditional pattern of capital mobilization and recruitment of managerial staff is becoming more and more an obstacle to any further expansion or shift in their industrial base. Consequently, competitiveness and productivity can be seriously affected as already shown in 1995-1996 immediately before the crisis.

There is little doubt that the role of the private sector, especially of these big groups and their related lobbying business associations (such as the Federation of Thai Industries), has grown rapidly along the FDI- and export-led industrialization in the 1970s and 1980s, which followed the ind strategy of the previous period. This evolution has left the kingdom with a class of local and dynamic (Chinese) entrepreneurs who have influenced the State with liberal ideas much more than in Singapore or Malaysia, where government has been rather autonomous in the absence of influential local private business circles.[5]

Thailand has implemented neither a laissez-faire nor a weak state regime, but a hybrid type of corporatist liberalism combining and overlapping public and private interests. This issue is further addressed in Part II of this book, where government policy vis-a-vis local SMEs is extensively discussed. Some authors like Silcok have perceived the Thai economy as essentially liberal, stating that policy outcomes would primarily result from ad hoc bargaining among elites pursuing divergent objectives.[6] Such liberalism is not so much a product of ideology, a search for economic efficiency, or the result of struggles among various segments of the elites, but is derived from ad hoc pluralism within the state organization itself, which explains its weakness. In that sense, it cannot be compared with the capitalist developmental states of Northeast Asia or of Malaysia and Singapore. More recently, Anand Panyarachun declared, before twice becoming Prime Minister, that Thailand's model could be best described as 'laissez-faire by accident'.[7]

Small Entrepreneurship and Development of SMEs

The ability to create large private groups may have helped Thailand to establish a presence, at least domestically, in sectors where economies of scale are particularly significant. On the other hand, dense networking among these groups and the big families involved may also have produced various forms of business and crony coalitions of interest, not so committed to producing additional wealth, as to using political power to influence the allocation of existing wealth. This phenomenon can produce significant market distortions, whose impact on other economic players, including SMEs, may be difficult to determine but are yet real as well illustrated in the case of the Korean conglomerates. The rise of Thai bureaucratic capitalism and the Chinese dominance of the private sector may have retarded the emergence of a business-oriented middle class.

Little room has been left for small and medium entrepreneurs, who have maintained a low profile and a modest role in modern manufacturing until the 1980s. However, like in most other countries, SMEs have been more dynamic and numerous in the retail and service sectors.

Since the early industrialization of 1947-57 under heavy military-related business control and patronage, manufacturing has remained underdeveloped. Very few private enterprises have notably contributed to industrial development. However, records at the Ministry of Commerce show that many investors, including Chinese capitalists and European traders, tried to establish manufacturing activities. Most enterprises founded between 1939-60 have remained small or medium-sized. Big investment was preferably in banking and insurance at that time. In manufacturing, private capital could hardly compete with military-related capital, which had access to political privilege. Therefore, manufacturing and technological development did not progress much due to the semi-paralysis of the large public companies.

During the 1950s, industrial growth was 7 to 8 per cent per year, and most of the industrial activity was carried out by a great number of small enterprises developing on the basis of family pluri-activism, especially among the Chinese community. But, in the late 1950s, the pro-state industrialization model (inspired by Pridi in the period 1932-57) was abandoned under the Sarit regime, close to the USA and the World Bank. Since then, Thailand has shifted to an export-led strategy and to reliance primarily on US and Japanese firms.

From the late 1960s and 1970s, local SMEs have not been economically and sociologically marginalized or separated from the rapid growth of the entire economy. The integration of local SMEs has gone through direct and indirect channels of multi-level subcontracting.

After a first phase of rapid urban-centered industrialization until the late 1970s, industrialization also started to disperse to provincial areas. In the last two decades, non-farm production and employment diversification (inclusive of part-time non-farming activities) in Central Thailand and even the Northeast have taken place in both the formal and informal sectors located in the main urban centers, the Bangkok Metropolitan Region in particular. According to a Japanese expert, the rural non-farm sector 'is closely woven into the urban market in the big cities, and it is the product of outside urban-centered capitalist development, rather than the product of indigenous rural development'.[8]

This means that the green industry does change where it still survives due to the impact of external structural shifts led by the urban and international economy. So called 'trickle down' effects have come to limits, and more important, most financial surpluses derived from agriculture have not been primarily invested in non-farm manufacturing activities. This is probably the most salient and specific feature of SME development in Thailand, also explaining why the traditional cottage industry seems to have rapidly declined. Multi-level subcontracting has either prevailed or even intensified in some traditional sectors (such as textiles and garments), or it has been a tool to disseminate modern production standards and technical know-how among most segments of the Thai economy. The number and types of manufacturing SMEs have been on the rise, and both the informal and formal sectors have contributed to flexible production by larger firms at the top of the production pyramid.

Table 1.2 shows a clear trend towards industrial concentration and the growth of large firms. However, due to the specific classification by the NSO, the important number of small and micro-enterprises below 10 employees cannot be assessed. In recent years, the rapid development of

Table 1.2 The Contribution of Manufacturing SMEs in Thailand: 1963, 1970 and 1996

(Unit: %)

	Year	10-19 Persons	20-49 Persons	50-99 Persons	100 or More	Total
Establish-ments	1963	49.4	34.9	9.1	6.6	100.0
	1970	38.5	33.5	12.5	15.5	100.0
	1996	40.8	27.6	12.4	19.2	100.0
Employees	1963	15.1	23.5	14.7	46.7	100.0
	1970	6.3	12.0	10.1	71.6	100.0
	1996	4.8	8.1	8.4	78.7	100.0
Value-added	1963	6.2	12.5	9.3	72.0	100.0
	1970	3.1	6.6	2.4	87.9	100.0
	1996	2.2	4.3	5.8	87.6	100.0
Wages	1963	9.7	17.1	12.2	61.0	100.0
	1970	3.1	6.4	7.1	83.4	100.0
	1996	2.9	5.7	7.2	84.2	100.0

Source: National Statistical Office (NSO), 'Report of the Industrial Census (Years: 1965, 1971 and 1997)'. SMEs defined according to NSO (more than 10 employees and less than 100)

medium-sized establishments with a few hundred workers cannot be well measured either. Over the last decades, the fruits of rapid growth have not been evenly distributed among all categories of producers, and public incentives targeting large domestic and foreign firms have aggravated the imbalance. Yet, SMEs have been able to develop and diversify along the path of overall development. This has become particularly true in the 1980s and 1990s, thanks to the strong dynamics and internationalization of the Thai economy.[9]

It may even well be that a segment of Thai SMEs has been more active on the export front than many large firms, preoccupied with taking over every corner of expanding domestic markets. However, the expansion of most manufacturing SMEs has remained primarily linked to booming domestic trade. Both the Chinese origin of most small entrepreneurs as well as the vitality of domestic transactions, controlled to a large extent by Chinese traders and moneylenders, has contributed to the start-up of simple but profitable activities in most consumption-oriented sectors. Other activities requiring higher technology and significant amounts of capital have been gradually launched in collaboration with foreign partners, especially from Japan. Several other specific factors have also come into the small business picture. At one extremity of the spectrum, small firms have been able to benefit not only from cheap rural labour but also from millions of seasonal or daily rural workers, especially during the dry season. At the other side of the spectrum, TNCs have de-localized some segments of their production, especially in the automotive and electronic sectors. Outsourcing to existing or newly established SMEs has rapidly expanded.

Though ignored by most analysts and policy makers, and neglected again at the time of the 1997 financial crisis outbreak, the expansion of the domestic market has been the key development factor in the case of local SMEs. This has been particularly true for household consumption products, construction materials, leather and shoes, textiles and garments.

The 1999 failure to launch an SME market (or second board) on the Stock Exchange of Thailand has demonstrated again the deeply rooted family-based culture of small entrepreneurship, even among the first class medium-sized firms and the so-called supporting industries to large corporations.

Contrary to anticipated results, the few available surveys dealing with the profile of SME entrepreneurs, such as the study conducted in 1994 by the Japanese International Cooperation Agency (JICA), have shown that the pure family business background is ranked as the first success factor in only one third of all cases. The vast majority of interviewed entrepreneurs tend to name first their previous working and on-the-job experience before deciding to become independent. Some of them have reached top management level through internal promotion by the SME family owners.

Vocational training and professional exposure play a significant role for most SME entrepreneurs involved in rather technological intensive sectors such as automotive, electrical, electronic and tooling components and parts. According to JICA, nearly 40 per cent have already been involved in technical work, whereas the others have had either a background in general affairs and accounting, or more seldom in marketing and sales. On average, SME entrepreneurs do not have beyond secondary school level education, but they have an average working experience of about 15 years before starting up their own business.

The secondary school bottleneck remains a major handicap to develop a wider reservoir of technicians and potential manufacturers. Only 9 per cent of the employed population has reached secondary or vocational school level, and the secondary school enrolment rate is only 30 per cent, even lower than Indonesia (39 per cent) and hardly comparable with Malaysia (53 per cent) or the Philippines (68 per cent). There is a major structural gap between the need of trained personnel and the actual supply. For instance in the automotive and electronic sectors, foreign firm affiliates have to import between one fourth and one third of their engineers owing to local shortage.

The Contribution of Thai SMEs before the East Asian Crisis

It is estimated that there were about 510,726 business establishments in Thailand in 1996. 400,000 were SMEs, defined as firms with up to 200 employees. Among 157,363 enterprises in manufacturing, over 98 per cent are SMEs contributing to 76 per cent of total industrial employment. Very small enterprises with less than 5 workers represent 74.7 per cent of the total manufacturing workforce.[10] The vast majority of manufacturing firms in Thailand are indeed small enterprises employing fewer than 10 workers, accounting for 88.5 per cent of the total. These figures do not take into account the high number of people employed as household-workers or working in the informal sector (textiles, leather, wood and furniture).[11]

Table 1.3 Working Experience and Education Background of SME Entrepreneurs

REGION	Working Experience	Bachelor Degree	Certificate /Diploma	Secondary School	Primary & Others
BMA	18 years	46%	12%	15%	27%
North	15	39	11	20	30
Northeast	13	21	15	19	45
South	13	14	18	27	41
East	11	29	10	7	54
Central	16	12	13	20	55
Average	15	28	13	18	43

Source: Industrial Finance Corporation (IFCT), 'Report to Ministry of Finance', December 1998, Bangkok Metropolitan Area (BMA)

Table 1.4 Number and Percentage of SMEs in Total Manufacturing by Size of SMEs

Total	1-4 workers	5-9	10-19	20-49	50-99	100-199	> 200
157, 363	117, 588	21, 666	8. 897	4, 662	1, 896	1, 195	1, 464
(100)	(74.7)	(13.8)	(5.7)	(3.0)	(1.2)	(0.8)	(0.97)

Source: 'Report of the 1996 listing of industrial and business establishments', National Statistics Office, Bangkok, 1998

There is a high concentration of employment in the textile and garments sector and in the agro-food sector. There are some discrepancies in lab statistics. Compared to the figures of the Ministry of Industry presented in Table 1.5, there are 4.65 million and 3.61 million employees active in manufacturing according to the National Statistics Office and the Ministry of Labour and Social Welfare respectively. The MoLSW claims that the manufacturing workforce is only 7 per cent of the total active population in Thailand, which is primarily concentrated in agriculture, commerce and other services.

If SMEs and large firms are combined, the average number of employees per manufacturing firm is around 102, and the average annual remuneration is below BHT 100,000 per person (below US$ 3000).

Table 1.5 Contribution of SMEs to Manufacturing Employment in Thailand (1997)

Sectors	Total employees	SME employees	% of SME employees
Basic Agro-industry	125,716	120,338	95.72%
Food	303,774	188,354	62.00%
Beverage	27,912	17,670	63.31%
Textile	273,048	176,828	64.76%
Wearing Apparel	223,842	210,623	94.09%
Leather & Footwear	103,089	67,968	65.93%
Wood & Wood Products	117,047	112,288	95.93%
Furniture & Fixture	67,094	63,189	94.18%
Paper Products	34,277	25,232	73.61%
Printing, Publishing	29,802	29,432	98.76%
Chemical Products	65,343	50,593	77.43%
Petroleum Products	8,260	4,943	59.84%
Rubber Products	76,940	57,751	75.06%
Plastic Products	130,859	105,937	80.96%
Non-metallic Products	158,037	128,950	81.59%
Basic Metal Products	49,472	38,647	78.12%
Fabricated Products	159,442	145,074	90.99%
Machinery	137,938	77,089	55.89%
Electrical Machinery	173,630	87,054	50.14%
Transport Equipment	160,228	128,982	80.50%
Other Manufacturing	213,542	170,854	80.01%
Total	2,639,292	2,007,796	76.07%

Source: SITE Statistic Compendium SSC 98, Bureau of Industrial Enterprise Promotion, Ministry of Industry, 1998

Table 1.6 Size of Firms by Sector of Production (in per cent)

Sector	Large firms	Medium firms	Small Firms
Food & Beverages	3.3	5.7	91.0
Textiles & Garments	10.5	30.6	58.9
Shoes & Leather	11.6	19.6	68.9
Electronic & Electr.	9.3	16.6	74.1
Jewelry	7.0	23.0	70.0
Timber & Furniture	1.8	8.3	89.9
Automotive	3.8	8.8	87.5
Plastics	3.5	11.2	85.3
Para Rubber Products	5.8	17.6	76.6

Source: Economic Monitor Journal, Bangkok, vol. 7, no. 1, Jan.-Feb. 1999, p. 2

The concentration of industrial activity is not as high as stated by the National Statistics Office, and the role of small firms and micro-enterprises remains predominant. The density of manufacturing SMEs in the Greater Bangkok Region stands particularly high.

Table 1.7 SMEs by Regions and Sectors (1997)

SMEs in	Total	BMA	North	Central	South	North East
Mfg.	90,122	50,141	8,713	13,478	7,479	10,311
Trade	134,171	59,607	17,681	17,019	15,896	23,968
Services	87,225	41,168	10,885	12,715	8,966	13,491
Total SMEs	311,518	150,916	37,279	43,212	32,341	47,770

Source: Ministry of Labour, Feb. 1998 (SMEs defined up to 300 employees).
Bangkok and Metropolitan Area (BMA)

According to various declarations by the Ministry of Industry, SMEs account for about 47 per cent of total value-added. However, there are very few figures available concerning the gross output and value-added of SMEs. Those provided by the National Statistics Office tend to be less optimistic than the Ministry of Industry: for instance, NSO claims in its 1997 industrial census that SMEs between 10 and 200 employees contribute only 19 per cent of total value-added, compared to 20 per cent for firms between 200 and 500 workers, 18 per cent for those between 500 and 1000, and 43 per cent for those above 1000 employees.

It is not possible in Thailand to find statistics on the contribution of SMEs to foreign trade, exports in particular, and to foreign exchange earnings. This is acknowledged by the Thai authorities and has been reconfirmed by a recent survey conducted by the ILO.[12]

Estimations vary enormously. According to the Minister of Industry, SMEs would contribute to nearly half of total exports, outperforming Korea (around 42 per cent) but not Taiwan (56 per cent). But according to the OECD in Paris, the figure would be around 10 per cent only![13] Our own estimation based on discussions and interviews with the private sector is between one third and one fourth of total exports depending on the sector involved.

The identification and number of exporting SMEs are not known either. This number does not exceed 20 per cent of all existing SMEs in Malaysia, which is more manufactured export-oriented than Thailand. The creation and development of SMEs are supported by internal and external sources of capital. Table 1.9 produced by the Industrial Financial Corporation of Thailand (IFCT) tends to inflate the role of the banking sector, which is also calculated from the total value of each granted credit line. It is also interesting to note that a public financial institution such as IFCT classifies both relatives and private moneylenders under the catch-all term 'Non-Systematic Financial Sources', though they are two very different sources of capital in practice.

Table 1.8 Average Value of Gross Output and Value-Added per Size of Enterprise

(in thousand BHT, US $ 1 = BHT 37)

Size of Enterprise	Gross Output per Enterprise	Gross Output per Employee	Value-Added per Enterprise	Value-Added per Employee
under 10 employees	NA	NA	NA	NA
10-19	6, 790	516	2, 310	176
20-49	21, 291	694	6, 606	215
50-99	70,798	1, 021	19, 832	286
100-199	160, 971	1, 148	43, 649	311
200-499	479,358	1, 565	132,818	434
500-999	1,122,069	1, 667	302,389	449
1000-...	3,755,452	1, 877	1,079, 327	539

Source: 'Industrial Census 1997', National Statistics Office, Bangkok

Empirical surveys, such as those presented in Part III of this book, indicate that most SMEs rely primarily on the capital of their own family and other private sources, which includes not only money lenders but also other types of business partners. In some specific sectors such as automotive or electronics, foreign direct investment might also represent more than just 1.4 per cent of total SME capital sources.

Table 1.9 SMEs' Sources of Capital

Sources of Capital	Capital Ratio (%)
Commercial Banks	44.6
Own Capital & SME Profit	32.3
Non Systematic Financial Sources*	9.6
State-Owned Banks	8.9
State Financial Institutions for Special SME Purpose	1.5
Foreign Investment	1.4
Finance & Trusts	1.4
Special Government Project Credit	0.3
TOTAL	100.0

Source: IFCT, 'Report to the Ministry of Finance', December 1998
* NSFS: relatives and private money lenders

Even if a majority of SMEs may have benefited from the spillover effects of rapid economic growth during the boom years, most public incentives were primarily targeted at large domestic and foreign firms. SMEs were yet gradually able to develop and diversify along the general dynamic path of the economy until 1996-97 thanks also to the entrepreneurial and financial capacities of a number of Thai business families (especially Sino-Thai ones) and some more modest households.

As long as the overall economic and financial situation of Thailand remained very favourable, the absence of specific government incentives, the low support from commercial banks, and the fragile linkages with suppliers and customers did not constitute major obstacles for SMEs, especially for subcontractors. But, when the macro-environment suddenly reversed, as it did in July 1997, SMEs were on the frontline of domestic recession. The subcontracting system in itself came under threat, since any significant market shrinkage is immediately felt by intermediate and final subcontractors.

Notes

[1] Suehiro (1989), p. 275. See also Phongpaichit (1992); Ueda (1995).
[2] For more details about the financial conglomerates, the industrial groups and commercial groups, see Suehiro, p. 219.
[3] According to the pre-capitalist *sakdina* system, the king is only one inviolable authority granting concessions to nobility and senior bureaucrats.
[4] Bualek (1987).
[5] Mcvey (1992).
[6] Silcok, T. H. (ed.) (1967), *Thailand, Social and Economic Studies in Development*, Australian National University and Duke University Press, Canberra.
[7] NPC Interview, Bangkok, 1987.
[8] Kitahara, A. (1999), *Development Possibility of Rural Small Industry in Central Thailand*, International Conference on SMEs at New Crossroads, USM, Penang, 28-30 September, and *Sustainable Part-time Farming beyond the Crisis of Asian Agriculture*, 1st Conference of Asian Rural Sociology Association, Bangkok. 29-31 January.
[9] Phongpaichit and Baker (1996).
[10] Liedholm and Mead (1998).
[11] Phongpaichit (1991). In 1998, informal sector SMEs are estimated to number around 700,000 (source: ILO).
[12] Allal, M. (1999), *Micro and Small Enterprises in Thailand: Definitions and Contributions*, ILO Regional Office, Working Paper no. 6, Bangkok, p. 50.
[13] OECD (1997).

2 Absence of SME Legislation and Loose Classification of SMEs

Lack of SME Legal Definition until 2000

Until the crisis, Thailand never passed any specific policy legislation concerning the SME sector. This is perhaps inspired by some kind of laissez-faire, like in Hong Kong, but remains quite surprising when compared with most other East Asian emerging economies like Korea, Malaysia, Philippines, Taiwan, and even Singapore more recently.

However, the need for a specific SME policy is challenged by the economic theory, and this point is extensively discussed in Part II of this book.

In Thailand, no national definition of SMEs has been proposed and commonly accepted, and various public agencies have used their own SME classification criteria, primarily to suit their respective institutional needs. Some of the concepts are confusing or unclear. For example, there is a lack of distinction between independent SMEs and so-called supporting industries. The latter category refers to medium-sized and even larger enterprises acting as suppliers and subcontractors to domestic and foreign corporations, and can be traced especially in the automotive and electronic sectors. Some of those supporting enterprises have even been created or co-founded as foreign direct investment ventures particularly popular among Japanese giant manufacturers, also attracting their closest subcontractors to venture into Thailand during the last 15 years.

In late 1998, the government recognized the need for a common definition of SMEs in order to facilitate statistical collection work, policy formulation and implementation, and the work of specialized agencies working together with SMEs.

Table 2.1, 'Thai SMEs Classified According to Total Assets and Number of Employees', shows the types of SME definitions applied by various national agencies until 1999-2000.

In the USA, Japan, or other emerging economies of East Asia, SMEs are classified as shown in Table 2.2, 'Definitions of SMEs in Various Foreign Countries'.

(Please refer to tables below.)

Table 2.1 Thai SMEs Classified According to Total Assets and Number of Employees

Organization	Medium-sized enterprises		Small-sized enterprises	
	Assets (million BHT)	Employees	Assets (million BHT)	Employees
The Small Industry Finance Corporation (SIFC)			Fixed Asset: below 50	N/A
The Small Industry Credit Guarantee Corporation (SICGC)			Fixed Asset: below 50	N/A
The Department of Industrial Promotion (DIP)	Fixed Asset: 20-100	50-200	Fixed Asset: below 20	below 50
The Federation of Thai Industries (FTI)	Total Asset: 20-100	50-200	Fixed Asset: below 20	below 50
The Industrial Finance Corporation of Thailand (IFCT)	*Fixed Asset: 100-500	N/A	*Fixed Asset: below 100	N/A
Japan International Cooperation Agency (JICA)			Fixed Asset: below 10	below 49
The Bank of Thailand (BOT)	Fixed Asset: below 500*	N/A	Fixed Asset: below 50	N/A

* for the loan from IFCT

Source: Department of Industrial Promotion, Ministry of Industry and Industrial Finance Corporation of Thailand (IFCT)

Note: SIFC was established by the SIFC Act in 1991;
SICGC was established by SICGC Act in 1992;
DIP was established by Improvement of Public Organization Act in 1942;
FTI was established by the Private Industrial Conglomerate Act in 1967;
IFCT was established by IFCT Act in 1959

Table 2.2 Definitions of SMEs in Various Foreign Countries

Countries	Sector	Criteria	Employees
Japan	Manufacturing Wholesale Retail & Services	-Investment Capital <100 million JPY -Investment Capital <30 million JPY -Investment Capital <10 million JPY	<300 <100 < 50
Taiwan	Manufacturing Others	-Registered Capital <60 million TW$ -Annual sales < 80 million TW$	<200 < 50
South Korea	Manufacturing, Retail & Services	-Fixed Assets < 80 million KRW	<300 < 20
Singapore	Manufacturing Services	-Fixed Assets < 15 million SG$ -Fixed Assets < 15 million SG$	N/A <200
Philippines	Manufacturing	-Fixed Assets < 60 million PHP	<200
Malaysia	Manufacturing	-Annual Sales < 25 million MYR	<150
USA	Manufacturing, Wholesale, Retail, Services	-Annual Sales < 5 million US$	<500
Canada	Manufacturing & Services	-Annual Sales < 20 million CA$	<500
Indonesia	Manufacturing Wholesale, Retail, & Services	-Fixed Assets < 1 million US$ -Annual Sales < 5 million US$	N/A
Australia	Manufacturing & Services	N/A	< 200
Hong Kong	Manufacturing Non-manufacturing	N/A	<100 < 50

Source: Department of Industrial Promotion, Ministry of Industry, Thailand, 1998

Towards a National Definition under the New SME Bill

As indicated in Part II of this book, the Thai government just started to realize in 1998-1999 that the SME sector had been deeply neglected during the last few decades. The magnitude of the crisis and its negative impacts on the domestic production structures have apparently convinced the authorities of the strategic importance of SMEs, if Thailand aims at reaching industrial maturity into the 21st century. Therefore, the need has been felt to harmonize the various definitions of SMEs, and to come up with one national definition as part of a 2000-2004 SME Master Plan under preparation.

On November 20th, 1998, Industry Minister Suwat Liptapanlop announced the drafting of an SME Act. On December 8th, 1998, a consultative committee was set up by the Prime Minister's Office and included representatives of the Ministry of Industry, Ministry of Finance, Ministry of Commerce, Bank of Thailand, Federation of Thai Industries, IFCT, SIFC, SICGC, Government Saving Bank, EX-IM Bank, Bank for Agriculture and Cooperatives, and the Thai Chamber of Commerce.

Two policy criteria have been tentatively retained:

- SMEs should have fewer than 200 employees, and
- SME fixed assets should be less than BHT 200 million.

On December 22nd, 1998, the Cabinet approved the indicator of net fixed assets as a third criterion to measure the size of enterprises. Then, on January 15th, 1999, it was decided to include under the new SME Bill under preparation the following definition:

- SMEs are considered as a single group;
- fixed assets are up to BHT 200 million for SMEs in production and services, up to BHT 100 million for wholesale trading SMEs, up to BHT 60 million for SMEs in retail trade;
- small enterprises have maximum fixed assets of BHT 50 million in the first three sectors mentioned above, and up to BHT 30 million for those in the retail sector; and
- production includes agriculture, manufacturing and mining.

Table 2.3 Classification of SMEs According to Fixed Assets

Sector	Medium-sized Enterprises	Small-sized Enterprises
Manufacturing	< BHT 200 million	< BHT 50 million
Services	< BHT 200 million	< BHT 50 million
Wholesale	< BHT 100 million	< BHT 50 million
Retail	< BHT 60 million	< BHT 30 million

Source: Ministry of Industry, Thailand, 1999 (land price is included in fixed assets)

The New SME Promotion Bill adopted by the National Assembly on January 12th, 2000 does not yet include these criteria, which have to be finalized by an inter-ministerial SME promotion committee.

Table 2.4 Classification of Enterprises According to Both the Number of Persons Engaged and Registered Capital

Enterprise size	BHT 1-9 million	BHT 10-49 mil.	BHT 50 mil.
10-49 employees	**75.4%** - 67.2%		
50-199		**14.9%** - 21.6%	
> 200			**9.6%** - 11.3%

Source: National Statistics Office (NSO), Bangkok, 1998 (the bold percentage refers to registered capital)

It is not known whether the government is aware of the difficulties in collecting reliable data on corporate assets, especially of SMEs. In a country like Thailand, where so many SMEs are unregistered or poorly registered, where most of them have two or three accounting books, where the whole family business is difficult to identify, and where even basic SME data is scarce, it is unrealistic to believe that this criterion can be effectively utilized as it is like in Japan or Singapore! At least, the current government tries to set up standards of good SME governance.

One will see whether the new SME Bill will be able to harmonize all previous definitions under the new one. In practice, analysts and researchers will have to continue to rely on the number of full time employees and the value of registered capital (when legally declared) as the only available indicators to measure the size of most local SMEs. In Thailand, even the evaluation of the SME workforce is not easy: the recent crisis has revealed the business cushion role played by millions of daily-paid and seasonal workers.

Registration and Taxation of SMEs: Red Tape and Malpractices

The Department of Commercial Registration (DCR) under the Ministry of Commerce is responsible for all types of business registration, and is therefore in charge of producing statistical data on such matters as corporate status, financial statements, dissolutions or mergers.

An 'ordinary partnership' (one owner or several jointly liable partners without limitation) can be registered or unregistered, and registration cost is limited to BHT 1000 (1999: US $ 1 = BHT 37). Micro- and small enterprises with a turnover of less than BHT 600,000 per annum are not required to register or pay tax. For limited companies, subscription of the entire share of the company requires payment of BHT 50 for every BHT 100,000 of capital, and registration requires additional payment of BHT 500 for every BHT 100,000 of capital.

Table 2.5 Average Amount of Registered Capital per Employee of SMEs in Thailand (Capital-Labour Ratio)

Sectors	1990	1995	1996	1997
Basic Agro-industry	0,28	0,38	0,39	0,4
Food	0,36	0,86	0,86	0,87
Beverage	0,43	0,66	0,68	0,78
Textile	0,22	0,3	0,31	0,31
Wearing Apparel	0,06	0,08	0,08	0,08
Leather & Footwear	0,18	0,19	0,19	0,19
Wood & Wood products	0,19	0,26	0,29	0,34
Furniture & Fixture	0,11	0,15	0,17	0,18
Paper products	0,59	0,85	1,17	1,19
Printing, Publishing	0,35	0,55	0,57	0,59
Chemical Products	1,1	1,64	1,74	1,97
Petroleum Products	0,81	1,08	3,32	2,99
Rubber Products	0,26	0,38	0,42	0,43
Plastic Products	0,29	0,44	0,46	0,53
Non-metallic Products	0,27	0,54	0,58	0,61
Basic Metal Products	0,55	0,74	0,82	0,87
Fabricated Products	0,36	0,42	0,47	0,5
Machinery	0,33	0,37	0,38	0,42
Electrical Machinery	0,33	0,44	0,48	0,52
Transport Equipment	0,35	0,42	0,46	0,51
Other Manufacturing	0,28	0,44	0,53	0,8

Source: SITE Statistics, SSC98, Department of Industrial Promotion, Ministry of Industry, 1998

The corporate population of Thailand was composed in 1997 as follows:

- 39 per cent of registered firms were sole ownership;
- 18 per cent were limited partnerships; and
- 43 per cent were limited companies.

There are also a number of different licenses and permits that are required depending upon certain types of business activity, locations and circumstances. Factory licensing under the Ministry of Industry

(Department of Industrial Works, Industrial Estate Office) is compulsory for manufacturers employing more than 7 workers and using machinery equivalent to 5 horsepower or more. But this second criterion is much outdated and rarely used: for SMEs relying on machinery, including imported ones, it is difficult not to declare it, but it can be undervalued in various ways.

Other licenses and permits are also issued by the Ministry of Public Health, the Ministry of Agriculture, and the Ministry of the Interior.

Compared to many other countries, and according to the rather liberal business environment in Thailand, SMEs do not complain too much about the overload of administrative controls and regulations. Micro- and small enterprises are kept rather free as a source of major employment, but also receive very little public assistance, if any.[1]

For the existing regulations and promotional instruments in favour of SMEs, the communication channels of state agencies are rather poor or ineffective vis-à-vis the small business community, which they hardly even know. On their side, most SME entrepreneurs are not informed and not very interested in government policy, which they have never trusted during the long years of political instability in the country.

Table 2.6 Format of SME Registration by Regions (in per cent)

Regions	Sole Ownership	Limited Partnership	Limited Company
BMA	5.6	20.1	74.3
North	40.5	26.0	33.6
Northeast	55.2	21.6	23.3
South	75.1	16.7	8.3
East	39.8	10.7	49.5
Central	78.5	11.6	9.9
TOTAL	39.1	18.2	42.7

Source: Industrial Finance Corporation, Report to the Ministry of Finance, December 1998. BMA stands for Bangkok Metropolitan Area

They also constantly fear that whenever some civil servants want to visit their factory, it has only a taxation purpose, including a corruption dimension in many cases. Therefore, red tape and corruption, or simple lack of business understanding and access to public services, are ranked as the first problems by most entrepreneurs. Compared to large firms, whether domestic or foreign, they do not have an easy and real access to middle and high levels of civil service.

There is also an over-centralization and sclerosis of the administrative apparatus in Bangkok, whereas many issues and problems could be more effectively handled at the provincial and tambon administration levels.[2] A real decentralization of power should take place and full time skilled civil servants should be recruited to provide local entrepreneurs with credible counterparts. Local or regional disparities should also be reduced through legislation and the way policies are implemented.

All registered SMEs are required to pay corporate income tax at a flat rate of 30 per cent of net profits, and net losses can be carried forward for a period of 5 years maximum. But how can their financial management be kept transparent when it has not even been the case for most large corporations, as shown during the 1997-1998 crisis?

Small entrepreneurs or their wives and relatives know well how to keep several types of books, but they have little knowledge of British style accounting as generally used in Thailand. The government has never provided any financial advisory facilities to SMEs, and the high number of SME non-performing loans has been the only reason behind the creation in September 1999 of SME financial advisory services under the Prime Minister's Office.

In January 1992, a value-added tax system (VAT) was introduced at an initial rate of 7 per cent, then increased to 10 per cent. Because of the crisis, it has been reduced to 7 per cent, but only in April 1999, and it remains highly unpopular, especially among small businesses.

Finally, for non-registered firms, every person receiving income from a business activity is supposed to pay the personal income tax. It can range from 5 per cent to 37 per cent, depending on net annual income between BHT 100,000 and 4 million.

Looking into the tax revenue statistics published by the Bank of Thailand, it is interesting to note that there is just a marginal difference between personal tax revenues and corporate income tax revenues. This indicates the size of fiscal avoidance and non-declaration, especially among the SME sector, both formal and informal.

For all these reasons, it is estimated that non-registered or illegal factories can represent up to one-fifth of the total industry in some sectors or sub-sectors of manufacturing.

Faced periodically with this problem, the Ministry of Commerce and the Ministry of Industry have developed a tradition of granting business amnesties, during which illegal enterprises can register. For instance, in the mid-1980s, more than 840 illegal plants have been identified in the spinning industry alone![3]

Over the years, a number of small entrepreneurs simply ignore legislation and controls, knowing from past experience that amnesties are periodically declared and that registration of new installation and machinery can then take place.

Drafting an SME Master Plan (1999-2004) without Proper Data

In the course of 1999, the Thai government has been drafting a rather ambitious SME Master Plan together with Japanese assistance under the Miyazawa Plan. This plan is expected to be a detailed complement to the first SME Bill, which has been finally adopted by the National Assembly on January 12th, 2000.

As explained in Part II of this book, the whole Master Plan exercise has an obvious political dimension. But its empirical basis and practical feasibility should raise concerns, if not fundamental questions. From the very beginning of its conception in late 1998, one should wonder how SME strategic planning could be seriously considered, when most of the basic knowledge regarding the real contribution of SMEs to the national economy was simply lacking. Thailand has a very severe overall data problem, which was criticized again in 1998-1999 by the most important bilateral and multilateral donor agencies. When it comes to SME data, segments of basic information are not available or in extremely poor shape, and Thailand is lagging behind most other emerging East Asian economies in this regard.[4] The problem has been officially recognized more than once, but has not been tackled so far.

For example, the Minister of Industry and the Director General of the Department of Industrial Promotion, in charge of the SME policy, quoted some symbolic figures in their frequent SME seminar briefings and speeches in 1999. According to them, SMEs represent over 70 per cent of total manufacturing output, 47 per cent of value-added and 50 per cent of total exports. However, such statistics are derived from occasional consulting work done for the Ministry of Industry, and the content is based on SME surveys very limited in scope and not supported by precise and targeted sample studies. In this context, even tentative estimations of the role of SMEs are hazardous.

There are also a few data impossibilities. For instance, how can the SME value-added contribution be calculated? A value-added tax system was introduced in Thailand only in 1997, and the taxation rate has been already modified twice. A huge number of transactions, especially among small firms, are not accounted for. The real output, not to mention the real value-added of most SMEs, is not communicated to the local district administration. SME entrepreneurs distrust local taxation officers, who they think do not understand anything about manufacturing and are only interested in collecting revenue, and lining their own pockets.

In addition to incomplete and unreliable SME official data, two other problems complicate the whole picture. First, the Industrial Census conducted by the National Statistics Office does not include small enterprises under 10 employees, which however account for 88.5 per cent of all existing manufacturing firms. Second, the contribution of unregistered SMEs belonging to the so-called informal sector is neglected, though it can be rather substantial, at least in a few labour intensive sectors such as textiles and clothing, leather goods, metal and wood work (including household work). According to the ILO, they may generate 3.5 time more jobs than the formal sector.[5]

For all these reasons, it can be understood why there is no published or even unpublished information dealing with the effects of the crisis on Thai SMEs. When the issue was raised by the Japanese donor agencies or by Joseph Stiglitz, World Bank Chief Economist, the Thai government had to confess its inability to provide any credible data.

The private sector does not seem in a position to supplement such deficiencies. Some major banks have a rough estimation of the number of non-performing loans belonging to SMEs, but their research departments have not conducted specific work on the subject. In January 2000, even such a big commercial bank as Thai Farmers Bank approached a major foreign consulting firm to help with its definition of SME credit policy.

Multilateral agencies and bilateral donors strongly denounced the situation in 1998 and 1999. According to the World Bank:

> It is clear that data availability and analysis of corporate financing and corporate governance represent major weaknesses in Thailand... Not only is the data on corporations, especially on SMEs, incomplete and of poor quality, there are also institutional gaps, as the responsibility for monitoring firm performance and behavior is scattered...Many databases already exist at NESDB, MOI, BOI, the IEAT, NSO and others, but the departments rather tend to guard them for their own use with scarcely any interdepartmental, horizontal exchange... Follow up work should aim at systematizing data collection on firms and performing more and regular surveys.[6]

Japanese aid, which has been the major contributor behind the drafting of the SME Master Plan in the course of 1999, is also particularly critical:

> It must be admitted that statistical data are limited to those of large scale enterprises and no statistical data are collected from small scale enterprises...The greater part of regional industrial activities is supported by small scale enterprises, and in this context, incomplete statistical data on small scale enterprises should be viewed as a significant impediment to obstruct planning of industrial development policy. The Ministry of Industry (MoI) had made it mandatory to force domestic factories to apply for and acquire operation permits. Application is usually submitted to the Provincial Office of MoI (PIO) and statistical data thereof are kept by PIO. However, since 1997, acquisition of an operation permit is no longer mandatory for factories with less than 20 employees, with certain special exceptions. As a result, statistical data of small scale

enterprises are no longer up-dated and the trend of the industry is no longer clear. On the other hand, the MoI has initiated announcements of monthly industrial dynamic statistics since January 1999...The MoI is therefore strongly urged to grasp the overall state of Thai industry as a whole by introducing annual statistical data and so forth. [7]

So far, the Thai government has not reacted. Chapter 3 suggests a few options for the build up of a sustainable SME data bank system.

Data and statistics presented in Chapters 1 and 3 have been compiled in three different ways:

- SME statistics are presented for a limited number of indicators when they are available from official sources;
- official or self-made estimations concerning some other SME indicators have been included as a second best option, when needed; and
- the lack of SME data for the period 1998-1999 has been compensated by the analysis of three industrial surveys conducted by the Japanese aid agency and the World Bank, and of course by a number of direct interviews of SME owners.

Exploring Alternative Sources of Information

Only three major industrial surveys have been conducted during the period of the crisis, two by the World Bank and one by the Japanese aid agency (JICA). Multilateral financial institutions such as the World Bank and JICA under the 1998 Miyazawa Plan for the East Asian economies affected by the crisis have been, in addition to the International Monetary Fund, the two external actors most involved in the structural adjustment and corporate restructuring programs designed for Thailand.

All three surveys were conducted in cooperation with the Thai Ministry of Finance and the Ministry of Industry. The 1997 and 1998 World Bank successive surveys were a joint research exercise involving a lengthy questionnaire and a number of surveyors. The 1999 Japanese survey was composed of two SME consulting reports supposed to help the drafting of the 2000-2004 SME Master Plan.

The World Bank surveys covered a total of over 700 enterprises in five sectors (textiles, garments, food, automotive and electronics). The sample did not only include a net majority of SMEs (over 60 per cent of the total), but made a clear distinction between SMEs and large enterprises (LEs) both in the structural composition of the sample and the presentation of the research results.

Worth mentioning here are a few non-deliberate characteristics of the sample:

- all enterprises were formally registered;
- the average number of employees was 58 for the surveyed SMEs compared to 736 for LEs;
- 38 per cent of SMEs were exporting (of which 18 per cent were highly export-oriented) against 79 per cent of LEs (48 per cent highly export-oriented);
- 11 per cent of SMEs had foreign capital participation and another 17 per cent were purely foreign affiliates, whereas the figures were 23 per cent and 45 per cent for LEs respectively;
- 26 per cent of SMEs had external debt, including 10 per cent with some foreign debt, whereas LEs were more indebted (52 per cent), with 34 per cent being exposed to foreign creditors.

The research methodology was debated, even among World Bank staff. Some critics were concerned about the whole approach and the questionnaire design. There were obvious limitations in taking only two successive pictures of the various impacts of the crisis at the micro-level. There was no intention to monitor the choice of each firm's product line or its management and productivity performance during the last two years.

The 1999 JICA/UNICO survey covered 244 firms and was specifically focused on the SME sector (201 respondents). Compared to the World Bank surveys, the Japanese approach focused more on the impact of the crisis at the SME internal management level. Therefore, more concrete and possibly more operational recommendations could be identified for the drafting of the SME Master Plan 2000-2004, which was also part of the terms of reference, unlike the World Bank surveys.

Notes

[1] Allal, M. (1999), *Micro and Small Enterprises in Thailand: Definitions and Contributions*, ILO Regional Office, July, Bangkok.
[2] There are 76 provinces, 876 districts, and 7,255 tambons or local governments.
[3] *The Nation*, 12 June 1987.
[4] Hall (1995) (1998).
[5] Wasuntiwongse, M. (1999), *Needs and Characteristics of a Sample of Micro and Small Enterprises in Thailand*, ILO, Bangkok, p. 91.
[6] World Bank Office and NESDB (1998), *Competitiveness and Sustainable Economic Recovery in Thailand*, volume I, Bangkok, pp. 43 and 62-3.
[7] UNICO International Corporation and International Development Center of Japan (1999), *The Follow-Up Study on Supporting Industries Development in the Kingdom of Thailand*, Draft Final Report, Bangkok, pp. 2-30 and 2-31.

3 The Effects of the East Asian Crisis on Thai SMEs (1997-1999)

Despite their flexibility, SMEs can only absorb market fluctuations up to certain limits. Their sponge function has often been demonstrated in the case of developed and developing countries, and Japanese SMEs have well illustrated this flexibility several times during the last decades. However, the intensity of the East Asian financial crisis and its deep spillover effects on the real economy hit the SME sector in Thailand rather badly as it did the other affected economies of the region.[1]

Not only the intensity and duration of the crisis, but also the management or mismanagement of its first most devastating waves, have caused the death or downsizing of a substantial number of SMEs. The first shocks of the crisis and the orthodox adjustment policy initially advocated by the International Monetary Fund rapidly affected the SME sector, while the large firms had not yet started their own restructuring. This may explain the sudden rise of unemployment as early as the beginning of 1998.

Collapse of Demand Preceding Credit Crunch

Since July 1997 and at least until mid-1999, the crisis can be associated with a drastic reduction of overall production and capacity utilization. This has been primarily noticeable in the domestic market, but also, and more surprisingly, on the export front, at least for about half of the existing export-oriented SMEs.

The three immediate implications have been:

- a sharp decline of domestic demand;
- a strong rise in input costs, mainly derived from the currency depreciation; and
- the surge of interest rates.

The sharp decline of domestic demand, both from individual and corporate consumers, has been the most immediately felt by producers, and SMEs in particular. Almost all interviewed SME entrepreneurs identify this factor as the main source of their concerns and as the main cause of production disruption or bankruptcy among a number of their local SME competitors.

Contrary to original claims in late 1997 and early 1998, the assumption that the credit crunch was the number one problem of SMEs has not been verified. In fact, the abrupt collapse of demand has been their main preoccupation, creating various financial management difficulties, which had little to do with the credit crunch in itself following the excessive debt exposure of the large banks and big corporations.

The sudden inadequate liquidity of SMEs and their lack of working capital have not been much linked to pure financial market constraints, but to depressed demand for goods both domestically and regionally.

As a matter of fact, most Thai SMEs have developed during the last two decades without relying much on commercial banks and other formal financial institutions, which were not interested in small business.

In addition, the 1998 and 1999 World Bank surveys concluded that there has been no proper credit crunch, and certainly no creditors' decision of that kind according to the definition. But, there has clearly been insufficient access to credit and supply of credit for various reasons, including high interest rates.

Until late 1999, the sheer number and very slow restructuring of the so-called non-performing loans (NPLs) has remained a major obstacle to lending fresh capital. This is, however, an issue between banks and large firms, as SMEs represent less than 25 per cent of total NPLs, and manufacturing SMEs a mere 10 per cent, according to Siam Commercial Bank and Thai Farmers Bank sources.

The assumption that the devaluation of the baht would favour all exporters has not been verified either. Many SME exporters did not benefit from the crisis due to rising input costs and loss of international competitiveness. This result also challenges the widespread belief that Thai exporters represent the major force behind economic recovery in the year 2000 and beyond.

Despite the large currency depreciation in 1997, less than half of all SME exporters have registered export increases, and the export effect of the depreciation has disappeared over time, taking into account the stabilization of the baht and even its re-appreciation in 1999-2000.

Domestic Demand in Disarray

Overall capacity utilization has declined for nearly 80 per cent of existing SMEs in manufacturing, and has increased for less than 5 per cent of them. Pure domestic market-oriented SMEs have been more drastically affected by the crisis–by more than -10 per cent on average–than exporting SMEs. The situation has been even more critical in some sectors such as automotive parts or electronic and electrical components, as they are particularly exposed to final product consumers' demand shrinking both domestically and externally.

The collapse of demand has been the main cause of financial difficulties for 85 to 90 per cent of all SMEs. Total revenue, but especially working capital, has been reduced for non-exporters, and even for exporters due to the decline of external demand (especially from East Asia, including Japan). It is estimated that about 55 per cent of SME exporters and 35 per cent of non-exporters were able to obtain some orders despite the recession, but they were not able to respond because of lack of cash flow.

Even though demand decreased by 30 to 40 per cent on average, and by 60 per cent to 100 per cent in certain sectors or for specific firms, only 60 per cent of surveyed SMEs mentioned that they were facing a very serious liquidity problem. The so-called credit crunch has therefore not been as severe and widespread as many had expected. In a limited number of cases, the concerned entrepreneurs worked out arrangements with their bankers. In most cases, they could identify various other sources of temporary financial support (themselves, the family, friends, suppliers, clients, private money lenders, foreign bankers...).

On average, the number of Thai SMEs facing liquidity difficulties has been significantly higher during the crisis than in Korea (50 per cent of all SMEs) or Malaysia (30 per cent).

SMEs Facing Credit and other Financial Difficulties

In general terms, the crisis had a mixed impact on the availability and cost of credit to SMEs. There has been a spillover effect from two factors. First, the reduction in aggregate demand and the higher interest rate policy have reduced the SME demand for credit, with most SMEs facing working capital constraints and decline in borrowing. Second, credit has become scarcer, not only from banks coping with the weight of non-performing loans, but also from suppliers of raw materials, intermediate products and services, who have drastically reduced the grace period for payment.

On the one hand, a majority of Thai SMEs declare that there was no overall credit crunch, especially from their suppliers. But on the other hand, two thirds of them indicate that they have been affected by a shortage of loans for working capital. The lack of availability and high cost of credit have been particularly acute problems for exporters not able to identify banking partners either domestically or abroad.

In late 1997 and early 1998, many foreign banks were reluctant to endorse export documents channeled through Thai banks. In addition, over

55 per cent of all SMEs–especially exporters–have criticized the high interest rate policy, even if they do not identify it as the main cause of declining output and revenue. According to World Bank sources, about 42 per cent of all SMEs have been handicapped by the reduction of their own internal funds, but at the same time 60 per cent have suffered a debt burden vis-à-vis banking or non-financial institutions.

The hot debate of whether a credit crunch has been imposed or not on the real economy is far from over in Thailand. It has had many political ramifications in the 1999-2000 pre-electoral period because banks have refrained from lending fresh money, and the injection of new credit has continued to decline.

There is apparently no clear evidence of a credit crunch since late 1997, even if a significant minority of SMEs tends to indicate the opposite. At least in theory, a credit crunch can be verified if two combined parameters can be detected:

- it can be established that there was indeed a close association between SME inadequate liquidity and the burden of debt serving and loans for working capital; and
- it can be confirmed that credit was rationed and that viable projects went unfunded. But this was not the case, according to the World Bank. In other words, the insufficient supply of credit does not mean that a deliberate rationalization of credit has taken place.

In our opinion, the late 1997 IMF prescription imposing high interest rates led to a de facto rationalization of credit. But the World Bank has adopted a cautious a-posteriori discourse:

> The widely perceived problem of a credit crunch, which can neither be confirmed nor rejected, may have in fact been just a problem of firms unable or unqualified to secure financing in the first place; this is different from the concept of a credit crunch where viable firms go unfunded. [2]

This argument tends obviously to protect the involved creditors and to hide their responsibility vis-à-vis the real economy and society at large. There was perhaps no credit crunch in the theoretical sense, but this is not what matters. The policy of the Thai banking community together with the blessing of the Bretton-Woods financial institutions led in practice to a rationalization of credit.

Even in late 1999, banks were not prepared to provide fresh loans to local SMEs. Their first priority remained how to handle large corporations' non-performing loans, and they continued to associate SMEs with poor management and high risk. Since the outbreak of the crisis, banks have also been criticized for collecting a lot of savings but for offering very low deposit rates in comparison to very costly credit. No wonder why a vast majority of SMEs have no trust in banks and prefer to rely on other formal and informal sources of finance.

SMEs Coping with Supply Constraints and Rising Input Costs

Besides the collapse of demand and financial liquidity problems, the crisis has had a third major effect in the rise of production costs for about 70 per cent of Thai SMEs.

The currency depreciation has increased the cost of imported inputs for two thirds of surveyed SMEs. It has revealed how far even those most traditional and labour intensive sectors such as textiles, footwear, metal work, and food products depend on specific imported inputs.

For instance, textile producers import machinery, polyester, and fine colour chemicals; footwear producers have to import specific glues and imitation leather; metal work relies on specialized alloys; food processing depends on specific preservatives and flavours. When it comes to mid- or high-tech sectors, SME import dependency tends to be extremely high.

In addition, differentiated tariffs have continued to heavily tax the imported components and parts used purely for domestic production, whereas export-oriented firms benefit from preferential rates. Domestic market-oriented SMEs feel discriminated against compared to other SMEs and especially vis-à-vis large firms.

The problem of rising labour costs has been mentioned by only a minority of SMEs (about 35 per cent). Due to the crisis, there was not much normal wage pressure. Many SMEs have tried their best to keep their employees, especially the most skilled and full-time workers. Others have limited pure layoffs and preferred to put some of their staff on temporary leave until normal orders resume.

On the supply side, no significant constraint has been registered. Very few SMEs have indicated any disruption of supplies or shortages of raw materials. Imports have continued to be financed somehow, considering that foreign exporters would not have shipped the goods before obtaining a payment guarantee from Thai importers.

However, due to cash flow problems, many SMEs had to negotiate payment delays and did not always obtain good deals. Apart from importing the necessary inputs, most SMEs looked into possible domestic supply alternatives, which were often not available or of poor quality. They have also refrained from buying new equipment and machinery from abroad until full recovery of the Thai economy is in sight.

SMEs in Distress: A Comparison with Large Enterprises (LEs)

Nobody can contest that the Thai government and the Bretton-Woods institutions have given full priority to the restructuring of the big scale corporate sector. Nevertheless, the World Bank industrial surveys demonstrate that the crisis has affected SMEs more than large enterprises (LEs). As the World Bank samples have primarily included so-called supporting industries (especially in the automotive and electronic sectors) and other SMEs of the upper-size category, and very few small enterprises (if any), it can be assumed that the distress of all SMEs has been even worse but has not been documented.

Decline of SME Output

A much larger proportion of SMEs (80 per cent) has experienced a decline of output against only 60 per cent of all existing LEs. However, the fall in capacity utilization seems to be more or less equivalent: -13 per cent for SMEs against -11 per cent for LEs. It has been particularly sharp for automotive parts and electronic components: -24 per cent on average for both firm categories.

SMEs have been much more sensitive than LEs to the drop in domestic demand, whereas there is not much difference when it comes to the negative versus positive effects of the devaluation of the baht.

Decline of SME Employment

As estimated by the International Labour Organization in 1998, the crisis has displaced over two million workers out of the formal sector. The vast majority used to work full- or part-time for SMEs, and only a minority has been able to be absorbed either by rural and seasonal activities or by the so-called informal sector. This has temporarily reversed the rural-urban shift in employment, especially in an agro-based economy like Thailand. However, the absorption capacity of rural birthplaces and villages has been over-estimated, and many unemployed have rapidly come back to urban centres, inflating the demand for petty or survival jobs below or just above the poverty line.

The slums in the Greater Bangkok Region have grown up and it is estimated that the situation could further deteriorate after the 1999 November harvest, when more labour returns from rural areas. It is very hard to draw more employment-creation funding from the public budget, whose deficit has already hit a record. In addition, the Japanese-backed Miyazawa social program will run dry in the first quarter of 2000. Budget cuts are also expected from the National Assembly, where a majority of

MPs tends to be against any kind of free lunch attracting further crowds into Bangkok from the rural world.[3]

SMEs and micro-enterprises can be envisaged as the only major job supplier, but so far most of them are still struggling and cannot obtain access to credit. Along the path of the recent but fragile economic recovery, they can at best re-hire some of their previous employees. Over 55 per cent of SMEs have reduced their staff against 45 per cent of LEs, mainly in the automotive, electronic and textile sectors, but these figures are certainly underestimated for what SMEs are concerned.

Downsizing LEs has also been a slower process, particularly in the public sector. SMEs had less capacity to rely on volunteer leave, severance compensation, seasonal working shifts, and reduction of working time. Wage reduction or temporary lay-offs have been the most common SME practice, especially to avoid firing anyone. The part-time or informal recruitment of seasonal workers and people working at home has been also considerably reduced.

SME Export Development versus Decline

Total exports of Thailand have decreased in 1998 by -6.8 per cent, and imports have dramatically fallen by -33 per cent. Both LEs and SMEs have faced sluggish regional export demand and rising import costs of components and parts utilized in exportable final products. According to the Japanese industrial survey, the SME export ratio has increased from 36 per cent to 39 per cent, but this is more the result of domestic market decline than a genuine increase in exports.

However, some SMEs have been able to increase their profits through substantial export growth in a limited number of sectors such as textiles and garments, processed food, wooden products, ceramics and glass products. Since the currency depreciation, 45 per cent of LEs against 38 per cent of SMEs have been able to increase their export performance, especially in textiles, garments and electronics. About 18 per cent of firms in both categories have been able to maintain the export level of 1996. Export development can be traced among those SMEs which could master the exchange rate volatility to accessing or reinforcing niche markets overseas, and to lower import costs. Among LEs, factors such as price competitiveness and marketing efforts have played a prevailing role.

SME export decline has resulted from poor regional demand (including from Japan), exchange rate fluctuations, high import costs and unstable political-economic conditions (especially in affected East Asian affected economies). The last three factors had much less impact on LEs.

SMEs Facing Domestic versus External Competition

Competition is primarily domestic for over 60 per cent of all SMEs, but only for 30 per cent of LEs. Less than one third of existing SMEs are fairly internationalized, primarily through export activities. After the domestic market, North America and Europe are the second biggest market for 24 per cent of SMEs, and East Asia for only 9 per cent. Contrary to widespread belief, low cost producers overseas are perceived as a competitive threat by only a minority of SMEs (15 per cent) and LEs (19 per cent).

Productivity and competitiveness of SMEs can also be measured according to their investment capacity, which on average lags behind LEs. Since mid-1997, 65 per cent of SMEs against 43 per cent of LEs have not introduced either new products or any kind of innovation. Fifty-eight per cent and 39 per cent respectively have not invested in any form of staff training, and 78 per cent versus 58 per cent in any form of research and development. However, on the positive side, a majority of SMEs would welcome investment incentives to up-grade standards of equipment and production. According to their own evaluation, their individual needs stand on average below US $1 million.

SME Revenue and Profit in Distress

Thailand has not published comprehensive official data on the death rate of SMEs during the crisis. In neighbour Malaysia, the powerful Ministry of International Trade and Industry has estimated that at least 10 per cent of existing SMEs have disappeared, even if it is not clearly reflected in the labour statistics.[4]

The profitability of most SMEs has declined. The number of bankruptcies is estimated to have at least doubled in 1998 compared to the 1996 level prior to the crisis. For instance, most construction SMEs and SME subcontractors have stopped their activity due to the crash of the real estate business. In plastics, 1500 registered SMEs went bankrupt between mid-1997 and mid-1999 according to the branch association.

Governmental statistics are very scarce on the subject and have to be analyzed with extreme caution, if not skepticism.

The Ministry of Industry (Department of Industrial Works) has only been able to document a slowdown in the establishment of new manufacturing SMEs from 6093 in 1996 to 5022 in 1997 and 3130 in 1998. The number of SMEs apparently continued to expand at an average rate of 6.1 per cent per year in 1996-1998, including during the period of the financial crisis, meaning that the number of registrations of new SMEs was greater than the number reported as having closed down.[5]

According to the Bank of Thailand, Southern Regional Branch, there were locally 509 and 773 closed-down SMEs in 1997 and 1998 compared to only 290 and 358 in 1995 and 1996. The number of new SMEs also slowed down from 3019 in 1996 to 1689 in 1998. But there are major discrepancies between national public or private sector data. For instance, the Industrial Finance Corporation of Thailand (IFCT) has declared that there were 3,391 and 2,544 bankruptcies among SMEs during the last quarter of 1998 and the first quarter of 1999, most of them in the Greater Bangkok Region (3,081 and 2,276 respectively!).[6]

Tracing bankruptcies is not an easy task. Many SMEs are not registered as explained in previous chapters. New bankruptcy regulations have been recently adopted, but are hardly implemented even in the case of LEs. Most SMEs tend to delay repayment to banks. Many entrepreneurs stop or change their business but do not de-register their previous firm, while registration can remain on the books of the Ministry of Commerce for at least three consecutive years. It is also not rare in Thailand that some businessmen change or shift activity under a new name and location to escape creditors.

Contrary to most SMEs, LEs have found various internal and external strategies to absorb the crisis, or at least to delay debt restructuring. Some of the most resilient ones have even been able to exploit new opportunities created by market turbulence. According to the World Bank, if profit margins have been drastically reduced for about 55 per cent of all SMEs, the same proportion of LEs have been able to maintain or even increase their profitability. Only 46 per cent of LEs have declared serious liquidity problems, and this figure corresponds more or less to the non-performing loans held by banks as of 1999-2000.

In 1999, due possibly to their flexibility and their emotional perception of the economic recovery, SMEs have been on average more optimistic than LEs about their short and medium term prospects. About half of them have anticipated a business increase against only 20 per cent a year earlier. LEs have remained much more cautious due to their heavy debt restructuring burden and slow growth forecasts until the end of the year 2000.

Credit and Debt Structure

By mid-1998, about half of all SMEs had to face some domestic debt but almost no foreign debt. Their total domestic debt was rather evenly distributed between short and long term debt, whereas LEs had primarily relied on short-term domestic and foreign debt.

According to the World Bank, the repartition among credit sources is also somewhat different between SMEs and LEs: domestic banks are the number one source for both (73 per cent versus 77 per cent), followed by family (45 per cent versus 24 per cent), suppliers (41 per cent versus 45 per cent), local lenders (28 per cent versus 22 per cent) and local partners (15 per cent versus 27 per cent). But the SME role of banks is much overestimated as indicated in Chapters 1 and 7.

Both manufacturing and service-oriented SMEs represent 25 per cent of high non-performing loans, but some private sources put the figure as high as 40 per cent.[7] According to Siam Commercial Bank, at least 60 per cent of the concerned SMEs are in trading and retail business, and about 60 per cent of them will not meet their short-term loan repayment obligations in 1999. According to the World Bank, over 30 per cent of all SMEs would not be able to meet their long-term credit obligations in 2000.

The Financial Advisory Center for SMEs, established in October 1999 under the Prime Minister's Office, states that only 10 per cent of SMEs' non-performing loans (about BHT 270 billion) will be restructured by the end of 1999 and reported to the Corporate Debts Restructuring Advisory Committee. Only three major banks, namely Thai Farmers, Siam Commercial and Thai Military banks, have started to take care of SMEs' NPLs in the course of the year 1999, while all other financial institutions have entirely focused on restructuring big corporate loans. Even in the case of an official request issued in March 1999 by the Ministry of Industry to lend fresh money to a hundred pre-selected SMEs, the largest state-owned bank, Krung Thai Bank, has declined, due to the financial fragility of those SMEs and the impossibility of getting company profiles.[8] Meanwhile, the irony is that the same bank has been accused of big corporate loan mismanagement, if not corruption, during the second half of 1999. This scandal has become one of the most controversial political issues during the ongoing pre-electoral campaign.

Notes

[1] Phongpaichit and Baker (1998).
[2] Waiquamdee, A. and other authors (1999), 'Corporates' Views of the Constraints to Recovery', in *World Bank, Asian Corporate Recovery: Corporate Governance, Government Policy*, World Bank Office, Bangkok, p. 14.
[3] *Far Eastern Economic Review*, 23 September 1999, p. 22.
[4] Mustafa, R. and Mansor, S.A. (1999), *Malaysia's Financial Crisis and Contraction of Human Resource: Policies and Lessons for SMIs*, Sun Yat-sen University, and *SME Administration of the Ministry of Economics*, APEC Human Resource Management Symposium on SMEs, Paper, Kaoshiung, 30-31 October.
[5] Watcharaphun, P. (1999), *Liquidity Problems of Small Business in Southern Thailand*, Paper presented at the International Conference on SMEs at New Crossroads: Challenges and Prospects, Universiti Sains Malaysia, Penang, 28-30 September.
[6] Bunmark, J. (1999), *Human Resource Management and Strategies of SMEs in Thailand to Fight with Asian Economic Crisis*, Paper presented at the APEC Symposium on SMEs, 30-31 October, Kaoshiung, p. B5-33.
[7] *Bangkok Post*, 1 September 1999.
[8] *Bangkok Post*, 17 May 1999.

4 SMEs Facing Survival and Competition Challenges

The Need to Create an SME Vulnerability/Resilience Index

Considering the rather substantial number of SME failures and the vast quantity of SMEs in distress in 1997-1999, there is certainly something to be learnt from the implications of the crisis as identified in the previous chapter. The industrial strategy of the last two decades should be reconsidered, and the real effects of policies adopted since July 1997 should be fully assessed, even if a fragile economic recovery is around the corner in the year 2000.

The first concrete action should be devoted to the construction of a systematic and reliable SME information system, but its feasibility and realization–if implemented–will take years for reasons extensively discussed in Part II of this book.

A second more realistic and rapid option would be to conduct regular SME sample surveys in targeted sectors or at strategic product levels, and to design a specific SME performance index. Based on the preliminary knowledge accumulated before, during and right after the recent crisis, such an index would be of great help for measuring the vulnerability versus the resilience of SMEs according to domestic and external market fluctuations.[1] It would also pave the way for anticipating possible business downturns and for designing the most appropriate anti-cyclical measures tailored to the real situation of local SMEs.

A First Option

The World Bank surveys of 1997 and 1998 already provide some background work regarding the empirical identification of the relevant SME variables. In these two surveys, eleven indicators measured the resilience of SMEs during the crisis. An intensity rating scale has also been utilized to differentiate four types of firms: SMEs and large corporations, domestic-oriented enterprises and exporting ones.

The sketch of a performance index is contained in figure 3.2 of the second industrial survey conducted in Thailand by the World Bank in 1998.

Following this kind of methodology, the elaboration of a SME performance index should be kept rather simple, so that not only the so-called SME experts but also the small entrepreneurs themselves can read it and deduce the right interpretations for their own benefit.

Table 4.1 Perceived Causes of Current Output Decline (SMEs and Large Enterprises) According to World Bank, Thailand Country Report 1999

(Rating Scale from 1 to 5)

Variables	Domestic Producers	Exporters
1. Change in Domestic Demand	5	4
2. Change in Currency Value	4	4
3. Change in Labour Cost	3.5	3.5
4. Change in Interest Rate	3	3.5
5. Change in Debt Burden	3	3
6. Change in Cash Flow	3	3.5
7. Change in Foreign Demand	2.5	4.5
8. Change in Credit from Suppliers	3	3
9. Change in Credit Expansion	2.5	3
10. Change in Cost of Raw Materials	3	3
11. Change in Delivery of Goods	3	3

Derived from the preliminary experience accumulated during the recent crisis, an SME index could contain:

- a set of indicators which would document in detail why exporting SMEs tend to be more resilient to market fluctuations, even though they do not represent the vast majority of existing SMEs in Thailand; and
- a set of indicators which would illustrate why the vast majority of domestic-oriented SMEs are particularly vulnerable to market fluctuations.

In doing so, both private and public decision-makers could determine how the promotion of SMEs could primarily target the domestic market, and where and when external market considerations could be also taken into consideration.

An SME performance index would also help in targeting priority sectors and sub-sectors, even groups of products, individual products and strategic components and parts. The lack of such a micro-industrial approach has been one of the weakest aspects of the 1997 and 1998 World Bank surveys, which have only brought up general conclusions of no direct use at the sector level and at the individual firm level.

A Second Option

The micro-enterprise methodology adopted by the Japanese surveyors in the mid-1999 JICA report suggests that an SME performance index could also be based on simple business monitoring and diagnosis, well adapted to the various categories of SMEs.

An SME evaluation matrix should include appropriate scoring of internal factors such as production, management, labour, and finance, and external factors such as supply purchasing, distribution and marketing, and after-sales service. Some comparative evaluation should be accumulated over time among autonomous exporting SMEs, contracting SMEs and SME joint ventures linked to foreign affiliates, and locally-owned SMEs that are primarily domestic market-oriented. As indicated in Part II of this book, the Thai government seems rather keen to develop some SME monitoring expertise throughout the country in the future.

A Third Option

A third option would be to review and evaluate the immediate responses and newly developed strategies of SMEs throughout the crisis.

Some of them, especially among the smaller ones, may have stopped their initial business before losing too much money or going bankrupt, and changed either their type of products or eventually their entire field of production.

Other SME entrepreneurs may have used various strategies to survive and recover. Their policy may have included a reduction in output and total working hours, a reduction in profit margin, a decrease in the quality or variety of products, a change of suppliers or a move to cheaper ones if available, a reduction of stocks, a shift in domestic versus external market orientation, a diversification of clients, etc.

The SME case studies presented in Chapters 9 and 10 show how some entrepreneurs have been able to find ways to overcome the crisis.

The three options presented above are not contradictory and can be combined. Of course, they are still sketchy ideas without enough flesh on the bone. But they provide scope for further analysis in order to develop the most appropriate instruments of SME evaluation. Down the road, public authorities and industrial branch associations could be equipped with better tools to promote the Thai SMEs in a more strategic and selective manner.

Competitiveness Recovery of the Thai Economy and the Possible Contribution of Thai SMEs

Looking into Downsizing versus 'Rightsizing' Strategies

As discussed from a theoretical point of view in the Introductory Chapter, the issues of whether, when and how to downsize SMEs (and large firms as well) are crucial to cope with any business downturn. In the first period of the Asian crisis and at least until mid-1998, the central debate has focused on ways to minimize the adverse social effects, especially unemployment. As mentioned in Chapter 3, a number of SMEs have tried various downsizing methods before being reduced to laying off workers.

However, due perhaps to the intensity of the crisis and other priorities focusing on the fate of large corporations, very little action has been taken beyond mid-1998 to supervise the more or less desirable aspects of SME downsizing taking place in practice. Previous international experience tells us that nine types of business downsizing have proved to be ineffective and damaging.

The first four involve a reduction of the workforce, the implementation of early retirement schemes, the decision for immediate across-the-board layoffs or gradual layoffs over time. There are four other types of downsizing methods focusing on the surviving workforce within the firm, and they include the placement of the remaining workforce in positions for which they do not have the right qualifications, the expectation that the remaining workers would work harder and longer, the emphasis on employee accountability, and the promise of financial rewards instead of career promotion. The last ineffective downsizing practice is to cut or eliminate training and development programs systematically.

A set of nine other practices has proven to be rather effective. The first four relate to manpower adjustment: reduction of the number of hierarchical levels in decision-making and production, consideration of the horizontal and vertical interdependent position of certain workers before cutting some positions, estimation of the appropriate business size before starting to cut staff, consideration of specific niche or priority areas in order to continue to hire and grow.

There are three additional measures concerning the remaining staff: workers with strong leadership should be protected and even promoted; maximum production flexibility and team work collaboration should be encouraged. In addition, core individual/collective competencies should be promoted and training/retraining programs should be utilized.

In other words, the cuts in human capital should be done as to not affect strategic competitiveness. Instead, the retrenchment activities should improve the firm's performance if cost and asset reductions are properly evaluated before implementation. More generally, the cuts should only affect those factors of production which are not related to core competitive advantage. If necessary or desired, that which has been cut should be rather easily re-hired or repurchased when the downturn is over. [2]

Therefore, local SMEs should have been encouraged during the crisis not to cut their staff expenditure to a minimum level and not to absorb wage and staff cuts among their friends and relatives alone, without evaluating short and longer term implications affecting the operations of the enterprise. The necessity of retaining quality and skilled employees has been particularly crucial. Thanks more to the Thai SME culture and to entrepreneurs' good common sense, and less to few government's appeals, a number of SMEs have been wise enough to act accordingly, as also shown in the case studies in Chapters 9 and 10.

The areas for divesting during times of crisis should be scrutinized with maximum care. The rightsizing strategy of any SME is the recovery response that should follow the retrenchment phase in order to secure a successful turnaround. [3]

In the case of Thailand, further investigation would be useful to study the effectiveness of downsizing among local SMEs, and also in comparison with other emerging economies in the region.

The Missing 'Middle': The Potentials of Supporting Industries and Other Types of SMEs

The declining competitiveness of Thai industry was already observed in 1995-1996, while the US economist Paul Krugman was criticizing the low productivity gains in East Asia. The crisis has underlined a few problems in the industrial structure of the Thai economy, as stressed in the course of 1999 by a number of foreign analysts and international agencies: [4]

- the top of the pyramid is made of a few large companies responsible for the biggest segment of high tech production and exports. Most of these firms are still family-owned and strongly linked to big financial institutions. But unlike the Japanese Keiratsu or the Korean Chaebol systems, they have not formed supplier chains and fostered the creation and growth of a wide spectrum of SMEs. Nor have they absorbed and

disseminated technologies and production processes to smaller entrepreneurs throughout the country;
- the middle of the pyramid, made of supporting medium-sized enterprises, is largely absent, contrary to Japan for example. In the case of Thailand,[5] it is not yet too clear why they are lacking to such an extent. The possible explanations could be related to lack of entrepreneurship, credit, skilled labour, etc; and
- at the bottom of the pyramid, SMEs and micro-enterprises are dense in number but most of them remain low tech, financially limited and still labour intensive. Therefore, their productivity and overall performance are rather poor, and they can hardly replace the missing middle, especially vis-à-vis large firms, whether domestic or foreign-owned.

The industrial structure of Thailand tends to be somewhat shallow, closer to the Philippines than to the four Asian newly industrialized economies, especially Taiwan where local SMEs are integrated in both domestic and international subcontracting networks which guarantee their market sensitivity and their technological sophistication.

Some would advocate that priority should be given to the promotion of small-scale cottage enterprises for employment and social reasons. But they cannot properly demonstrate whether and how far this strategy could lead to the needed restructuring of Thailand's rural economy, where neither domestic nor foreign capitalists have invested very much so far.

The promotion of SMEs, particularly the missing middle and other types of SMEs upstream or downstream the production of large corporations, seems much more urgent to remedy the structural productivity problems and to meet the regional and global competition challenge, especially in growth sectors (including the processed food sector). It should be noted here that the so-called supporting industries consist of two segments:

- technical equipment and machinery; and
- components, materials and parts.

In Thailand and many other emerging economies, supporting industries are generally concentrated in the manufacture of plastic injection moldings, metal parts, and moulds and dies.

The development of supporting industries could ease the balance of payments of Thailand weighted down by imports of intermediate goods and technology transfers. It would improve international competitiveness and (a) reduce imports and increase the value-added of domestic production, (b) strengthen the industrial base and diminish the structural segregation between export industry and domestic industry and (c) stimulate entrepreneurship through increased business opportunities for local industry.[6]

Imports of intermediate goods have significantly increased since a big number of Japanese firms have set up export-oriented operations in Thailand since the mid-1980s and following the sharp rise of the yen. The further appreciation of the Japanese currency since 1993 has prompted many Japanese business players to trim costs and expand their imports of intermediate goods and parts from third-country sources. Similar moves have been observed among South Korean and Taiwanese companies, delocalizing intensive-labour activities to Southeast Asia, and Malaysia and Thailand in particular.

Such supporting SMEs are manufacturers of finished goods and/or suppliers of large firms, and they introduce an above average number of simple or more sophisticated production innovations (self-autonomous ones or inspired by large firms). They are either entirely Thai-owned or real minority joint ventures with foreign operators already well established in the country.

For example, the case of the die and mold industry plays a horizontal supporting role in providing vital machinery to different industries. In 1998, most moulds were imported in pieces for a total cost of BHT 14,5 billion, and assembled locally. The Thai Die and Mold Making Industry Association estimates that about half of this amount could be saved by manufacturing such moulds in Thailand.[7]

Some case studies also illustrate this point in Chapters 9 and 10. For instance, there is no good quality local supplier of wire to the electrical industry. In the agro-food sector, there is an absence of local producers specialized in the colour and flavour sub-sector. Even in the automotive sector, it is rather surprising to consider that at best one or two local SMEs are able to supply some specific but rather simple molded parts.

In conclusion, the debate on the future of supporting industries in Thailand is far from being settled. In both the automobile and electronic sectors, the creation of pure local supporting industries has not much taken place. Loose industrial content policy and strong Japanese lobbying have led to a situation in the 1980s and 1990s where Japanese giant firms and their integrated upstream and smaller suppliers have massively moved to Thailand. They have not contributed to the real development of Thai SMEs but to the consolidation of Japanese control over the domestic market in a first phase (1980s), transforming Thailand into a regional production base in a second phase (1990s).[8]

The situation has not significantly changed since the early 1990s, when UNIDO wrote 'The weakness of Thai supporting industries often compels foreign investors to either source from abroad or to encourage their traditional suppliers to move to Thailand'. Indeed, given the weakness of the educational and technological infrastructure, even local leading firms acquire technology and know-how from outside. Very few Thai firms and almost no SME have been able to develop their products by themselves.[9]

Contributions of SMEs to Economic Recovery

By the third quarter of 1999, the IMF had predicted that Thailand's GDP should rise at least 3 per cent after contracting 9.8 per cent in 1998. Disbursements of new loans should follow, and the successive stimulation packages announced in 1999 by the government should also be able to boost the recovery.

However, many observers remain unconvinced either by the timid nature of the current recovery or by its too slow pace.

First, a GDP rise does not mean the end of the economic crisis or its impact, especially for SME manufacturers. Due to the debt burden on the entire economy, regained but modest growth, from a much-lowered 1998 base, will not immediately translate into a general corporate recovery.

Second, although the ongoing debt restructuring efforts are of high necessity (total debt stood at US$81 billion in mid-1999 compared to 93 billion at the end of 1997), most measures announced under the stimulation packages fell short of reviving domestic demand, which has been demonstrated as vital for the survival and rebirth of most SMEs affected by the crisis. Moreover, any sustainable SME rebound cannot be primarily export driven, except possibly for a few sectors or sub-sectors in which SMEs have performed even better during the crisis than before–the food sector for example.

Thirdly, manufacturing has started to show signs of recovery during the first two quarters of 1999, but the majority of foreign investment has so far gone to financial institutions, mainly due to the ongoing 1998-1999 bank re-capitalization. In manufacturing, due to internal difficulties, Japan has been temporarily replaced by investments from the EU and ASEAN. These new investments have fewer spillover effects on supporting industries and other local SMEs than the Japanese ones that poured in during the 1980s and early 1990s.

Fourthly, net private capital outflows have not only more than offset foreign investment inflows, but have remained high at over US$ 8 billion in the first semester of 1999. As in 1998, this is due to continued large banking outflows to repay short-term debt and an increase in foreign assets held by foreign banks.

Fifthly, as recognized by the IMF and the World Bank themselves, unemployment is expected to rise further in 1999 (up to 1.7 or 1.8 million: 5.7 per cent of the total labour force) reflecting lags in the pace of adjustments, and output growth will not be strong enough to absorb new entrants to the labour force.

SMEs' Non-Access to Banks as a Major Obstacle

Until the outbreak of the crisis, a number of SME entrepreneurs could not resist the temptation to expand their manufacturing business into other types of activities, as bankers or other fellow businessmen repeatedly called with offers of cheap money and fast return. The cost of those loans and promises became exorbitant after the crisis.

For instance, let's consider an SME that contracted a US$1 million (BHT 25 million in early 1997) foreign-currency loan to purchase new machinery. The creditor hastily converted the loan into the local currency after the mid-1997 plunge of the baht. The amount of the loan suddenly became BHT 50 million and the bank refused to revise conversions, although the currency has been trading around 38 to 40 vis-à-vis the dollar in 1998-1999. Combined with the slump in sales, the concerned SME could not face its external debt, and not only were its credit lines cut but creditors also imposed penalties for repayment delay, increasing the SME's indebtedness even faster. To maintain minimum cash flow, the SME reduced salaries, negotiated new credit terms from its suppliers, and turned to blackmarket lenders at 2-3 per cent a month to pay for foreign-source supplies. All this means no profit for the next 2-3 years!

This strategy should worry banks, since they did not save many SMEs from bankruptcy and have provided so far very few new loans even to well-managed SMEs. This has two types of structural consequences.

Thai banks tend to drop to last on the list of those loans to be repaid by SMEs, and small entrepreneurs may follow the example of Bangkok's big firms notorious for their refusal to honour their debt obligations. Even more serious, the proportion of SMEs that consider banking institutions irrelevant has never been as high as it is now. As revealed in 1999, a few financial scandals, involving some of the most prestigious state banks, and possibly involving the family of the Minister of Finance himself, have certainly not eased this kind of attitude.

At the core of a real and sound business recovery, renewed access to traditional sources of operating capital should be considered as a high priority. Distribution and efficiency of credit allocation to all categories of firms–not only a few large ones at the top–has to be drastically improved. Banks cannot be paralyzed by their large corporate non-performing loans if they want to maintain some credibility among SMEs and private individuals. However, NPLs are expected to haunt banks at least until 2003.[10]

Rescheduling NPLs by banks may also lead to NPLs rising in the mid-term future. The available statistics on the reversion of restructured loans of NPL status suggest, according to the World Bank, that banks are mostly rescheduling their NPLs in order to reduce provisions for losses required by the regulator. The Bank of Thailand allows a rescheduled loan to be immediately reclassified as performing without any repayment history; rescheduling involves stretching out due dates on loan payments. Instead, the NPLs need to be restructured in such a way that loan payments are reduced to levels sustainable by the borrower's underlying cash flows.[11]

A clear contradiction is emerging between the continued non-availability of funds for the so-called risky SMEs and the rather high levels of poorly remunerated savings collected by banks from the general public in 1997-1999. When compared to the same period in 1998, and due to debt repayments and NPL provisions, commercial bank credit continued to decline at a monthly rate of over 6 per cent during the summer of 1999, whereas deposits grew by nearly 6 per cent! This situation has not changed during the last quarter of 1999. It is feared that in addition to maintaining high lending rates, banks have been tempted to use part of these funds to compensate some of their losses on other fronts instead of injecting fresh money into the sluggish economy.

In mid-1999, the Bank of Thailand seemed inclined to use tax payers' money to rescue a major financial company closely linked to Thai Farmers Bank. Therefore, it remains to be seen whether the government, and the Prime Minister's Democrat Party in particular, are primarily committed to the recovery of big business first.

Is there real backing behind the newly announced SME policy or is it window dressing? This is now the topic of the investigation proposed in Part II of this book.

Notes

[1] Preeyanuch (1985).
[2] Michael, S.C. and Robbins, D.K. (1998), 'Retrenchment among Small Manufacturing Firms during Recession', *Journal of Small Business Management*, July, vol. 36, no. 3, pp. 35-45. Dedee, J.K. and Vorbies, D.W. (1998), 'Retrenchment Activities of Small Firms During Economic Downturn: An Empirical Investigation', *Journal of Small Business Management*, July, vol. 36, no. 3, pp. 46-61.
[3] Enright, M.S. and Leung, E. (1999), *Hong Kong's Competitiveness beyond the Asian Crisis: An Overview*, Hong Kong Trade Development Council, Government Printer.
[4] OECD (1999), *Industrial Restructuring in the Asian Economies*, DSTI/IND(99)2, Paris, p.5.
[5] Kawabe (1996).
[6] Kawabe (1996), pp. 130-31.
[7] Leopairote (1999), p. 8.
[8] Bello (1998), pp. 61-4, Yamashita (1991), pp. 179-80, and Thai Development and Research Institute (1991), *The Barriers to and Strategies for Technology Acquisition*, TDRI, Bangkok. p.173.
[9] UNIDO (1990), p. 31.
[10] *The Nation*, 17 September 1999.
[11] World Bank, *Thailand Economic Monitor*, 2nd Quarter 1999, p. 13.

PART II

STRUCTURAL ADJUSTMENT UNDER THE INTERNATIONAL MONETARY FUND AND SME GOVERNMENT POLICY

5 Thai SMEs: The Role of the Private and Public Sectors Before the Crisis

The Need for an SME Policy: An Open Debate

As shown in the Introductory Chapter, there is plenty of argument regarding the importance of SMEs in economic and social development. But, this interest has not necessarily led to the conclusion that the government should mobilize public resources to promote SMEs. Some say that the matter can be left to the market economy. Others express the view that since SMEs are profit centers like any other types of enterprises, it is not crystal clear, except perhaps from a social and welfare perspective, why public funding should selectively support either the most promising or the weakest ones.

In theory, the market economy is supposed to provide an efficient allocation of resources to produce goods up to the utility possibilities frontier, which is determined by technological and other resource limits. However, there is at least one major argument in favour of government intervention in order to maintain, if not increase, overall welfare. This argument is based on the many causes for markets to fail and prevent demand from matching supply. It may be generally accepted that SMEs tend to be dismissed from competition by large domestic and foreign firms, and that the entire economy can suffer from such market distortions. The East Asian crisis can be attributed to a market failure of such a magnitude that local authorities felt the obligation to boost the traumatized corporate sector, the hard-hit SME sector in particular. SMEs may be regarded as a traction engine which needs to be fuelled for the benefit of the entire economy, whereas the cottage and smaller businesses or so-called informal sector should be left to social and welfare considerations.

In a country such as Thailand deprived of any significant SME policy until the 1990s, policy-makers would like to know in advance how effective the possible forms of SME promotion are in order to select the most cost-effective ones in the face of severe budget constraints under IMF adjustment commitments (Phodhivorakhun, 1999). Evidence available from both OECD and emerging economies is generally inconclusive (Bridge, O'Neill and Cromie, 1998, p. 276):

There appears to be no strong body of evidence to say that intervention works, but also there is no clear evidence that it doesn't.

Some interventions have had or can have a positive effect, but research data and evaluation are mostly imperfect, ambiguous and sometimes even contradictory. As private firms, SMEs do not generally undergo an accounting of costs and benefits beyond their own financial feasibility. Yet, if they are to be promoted through public investment, the whole exercise merits some economic valuation, which should according to Chan[1] either be directed at possible optimum policies or directly at the production function of the concerned SMEs themselves:

> Still, the expected realization of actual outcomes will more likely be second best solutions. Implications over government regulations, production efficiency and returns to scale must be carefully considered.

At best, government may be able to perform a facilitation role to ensure the existence of a wide range of production activities by stimulating the growth of missing industries–especially the so-called supporting ones and SMEs–to supplement the numerous product niches already filled by large domestic and foreign private investors. But there is little evidence that government is particularly well equipped to understand small private entrepreneurship and to provide the right inputs. At best, it can provide supporting infrastructure and create good business environment conditions.

In the absence of any long experience in promoting SMEs in Thailand, it remains to be seen how far the effects of the East Asian crisis can militate in favour of pro-SME intervention, and whether the new SME policy in the making indicates real public commitment or only mere political expediency.

The Role of the State during the Pre-Industrialization Period

Historically, the royal state relied on European trading and financial companies and on local and oversea Chinese business families to look after the economic interests of Siam in the 19th and early 20th centuries, with the patronage and support of the royal bureaucracy and nobility. This situation continued until Thailand regained customs sovereignty in 1927, and until the end of the absolute monarchy in 1932. Until then, there was no independent governmental organization responsible for formulating industrial policy.

There were two periods of rather strong state intervention during the pre-industrialization history of Thailand, namely in the 1930s and 1950s (Ingram, 1971; Wonghanchao and Ikemoto, 1988).

In the mid-1930s, the first Phibun government put more emphasis on promoting the manufacturing sector in order to counterbalance the role of foreign capital and Chinese merchant capitalists. As elsewhere in Southeast Asia, there was too little pure Thai capital to think of any other alternative. In 1936, the Industry Division was set up under the Department of Commerce, Ministry of Economic Affairs, and it expanded in 1943 into a specific Ministry of Industry in charge of the promotion of manufacturing activities.

The first state factories were launched in sectors such as sugar, tobacco, and handicrafts. The Thai Industrial Development Co. (TIDC) was established as the biggest pre-war holding state enterprise for both existing and newly formed manufacturing plants. In the financial sector, senior politicians and bureaucrats initiated the Bank of Asia, the Bank of Ayudhya, the Safety Insurance Co., and the Thai Life Insurance Co. But as Suehiro (1989, p. 133) notes:

> Those who really entered into profit-producing industries were recruited from political groups which dominated the power structure, and not the Thai common people or indigenous merchants who were supposed to be promoted in its original economic programmes (...) The first Phibun government not only enhanced state control over the economy in general, but also promoted a new 'bureaucrat capitalist class' rather than indigenous capitalists in Thailand.

During a second phase of state control development in the 1950s and early 1960s, the leading groups representing bureaucrat capitalists changed from the former People's Party group (in the late 1930s) to new military leaders. They especially came from the Army Commander-in-Chief Phin's faction, that had emerged from the 1947 coup and the so-called silent coup in 1951, and then from Sarit's faction leading the 1957-58 coup and so-called revolution. After 1951, military commands and politico-bureaucrats openly began to take part in private and state business activity, establishing new firms and holding directorships in existing Chinese-owned enterprises. Military leaders were invited to become board members and shareholders and monopolized some of the most lucrative businesses. Suehiro (1989, p. 138) estimates that 61 of them were involved in 107 key firms in all sectors of manufacturing and services during the period 1932-1962:

> Although several distinguished Chinese families formed giant business groups by the early 1950s, it was impossible for them to continue and develop their enterprises without the political patronage of the military command. The dominant capitalists in the 1950s were comprised of the army, the politico-bureaucrats and their Chinese business collaborators, and they were all consolidated into a system of capitalism.

However, according to him (p. 183), this system of flourishing military-related business and prevailing monopolies did not contribute much to any rapid development of manufacturing:

> We can arrive at the simple conclusion that Thai manufacturing industries in the private sector had experienced no remarkable change throughout the 1950s, although the Phibun government had attempted to introduce modern industries under the leadership of state enterprises.

In most sectors, the 'raison d'être' of the bureaucratic capitalist system and of the military involvement aimed at exploiting and appropriating the economic surplus for political purposes (Phongpaichit, 1992). Sarit's coup and 'revolution' in 1957 was the starting point of a new policy, and industrialization became a higher priority. Planning was introduced in 1959 with the creation of the National Economic Development Board (becoming NESDB in 1972). Under the Industrial Act of 1960, the newly established Board of Investment was put in charge of industrial promotion through selective incentives for domestic and foreign investors. During the 1960s, manufacturing rose from 12 to 16 per cent of GDP, and 607 import-substitution enterprises were promoted, especially in textiles and garments, but only 225 were wholly Thai-owned. Tariff restructuring was encouraged to protect infant industries, defined as domestic and foreign ones producing in Thailand, but no additional state intervention was decided on in sectors or sub-sectors already exposed to private competition.

Dual Industrial Policy and Positive Discrimination of SMEs

In the pre-industrial context and until the 1960s, most small-scale factories remained in the hands of the so-called foreign and essentially Chinese capitalists. Many had not even changed their nationality, contrary to the big Chinese business families dragged into collaboration with the Thai ruling elite during and beyond the Phibun government.

Sarit's new industrialization policies had a concrete impact with the rise of industrial concentration through large firms (Hewison, 1989). During the 1960s, according to the National Statistics Office, the proportion of enterprises employing more than 100 employees jumped from 47 to 72 per cent, whereas small firms under 20 employees dropped from 15 to 6 per cent (see Chapter 1).

The new industrial policy was not neutral vis-à-vis the SME sector, but created a dual industrial system, discriminating at least implicitly against small entrepreneurship. The Board of Investment (BOI) promoted large import-substitution firms in priority sectors such as textiles, automotive assembling, electrical appliances, steel products and food processing. One-third were affiliates of foreign transnational corporations, and two-thirds were domestic firms controlled by the Sino-Thai merchant class (Bunjongjit and Oudin, 1992).

Smaller local enterprises, when existing, remained underdeveloped technologically and financially, and were barred from moving into the promoted industries. The Board of Investment encouraged only larger firms by regulating either the minimum amount of initial investment or the minimum production capacity required. The intention was to develop the selected firms in the shortest period possible to catch up with international competition.

For instance, a promoted spinning firm was required to equip itself with no fewer than 3,000 spindles, while a promoted glass manufacturer was asked to invest no less than 10 million baht. In textiles, the promoted firms were invited to introduce new types of products such as polyester-cotton mixed yarn or polyester-rayon mixed yarn, both of which enjoyed an expanding market, instead of pure cotton fabrics. But the small weavers were forced to continue with their traditional production, which appealed only to a limited and domestic rural market. Therefore, they experienced a drastic reduction in their proportion of total production volume of textiles from 48 per cent in 1961 down to 16 per cent in 1975.

In addition to significant inflows of foreign direct investment, from European and American origins, but also and more and more from Japan, domestic groups transformed themselves into both industrial and service-oriented conglomerates. Industrial policy was the chief cause of new investment by the local merchant class into import-substitution industries and gradually into assembly joint ventures with foreign partners, especially from Japan. Statistical evidence during the 1970s and early 1980s shows that over 70 per cent of the large manufacturing firms, both local and foreign, enjoyed various incentives and privileges granted by the BOI. For instance, among the textile firms receiving investment privileges between 1960 and 1976, more than four-fifths were joint ventures in which Japanese firms held some equity.[2]

In brief, it can be said that credit extension from both government and large commercial banks has been directed with foreign support to highly capital-intensive sectors in both manufacturing and services. The integration between the emerging conglomerates and foreign capital has been the driving engine of Thai industrialization, simply because the local merchant elite could arrange through government connections various BOI privileges in exchange for foreign technology and marketing know-how, which they had not accumulated historically (Phipatseritham and Yoshihara, 1983; Piriyarangsan, 1983 and 1990).

In conclusion, and contrary to Japan for example, there was in Thailand no comparable development of small and/or gradually larger native industrialists among the local group of technical experts and factory owners, like the founders of Hitachi, Sony, Toyota, Nissan. In the absence of a strong or potential class of local private manufacturers, industrialization developed primarily in the face of the following realities:

- the Board of Investment and other state agencies supported a small group of large firms. The existing small factories and workshops were automatically excluded from the support programs;
- large importers had access to foreign exporters and hence to foreign manufacturers, who became partners in setting up the modern industrial activities of today's Thailand. The existing local factory owners did not have such contacts and no public instrument was introduced as a facilitator;
- the Thai commercial and industrial conglomerates were able to enjoy oligopolistic status in those sectors selected by the BOI. This position resulted from quick expansion of their activities under various BOI privileges and active promotion of vertically integrated production systems; and
- some conglomerates developed into domestic market monopolies under various official or informal and non-transparent discrimination policies and protective measures of the government, but never under pure movements of private capital alone.

For these reasons, Thailand was left neither with a strong local SME sector, nor with large highly competitive and non-foreign controlled manufacturers. Even the monopolistic and highly privileged conglomerates did not reached significant international market weight. They were able to control only a small domestic market in Thailand, meaning that they remained small in size and primarily unknown at the international level, for instance in terms of recognized brand names.

Big Business, SMEs and Politics

For the reasons explained above, and despite a few measures targeting the supporting industries (such as the BUILD program under the BOI), there has been no comprehensive SME policy in Thailand, either during the pre-industrial period or during the last few decades of rapid economic growth.

The SME issue was put on paper in the Fifth Plan (1982-86). This plan preached in particular for a more balanced distribution of industry throughout the country, whereas the Sixth Plan was the first one to address the development of supporting industries–whether SMEs or larger firms– especially in the automotive and electronic sectors.

Only the Ministry of Industry has tried to make use of its Provincial Industrial Offices (PIOs). The PIOs have been responsible for registering industries, to implement governmental regulations and to provide assistance to local firms, without a particular focus on SMEs. In practice, due to limited staff in particular, PIOs' activities have concentrated in regulatory work and not much in providing support services to the local private sector (ILO, 1993, p.25).

Within the Ministry of Industry, The Department of Industrial Promotion (DIP) has framed up a policy and has envisaged to become a one-stop service in the absence of a better solution. The creation of Regional Industrial Promotion Centres (RIPCs) has targeted the promotion of local SMEs and cottage industries. However, until 1997-98, the RIPCs have mainly consisted of coordinating and channeling services from various divisions of the DIP in Bangkok, of relying on other public agencies to provide any specific service and of involving very little participation from private sector organizations or NGOs. Their activity has concentrated in the delivery of various entrepreneurs' development training programs (EDPs), but has not been supplemented by formal assessment and impact evaluation procedures in most cases.

It is revealing that most SME entrepreneurs interviewed in the frame of various independent surveys–even in Bangkok– were not capable of tracing any concrete governmental support extended to them in the 1980s or 1990s, despite the efforts of the Board of Investment (BUILD Program), the Ministry of Industry or the Small Industry Finance Corporation (SIFC).[3]

This kind of benevolent neglect is rather similar to the lack of industrial policies in some other East Asian economies such as Hong Kong or the Philippines. But it diverges from the experiences of Japan and most leading emerging economies in East Asia such as Korea, Malaysia, Singapore,[4] Taiwan and even coastal China more recently.

The socio-cultural, economic and political environment prevailing among the Thai elite has not been particularly aware of the potentials and problems of small entrepreneurs.

First, the dual pattern of Thai industrialization, as described above and in Chapter 1, was reinforced during the 1980s and 1990s due to the acceleration of foreign direct investment and other investment inflows in a few key sectors. In addition to the classical divide between large firms, whether domestic or foreign ones, and the local SMEs, Chapter 4 has stressed that another divide has rapidly emerged between foreign affiliated supporting industries, which are on average medium-sized firms, and domestic market oriented SMEs. The intimacy between top business leaders and the political and military elite has further grown, induced by the rapid acceleration of financial and economic wealth concentration. This has left very limited business options for autonomous development of SMEs, and very limited access for small entrepreneurs to powerful business or governmental decision-makers.

Second, the number and diversification of SMEs has obviously increased, induced at the macro-economic level by the rapid growth of the economy in the 1980s and early 1990s, and at the micro-level by multi-level subcontracting and decentralized production activities. But the SME sector has not been able to expand much in high tech and intensive capital sectors, and to improve significantly the local content into final sophisticated products. This situation has certainly not inclined government and big business to pay more attention to the potential of local SMEs, and top priority has remained to attract large-scale foreign direct investment and foreign expertise.

Thirdly, institutionalized and transparent consultation between the public and private sectors has never been a strong feature of Thai governance. The lobbying track record of leading private institutions such as the Federation of Thai Industries or the Thai Chamber of Commerce has not occupied the front scene and has been systematically biased by the conglomerates and other large firms, both at the national and provincial levels. Therefore, local SMEs have never been well represented at any level of Thai society and decision-making.

Fourthly, until the adoption of the New Constitution in 1997 and the beginning of the East Asian crisis, no political faction or party had ever identified the SME sector, either at the employer or the employee levels, as an attractive constituency. The societal influence of small entrepreneurs is normally associated with a strong middle class, which has remained a rather limited phenomenon outside the Greater Bangkok Region in the case of Thailand, and also when compared to other emerging economies such as Korea and especially Taiwan. In many ways, Thai society remains bipolar, with a narrow middle.

Notes

[1] Chan Huan Chiang (1999), *Government Intervention and Small-Scale Industries: Theoretical Implications*, University Sains Malaysia, International Conference on SMEs at New Crossroads, Paper, Penang, 28-30 September.

[2] Yoshino, M. (1976), *Japan's Multinational Enterprises*, Harvard University Press, Cambridge, p. 72.

[3] SIFC was established in 1992 after the merger of the SME finance departments of the Ministry of Industry and of the Industrial Finance Corporation of Thailand.

[4] Singapore is primarily dominated by transnational corporations compared to the other newly industrializing countries and emerging economies of the region. However, a first SME Master Plan was introduced in the aftermath of the 1984-1985 brief recession ever experienced by the small island republic. This policy has been expanded consistently and the Singaporean Government has the ambition to double the number of manufacturing SMEs in 2000-2005.

6 Thai SMEs and Structural Adjustment Policy (1997-1999)

Since late 1998, the Thai Government has given the impression of assigning more importance to the promotion of the SME sector, with the expectation that it can make a positive contribution to sustainable growth recovery. For the first time in Thai modern economic history, a package of rather ambitious policy measures and related support mechanisms has been formulated in favour of SME creation and development. On January 12th, 2000, an SME Promotion Bill was adopted just one year after it was proposed by the Thai Cabinet.

SMEs in Distress but Absent from the Emergency Rescue Agenda (1997-1998)

It is symptomatic to note that under the original 8th National Economic and Social Development Plan (1997-2001), the SME issue was hardly mentioned. There was only one minor item recommending the promotion of an SME industrial estate on the East Coast.[1]

During the first phase of the crisis between mid-1997 and mid-1998, the importance of the SME sector was recognized only on paper, under the revisions to the 8th National and Economic and Social Development Plan, and more specifically the National Industrial Restructuring Plan to be coordinated by the Ministry of Industry.[2] In the planning document titled *'Strategies for Incubation and Strengthening of SMEs under the Five Year IRP 1998-2000'*, a new SME strategy is supposed to target:

1. Development of an enterprise culture.
2. Promotion of industry associations and business linkages.
3. Delivery of various incentives and access facilitation to financial services.
4. Reform and efficiency of the Small Industry Finance Corporation (SIFC).
5. Access facilitation to technical assistance and business services.

6. Development and strengthening of public organizations and SME development agencies.

This strategy includes some innovations departing from the usual Thai public policy context. On the one hand, it implies the delivery of business development services by associations of enterprises and through private sector linkages, provided that such private institutions not only exist, but can also effectively deliver. However, on the other hand, some debatable reinforcement of state agencies and the setting up of new organizations are also suggested, which are contradictory to the so-called official policy calling for 'less government' and 'more private sector empowerment'.[3]

Beyond such contradictions, which may reflect the absence of consensual viewpoints within the bureaucracy, it must be strongly underlined that the fate of local SMEs did not interest the Thai elite and did not become an issue at all during the first twelve months of the crisis. A number of conjuncture and structural reasons were possibly behind this sad reality, but do not necessarily excuse it.

From the shock of July 1997 onward, the Thai government was entirely occupied together with the IMF in designing and implementing a first rescue package to restore macro-financial stability and credibility as soon as possible. On this front, the adjustment policies have proven to be rather effective, as can be seen from the rapid stabilization of the national currency. They have provided the bases for a business environment moving from the worst to the better, mainly to ease the poor performance of Thai and foreign large firms operating in manufacturing or services, both domestically and internationally. Positive medium-term spillover effects were also expected in 1999-2000, and were correctly anticipated at least to a certain extent as discussed in the Conclusive Chapter.

Consequently, industrial policy at large and SME-focused measures in particular have not been at the top of the agenda, first of all due to the pure financial nature of the crisis affecting the traditional emphasis on large enterprise development. The distress of the non-financial corporate sector, especially manufacturing SMEs, remained in 1998 totally neglected by the two major fire brigades, namely the Ministry of Finance and the Bank of Thailand. Due to such lack of interest and also due to the absence of monitoring data, the capacity of local SMEs to withstand the crisis has been totally out of top decision-makers' sight. There was, however, a strong controverted policy debate in 1998 on how to save the real sector instead of concentrating on the financial sector.

In addition, as illustrated in detail in Part I of this book, the initial restrictive adjustment policy prescribed by the IMF may well have amplified the financial distress of local SMEs. The late 1997 raise of taxes and interest rates to discourage consumer purchases and provide a budget surplus have certainly aggravated the slump in domestic demand and the credit crunch.

The sudden burst and magnitude of the financial crisis has obviously taken the Thai authorities by surprise. But the nature and content of their immediate reactions met the preoccupations of the international and domestic financial community, with the blessing of the IMF and the United States in particular. SMEs, representing the overwhelming majority of existing firms, were left on their own to face the depression. No timely assistance of any kind was provided to rescue–at least temporarily–those going bankrupt or interrupting production from one day to the next. The explosion of unemployment was left to start, unchecked, early as January 1998.

The Rationale and Implementation of a New SME Policy

In the course of 1998, the adjustment policy considerably shifted, thanks to strong international lobbying and the recognition by the IMF of the too restrictive nature of its initial prescriptions. It was realized that not only financial market liberalization weaknesses, but also structural corporate problems were behind the crisis. The SME sector was apparently not forgotten in the series of economic and financial stimulation packages delivered by the government in 1999.

The Rationale

A combination of internal and external considerations may have contributed to this new policy trend.

Domestically, the multiplication of businesses' drastic downsizing or bankruptcy and the very rapid rise of unemployment during the first quarter of 1998 have been mainly attributed to the badly hit SMEs, in comparison to large firms. Within the ruling democratic coalition, but especially among the opposition (notably the Thai Rak Thai Party), the SME distress has been identified as a sensitive political issue, able to hurt or pay off in the context of upper house and lower house elections due in the year 2000. Prime Minister Chuan Leekpai's Cabinet has been criticized for pouring help into the financial institutions at the expense of the real industrial sector, including SMEs and the millions of unemployed. The fragile and slow pace of economic recovery has increased tensions both within and outside the ruling coalition, contributing to the erosion of urban middle class confidence and the possible lack of support from the rural hinterland, which accounts for the majority of the workforce and voters.

Externally, international financial assistance has also started to target the SME sector in Thailand. The initiative has not come from the IMF or the World Bank, which have continued to work primarily at the macro-policy level, but from the number one bilateral donor, namely Japan. Following a visit by the Thai Prime Minister to Tokyo in October, a first so-called Miyazawa Loan Facility of US$2.35 billion was announced on December 16th, 1998. It was expected to become operational in March 1999 as part of a US$30 billion regional recovery plan proposed by Japan.[4]

Under the Miyazawa Facility, half of total funding should be devoted to the stimulation of investment and job creation, notably in the SME sector. Such aid from Japan is not a pure act of philanthropy. Regarding the weight of Japanese multinational corporations and related supporting SMEs in key sectors of the Thai economy such as automotive and electronics, there is little wonder why SME suppliers and subcontractors among other SMEs stand rather high on the Japanese cooperation agenda. As a matter of fact, the announcement of the so-called Miyazawa Plan for Thailand has been very timely. Internationally, it has come as a micro-policy supplement to the criticized IMF adjustment macro-policy. The Japanese have kept a lasting memory of the USA and IMF refusing, one year earlier, their anti-crisis proposal to set up an Asian Monetary Fund.

Internally, international finance assistance met some of the Thai Cabinet's preoccupations in a pre-election context. It served as a counter-offensive instrument vis-à-vis some aggressive politicians of the opposition responsible for the early crisis mismanagement in mid-1997. There is little doubt that Japan has been supporting the current democratic government more than any previous semi-authoritarian one in the recent past.

Would it be exaggerating to suggest that the new Thai SME policy has been suddenly designed thanks to Japanese financial aid? It is unrealistic to believe that the announcement of the Miyazawa Plan and the Thai SME Policy in late 1998 were just pure coincidence. The tradition and size of Japanese aid and business influence should not be underestimated in Thailand. The Japanese dual industrial model and the role of its SME sector both at home and overseas have regained attention among the Thai senior technocrats addressing Thailand's competitiveness challenges beyond the East Asian crisis and into the 21st century.

The Implementation

Despite the obvious influence of external partners, such as Japan, credit must be given to the current administration, particularly to Industry Minister Suwat Liptapanlop and his team at the Department of Industrial Promotion (DIP), for having tried to use the crisis to create fresh ideas, such as a new SME strategy. It is also suggested in Chapter 7 that there are political motives behind such moves.

Thanks to DIP Director General Manu Leopairote, promoted as Permanent Secretary of the Ministry of Industry in October 1999, the New SME Policy is significant in view of its convergence with the prevailing opinions of international SME experts. With the help of a Joint Public and Private Sector Consultative Committee, which should lead to the creation of a centralized pluralistic policy-making body, it seeks to create public-private partnerships with more co-decision making for planning, implementing, monitoring and evaluating SME development programs (Leopairote, 1999).

This concept was formally endorsed on December 22nd, 1998, when the Cabinet approved in principle and for the first time the draft of a SME Promotion Bill proposed by the Ministry of Industry.[5] An SME Promotion Committee, chaired by the Prime Minister and co-chaired by the Ministers of Commerce and Industry, was set up to consult several ministries (Agriculture, Commerce, Finance, Industry), specialized agencies and the private sector. At the same time, with the back up of the Miyazawa Plan, a first financial package of BHT 35 billion (about US$945 million) was announced to facilitate the financing of SMEs through the existing specialized financial institutions. An additional BHT 5 billion (US$ 132 million) and BHT 2.1 billion have also been allocated to support the drafting of a so-called SME Master Plan and the establishment of an institute for SME development (ISMED).

Due to the need for several legislative readings, it was expected that the SME Promotion Bill would have been promulgated by the end of 1999, but it was delayed until January 2000 due to a motion of censure right before Christmas. In the meantime, the SME Master Plan was drafted during the first semester of 1999, with considerable advisory inputs from Japanese specialists. After the adoption of the SME Promotion Bill, the Draft SME Master Plan is supposed to be used as a working document by a newly established SME Promotion Office responsible for revising the definition of SMEs and for formulating a final SME Promotion Action Plan.

The global objective is ambitious, if realistic at all, as it aimed in 1999-2000 alone to support 8,400 existing SMEs and train 24,000 new entrepreneurs. A few positive and rapid implementation signals were given with the creation of ISMED in June 1999, and the creation of decentralized SME Financial Advisory Centres in October.[6] The first stimulation package of March 30th, 1999 did not target the SME sector in particular. But the second one adopted on August 10th, 1999 has been aimed at encouraging private investment. Among four priorities, one targets financial measures in favour of SMEs. It involves tariff reductions on imported raw materials and machinery. It also includes a proposal for three capital venture funds to be set up by the end of 1999.

A Critical Assessment of the New SME Policy (1999-2004)

An Ambitious but Comprehensive Master Plan

The Draft SME Master Plan has been mainly formulated by the Department of Industrial Promotion with some Japanese technical assistance led by Mr.

Shiro Mizutani, an ex-senior official of the powerful Ministry of International Trade and Industry (MITI), who has been appointed as SME senior advisor to both the Thai Ministry of Finance and the Ministry of Industry.

The plan is subdivided into a number of strategies and specific instrument recommendations, with some indications for implementing public/private agencies on the one hand, and supporting ones on the other.

Six core strategies are envisaged, but it would be too tedious for the reader to present them here in detail. They are titled as follows:

1. Strengthening Financial Support to SMEs (Strategy S1).
2. Upgrading Technology and Management Capability of SMEs (Strategy S2).
3. Development of SME Human Resources (Strategy S3).
4. Securing Markets for SMEs (Strategy S4).
5. Improvement of Business Environment for SMEs (Strategy S5).
6. Promotion of Supporting Industries and Industrial Linkages (Strategy S6).

Strategy S1 In 1999, some initial implementation moves have been taken under S1. Such focus has been a matter of urgency due to the so-called SME credit crunch still prevailing in the local banking system, and also considering the obligation for the Thai authorities to utilize within the 1999 fiscal year the short term funding made available under the Miyazawa Plan. The two economic stimulation packages announced by the Cabinet in March and August 1999 included some financial provisions targeting the SME sector such as the delivery of specific credit lines under existing state institutions, the establishment of SME equity funds and venture capital, and the setting up of SME financial advisory services.

Strategy S5 Some other concrete measures have been adopted in relation to S5, such as the reduction of the VAT tax from 10 per cent to 7 per cent (March 1999) and the reduction of import tariff barriers on various raw materials and parts utilized by local firms (August 1999), SMEs in particular.

Strategies S2 and S3 A few more initiatives have also been taken under S2 and S3 with the creation of new research and training institutions such as ISMED (Institute for SME Development) and the Automotive and Electronics Institutes.

Strategy S6 Under S6, The Board of Investment could further develop its BUILD industrial linkage program between large manufacturers and supporting SMEs in the same two sectors.

The Innovative and Strongest Aspects of the SME Master Plan

At the macro-level, in addition to newly desired public/private cooperation, several other innovative and strong aspects of the plan are:

- a declared intention to clarify objectives, to select instruments for action and channels for operational implementation, and (what is totally new in the Thai context) to monitor and evaluate both the effectiveness of the delivered assistance and its real impact on those targeted SMEs;
- a declared intention to set up an autonomous SME Promotion Office in charge of the overall coordination of SME policies; this office would probably take over some of the current activities of the Department of Industrial Promotion (DIP) under the Ministry of Industry;
- a declared intention to decentralize the current bureaucratic system in charge of enterprise and SME promotion; for instance, the DIP Industrial Productivity Division has been transformed into a private and consultancy body: the Foundation of Thailand Productivity Institute (FTIP); the Thailand Textile Institute and the National Food Institute have been invited to adopt a state enterprise management profile;
- a declared intention to decentralize SME promotion and coordination decision-making in favour of local governments (tambon administrations) and to network with local entrepreneurs, relevant NGOs and non profit organizations in charge of community and local development.

At the micro-level, a few interesting aspects of the SME Master Plan merit mentioning such as:

1. Establishment of an SME equity participation system under S1.
2. Establishment of an SME factory evaluation system and the introduction of an SME technical guidance system under S2.
3. Establishment of certified skill-standards in cooperation with the private sector under S3.
4. Promotion of supporting industries under S6.

Strategy S1 Under S1, some innovative financial instruments are supposed to materialize.

First, at the beginning of 1999, the upper-size segment of SMEs (between BHT 40 and 100 million in registered capital) was invited to be listed on a new trading board to be established by the Stock Exchange of Thailand. The newly listed SMEs were promised total exemption from capital gains tax.[7]

Second, two venture capital funds were announced as part of the stimulation package of August 1999. A Thailand Recovery Fund, targeting medium-sized firms with initial capital of US$100 million, is to be set up with the support of the Asian Development Bank and possibly Japanese bilateral aid. Another SME investment fund will be started by the Ministry of Industry with a 10-year closed-end capital of US$35 million, including a possible contribution of US$15 million by the Bank of Taiwan.[8]

Thirdly, a SME Financial Advisory Centre (SFAC) started operation in October 1999 to tackle SME non-performing loans, which are not being cleared rapidly enough according to the Corporate Debts Restructuring Advisory Committee.[9] Ten provincial advisory offices will gradually be opened with a budget of about US$3 million. During its first month of operation, SFAC received 422 SME inquiries and pursued 125 deeper consultations among them.

The Ministry of Industry has also been studying ways to increase the lending capacity of the Small Industry Finance Corporation (SIFC) through soft loans secured by the Ministry of Finance. However, the performance of SIFC has been criticized in various circles, considering that it has only one office in Bangkok and has been able to lend over BHT 3 billion so far against an annual target of BHT 10 billion.[10] In December 1999, the Asian

Table 6.1 Lending to SMEs by State Financial Institutions (1999)

Institution	Lending Line	Total (m)	No. clients	Type of Credit
Industrial Finance Corporation	up to BHT 100m	12,000	506	general
Small Industry Finance Corp.	0.5-25m	3,000	600	export community industries
BAAC	up to 5m	2,000	10,000	agriculture
Government Savings Bank	0.2-10m	1,000	433	general
Export-Import Bank	No limit	5,000	115	export
Bank of Thailand	up to 100m	12,000	1,733	general
SICGC	Guarantees up to 10m	500	300	general
TOTAL		35,500	13,687	

Source: Bank of Thailand, 1999; Bank of Agriculture and Agricultural Cooperatives (BAAC); Small Industry Credit Guarantee Corporation (SICGC)

Development Bank and the Thai government have agreed that both SIFC and SICGC should be–among other public specialized financial institutions–completely reorganized. Restructuring work should start in May 2000.

Strategy S2 Under Strategy S2, the Bureau of Supporting Industry Development (BSID, Ministry of Industry) and the Thai Productivity Institute together with the Technology Promotion Association of Japan were appointed in March 1999 to launch an SME management and technology evaluation scheme in order to boost competitiveness and productivity of about 2,000 selected SMEs.

An SME monitoring and training system (providing training for SME evaluators) should be implemented, and a register of certified SMEs gradually developed in 2000-2004. The monitoring component should facilitate the access of promising SMEs to external capital sources based on each SME's performance records well documented by skilled evaluators.

In addition, technical guidance and total quality management (TQM) should be provided by rotating teams of highly experienced professionals dispatched to the targeted SMEs. The type of TQM concept prevailing in Japan and other OECD economies does not necessarily match the business culture and customs of Thailand, especially among small firms. Therefore, it is not expected to take root in its imported form, but a Thai system of TQM has to be derived from regular SME monitoring and evaluation standards.

Strategy S3 Under Strategy S3, a certified skill-standard had been already proposed by the Japanese cooperation in 1995 in order to promote vocational training in Thailand. The concept re-introduced in 1999 is to outsource official skill certification to the private sector, in particular to training programs made available at large corporations, including TNCs and their local subsidiaries.

Strategy S4 Behind Strategy S4 lays the obvious need to improve the quality of most SME products up to international standards. Voluntary or compulsory standards in use in Thailand are not yet fully harmonized with international requirements, especially new norms like ISO 9000 and ISO 14000. Thailand has not invested enough in an appropriate laboratory infrastructure for accredited testing and calibration in spite of significant inputs by foreign inspection firms such as French Veritas or Swiss SGS. Eleven major international and local certification bodies are registered, but their capacity and outreach are still far too limited. Local SMEs are notably weak in production planning, quality management, processed control systems, and corrective and preventive action.[11]

Strategy S6 The promotion of supporting industries is nothing new in Thailand, but under Strategy S6 it gains further importance as indicated in Chapter 4. This phenomenon is linked to the emergence of global competition among the supporting industries of Japan, USA and Western Europe and their worldwide investment strategy to synchronize the local production needs of the final automotive and electronic assemblers.

The Possible Weaknesses of the SME Master Plan

The absence of any emergency plan to rescue the hard-hit SMEs in late 1997/early 1998, and the slow drafting in 1999 of the SME Promotion Bill and Master Plan have to be criticized. After the adoption of the SME Promotion Bill early 2000, there is still a long bureaucratic road before concrete action is not only implemented but also felt by potential recipients throughout the country. No wonder most of the interviewed small entrepreneurs continue to distrust government policy.

Is the Chuan administration genuinely interested in SMEs? The answer is most probably negative, except for a few leading personalities at the Prime Minister's Office and mainly at the Ministry of Industry (Sevilla, 2000). SME employers and independent observers go as far as suspecting that the new SME policy is little more than political rhetoric and lip-service to gain votes in the next election. This view is perhaps extreme, but yet prevailing. For the moment, the SME policy is used at least as a vocal tactic to speed up corporate debt and non-performing loan restructuring among all categories of firms, including SMEs.

Macro-level criticism The most striking observation is that the Ministry of Industry is almost exclusively the sole agent to be responsible for SME development. Of course, under the Master Plan the MoI will coordinate with other public and private institutions, but it is quite revealing that no other major government agency shares the SME promotion responsibility.

Looking at the draft of the SME Master Plan from a macro-perspective, there is some obvious complacency with the general discourse of good economic governance replicated at the new SME policy level. The draft text is meant to please bilateral and international donors coming to the rescue of the kingdom since July 1997, but some question marks remain. For example, the call for OECD-inspired and public-private partnership targeting SME promotion sounds fine on paper. However, one wonders how it can operate in the Thai context of business and politics, and whether it will really benefit SMEs. This point is further developed in the Conclusive Chapter.

Another illustration refers to the striking similarity between the key concepts of the draft plan and the Japanese SME development experience during the last decades. Today, some aspects of the so-called Japanese industrialization model may be less appealing,[12] but no bilateral or multilateral donor besides Japan has invested so much in Thai supporting SMEs. The Japanese private sector seems determined to continue to do so for the obvious reason of economic self-interest.

Micro-level criticism Some other weaknesses of the Draft SME Master Plan lie in the omission or negligence of several crucial micro-issues.

First, the promoters of the plan do not seem to have conducted any critical review of the myths and realities of SME promotion. Let us take a simple example. They have wisely revised the definition of Thai SMEs to match the international standard definition (by number of employees and, when available, by corporate fixed assets). But they have not addressed how fixed assets can be measured, when Thai SMEs–and especially small ones or supposed small ones–are not even obliged to properly register their paid-up capital.

More troublesome, they have not reflected, at least in the text of the draft plan, on the newly emerging features of 21st century SMEs. The new policy seems completely indifferent to issues of SME ownership, which are yet so crucial to anticipate possible dynamics in local versus foreign entrepreneurship capacity and to identify various paths of capital mobilization. The evolution of SMEs in sole ownership, the management of family businesses and their succession, their formal and informal financial links with large domestic and/or foreign investors are surprisingly not addressed.

In the field of new technologies and services in particular, more and more SMEs will be able to remain physically small in terms of occupational space, number of employees and declared minimum capital. However, these indicators may hide rapid growth of turnover and high returns on investment, as well as dense networks of external collaboration and subcontracting, and sometimes even strong potential to be listed on the stock exchange. In the case of Thailand, the local press reports about the very recent emergence of a few such SMEs in E-commerce for example. Gradually, especially through extensive regional and global networks among oversea Chinese entrepreneurs, a new generation of SMEs is expected to develop and differ from the classical profile of SMEs which both government and large firms have been used to in the past. It should be the responsibility of SME promotion planners, in Thailand as everywhere else, to anticipate such evolutions.

Second, the envisaged range of SME development services is rather comprehensive under the draft plan, but it is exclusively 'supply-driven' based on a 'government knows best' attitude. The demand side and its tentative assessment are totally neglected, and no precise manufacturing sector or sub-sector is targeted.[13] This is not too surprising, when the operational arm of the Ministry of Industry is believed to have direct access to only 3 to 4 per cent of all manufacturing SMEs.[14] Believe it or not, the draft plan does not contain one single word on the thousands of SMEs having gone bankrupt or stopped production in 1998-1999. It also does not anticipate the possible implications on market structure and competition, both domestically and possibly externally.

Thirdly, despite criticism expressed at the highest level by the World Bank and by the Japanese cooperation, the draft plan does not contain a single concrete proposal for building a coordinated and sustainable SME information system, including a data bank tracing SMEs' life and death cycles. How can such an indispensable instrument be totally ignored when drafting the very first SME Master Plan for Thailand? What kind of credibility can such a Draft Master Plan achieve even before its legislative adoption and final publication in the year 2000? As stressed in Chapter 2, some of the most basic indicators are simply not available, like the SME contribution to total manufacturing and exports, sector by sector, and even more interestingly at the sub-sector and product levels. In 1987-1988, an UNIDO textile mission already noted that the lack of information was so great that the Ministry of Industry was subject to manipulation by rent-seekers.[15]

Furthermore, the draft plan does not cover any sensitive issues. The registration, taxation and red tape climate for SMEs is not mentioned. Nor is the access to non-banking or informal sources of finance for SMEs, which is yet so crucial for a great number of them. The necessary reform of SME-oriented state banking and credit guarantee institutions is hardly mentioned because their selective recapitalization or closure is controversial and unsettled. When it comes to the lending versus non-lending responsibilities of commercial banks vis-à-vis SMEs during the whole duration of the crisis, there is an embarrassing silence.

Finally, the draft plan obliterates some other crucial subjects, though they are among the first chapters of any textbook dealing with entrepreneurship.

For instance, rather ambitious entrepreneurial incubation programs are proposed such as the training of existing entrepreneurs and training of new ones. But there is not a single mention of the cultural and family background of Thai entrepreneurs, of their educational and professional profiles, of their networking attitudes and behaviours, and which aspects should be promoted.

Another example relates to the promotion of a more efficient vocational training system, which is recognized as a major human resource development problem in Thailand. However, the draft plan does not discuss the fundamental adjustment linkages between production and on-the-job training on the one hand, and between vocational training and more classical technical education on the other. This is particularly astonishing not only from a conceptual point of view, but also in relation to the ongoing controversial reform of the whole educational system and the gradual privatization of higher education, partly imposed by the World Bank and the Asian Development Bank since the beginning of the crisis.

Dual educational and vocational systems as experienced in some OECD countries are not envisaged, even though these countries already provide some SME training assistance to Thailand. This is the case, for example, since 1996 of the German development cooperation (GTZ Agency) and the Department of Industrial Promotion (Ministry of Industry), which have trained or retrained more than 4000 small entrepreneurs so far. On-the-job training, and not even vocational training in the proper sense, may be particularly strategic in some key labour intensive industries such as textiles and garments, leather and footwear, wood and furniture, which essentially involve micro and small firms in Thailand. However, as stated by the ILO in 1999, this category of SMEs is more or less ignored by the draft plan.

Review of Proposed Micro-Strategies

Turning to the micro-level strategies as drafted so far under the SME Master Plan, a number of points should be discussed by both the local business and scientific communities. But so far, the whole plan has not attracted much attention outside government circles. And there is not one single full time academic position specializing in small enterprise economics and management at the two most prestigious universities in Bangkok.

Strategy S1 (Strengthening of SMEs financing) This strategy, conceived as the first ranking priority in the draft plan assumes that the number one problem of SMEs is finance.

This argument may have been reinforced by the pure financial nature of the East Asian crisis at its beginning, by the prevailing debate of a so-called credit crunch in the case of Thailand, and also by the leading role of financial powerhouses such as the Ministry of Finance and the Bank of Thailand throughout the entire duration of the crisis. However, most international SME specialists advocate that financial capacity is not the driving engine of small entrepreneurship dynamics. It is rarely the central preoccupation of small entrepreneurs, paradoxically both in developing and developed nations, and in more or less risky business environments as well. Even in the case of a sudden crisis, Chapter 3 has shown that Thai SMEs have been primarily affected by a decline of domestic demand, which has only indirectly produced working capital problems for those purely domestic market-oriented SMEs. In general, the financial situation has been highly contrasted among SMEs, a relative number of firms having performed even better than before July 1997.

Nevertheless, some structural financial difficulties could delay the implementation of the SME Master Plan in the year 2000.

First, the proposed restructuring of banking support and credit guarantees in favour of SMEs is far from convincing. Re-capitalization is supposed to take place at various state institutions such as the Small Industry Finance Corporation (SIFC) and the Small Industry Credit Guarantee Corporation (SICGC), but some of them have been so inefficient in the past that they could or should be downsized or simply suppressed.

For instance, the Thai Textile Association complained in September 1999 that most of its SME members could not get access to the new machinery preferential loan scheme set up by SIFC together with the Export-Import Bank.[16] During our own interviews, some SME entrepreneurs complained that SIFC would charge interest rates above market level, when the opposite was expected under existing state regulations.

Therefore, the announcement on December 21st, 1999 by the Thai Cabinet together with the Asian Development Bank of a project titled 'Restructuring of Specialized Financial Institutions' came as little surprise. Restructuring is supposed to start in May 2000 and both SIFC and SICGC are among the four targeted institutions. The objective is to clarify appropriate institutional mechanism and strategies for SME financing. SME corporate governance framework and the redefinition of the role of the public financial sector in particular will be looked after.

Second, the low credibility of banks and guarantee institutions has not been affected only by their own self-imposed credit crunch. Until the anti-government censure motion in December 1999, persistent allegations of state banking mismanagement and possible corruption circulated, particularly against Krung Thai Bank, and indirectly its former president, Finance Minister Tarrin Nimmanahaeminda's own brother.

Thirdly, the opening of a second or so-called alternative board on the Stock Exchange of Thailand (SET) was a complete failure in 1999.[17] About 68 SMEs had originally expressed their interest. But before final selection and in order to attract investors, these SMEs were required to meet the same standards in reporting their performance to SET, including reporting transparent balance sheet information, as companies listed on the main board. In the end, not one single SME agreed to meet such criteria. This has come as a severe blow to SET and financial regulators, who have neglected to accommodate the local SME business and financial culture, and who have overnight expected high accountability of family-run enterprises.

Fourthly, since October 1999, the creation of decentralized SME financial advisory services has encountered some problems. Their concentration on SME non-performing loans can be understood as a tool to accelerate the cleaning up of the banking system, but has not been conceived within the wider multidisciplinary objective of revitalizing the SME sector. The need for such services is far from clear considering the fragmentation of financial institutions already in existence, including those mentioned above which are supposed to deal with SMEs. Their location at provincial universities (Departments or Faculties of Accounting, Commerce, and Management) is also questionable. It is feared that political patronage may interfere with the selection of sites and personnel, just as in the case of ISMED a few months earlier.

Strategy S2 (Upgrading of Managerial and Technological Capability) The most serious vulnerability contained in S2 relates to the government's intention to support entrepreneurial incubation packages, in other words to assist potential entrepreneurs in starting their own business.

First, the target group remains extremely vague ('people who intend to start a new enterprise'). Second, incubation-training programs are difficult to tailor, require costly inputs with very low return on investment, and do not often produce tangible results. Thirdly, such programs can hardly perform well when handled by public bodies alone like the Small Industry Finance Corporation (SIFC) together with other institutions, which either do not exist yet (such as SME venture capital funds), or have no record (such as the recently created ISMED). One real source of entrepreneurship should be the established private sector in Thailand. Forty to 70 per cent of new entrepreneurs–depending in which sector or sub-sector–have previous professional exposure in existing SMEs or large firms (see also Chapter 1).

Another concern is related to the rather vague concept of enhancing technology transfer from large firms to SMEs. According to the Japanese consultants behind the draft plan, promotion here will focus on the automotive and electronic sectors, and more specifically the so-called supporting industries. This is nothing but a repetition of previous industrial strategies to attract some foreign/mainly Japanese direct investment having such industrial linkage characteristics. As a matter of fact, the automotive giant Toyota has confirmed during the third quarter of 1999 that Thailand will become its major production hub in developing Asia.

Chapter 4 has underlined that supporting industries are mainly FDI-driven and should be distinguished from pure local SMEs facing difficulties to attract technology transfer and to adopt international best production practices. Therefore, once again, the Thai government is suspected of promoting not so much small industrialists but large domestic business groups to venture with foreign supporting industries and capture high tech components and parts assembling expertise.

A 1998 survey has estimated that only 8 per cent of all SMEs had received support from the Board of Investment (BOI) since the beginning of the crisis.[18] Only 500 SMEs have been registered so far under the BUILD program of the BOI promoting close linkages with large manufacturers.[19] Apart from the BOI, most state agencies do not seem preoccupied by the growing market entry barriers separating transnational corporations (TNCs) from local enterprises, SMEs in particular. Both demand and supply-linkages commanded by TNCs should be effectively considered in terms of economic and employment spillover effects. Such flows of outsourcing may increasingly affect local market competition and the adaptability or resilience of local economic agents vis-a-vis external forces.

A final observation is that technology is not the monopoly of large firms. However, the draft plan does not include any provision regarding innovating SMEs. Large firms may have a disincentive to invest in radical innovation due to gradual obsolescence of their central competencies. Some SMEs can concentrate on their flexible and niche abilities to match technology with specific customer's requirements. The strategy of the most advanced SMEs is systematically to upgrade their products and after-sales services from the feedback provided by their clients.

Strategy S3 (Development of Human Resources for SMEs) The formulation of this strategy raises a first question related to ISMED. The Institute for SME Development (ISMED), created in June 1999 after the model of the Japanese Institute for Small Business Management and Technology Institute (JSBC), has not started its activities on the right foot.

There is not so much controversy about either its functions of initiating and coordinating SME grassroots training activities all over the country, or its transitory location at the Department of Industrial Promotion (Ministry of Industry). However, the structure of ISMED seems less ideal. Reliance on a dozen universities and on individual academics to activate SME information networks and training may not be the most optimal way since academics are not primary stakeholders (Sevilla, 2000). The initial budget of ISMED was also generous, thanks to Miyazawa Plan funding, but local or provincial constituencies of SMEs were assigned to universities, where professors did not even know what to advise or teach to them!

There was also a total lack of transparency in the nomination of the first director of ISMED, a lawyer and former Vice Rector of Thammasat University, a person with no background in entrepreneurship and SME experience. In fact, this political appointment was inspired by the Minister of Industry and the Rector of Thammasat. As stated in March 1999, their joint decision was that ISMED would be located at the new Thammasat University Rangsit Campus. The first director of ISMED was chosen because of his business and political connections. Previously, he was in charge of supervising the construction of extensive facilities to host the 1998 Asian Sport Games. It is certainly no accident that these facilities are due to be used by Thammasat University and that the newly-born ISMED should be accommodated at the Rangsit Campus near the International Airport. Whether the first director of ISMED was or was not the right person for the job does not matter any more. He suddenly resigned in November 1999, and the Board of ISMED accepted his departure after only 4 months in office! The Deputy Director General of DIP, and acting Director General, has assumed the interim post while an open and more transparent competition has been organized to select a new director and a deputy director whom were appointed in January 2000.

The concrete activities to be performed by ISMED are still unclear. Together with eight academic centres, it is supposed to extend business development services closer to the location of SMEs throughout the country. So far, a few short SME training sessions have been organized in cooperation with leading faculties of engineering. But, there is no mention of the need for ISMED to coordinate with the newly created sectoral institutes also recommended by the draft plan, namely the automotive, electronics and textiles institutes. Even more embarrassing, there is no close linkage with the SME monitoring system envisaged under Strategy S2, even though monitoring and training could be considered as complementary. Thirdly, concrete channels of communication and funding between ISMED and the private sector are not strongly established, and the Miyazawa Plan's initial support for ISMED may not be renewed in the medium term.

The second critical element to be mentioned under S3 is the low consideration given to the treatment of crisis and post-crisis employment. The SME draft master plan cannot politically state that labour should be left entirely to private forces. But its language remains extremely loose. State intervention should secure appropriate manpower for SMEs, but this task is left to the weak Ministry of Labour and Social Welfare (MoLSW). There is no indication of the types of labour market distortions to be introduced by the state in order to achieve this objective. The need to consult and coordinate with employers and labour unions is not mentioned, although a tripartite approach, mentioned as earlier, should be the top macro-economic principles behind the draft plan.

The MoLSW, and more specifically its Department of Skill Development (DSD), are also named under S3 for promoting the delivery of vocational training (VT) and retraining workers through the implementation of a so-called National Skill Standard Certification Scheme. VT remains a crucial problem in Thailand, which lags behind most other East Asian emerging economies, and the DSD has not been particularly able to remedy the situation during the last two decades. The SME Master Plan would have probably been better inspired to suggest that public institutions (such as MoLSW and MoI) try to work out concrete VT actions together with the private sector concerned, represented for instance by the Federation of Thai Industries (SME Committee). It should also operate some distinctions among various types of training such as on-the-job training, training at the workplace but off the job, and part-time training outside the workplace.

A pragmatic skill certification system could be based on the vast training experience of the private sector, including a number of SMEs, and worked out with some public regulatory agency. Furthermore, S3 should anticipate the effects on VT activities following the diminishing role of the state in higher education and its focus on primary and secondary education in the near future.

Strategy S4 (Securing Markets for SMEs) Behind S4, there is the implicit assumption that the promotion of exporting SMEs should be given the priority. In August 1999, the DPI selected 500 SMEs among 1,008 applicants. They were expected to receive advice for 'quality export' from six different academic and state institutions.[20]

In principle, such a policy sounds like just a continuation of the traditional export–led industrialization followed by Thailand during the 1980s and 1990s. However, most Thai SMEs are primarily domestic-market oriented. They also happen to be the ones, as shown in Chapter 3, which need some temporary assistance to recover from the collapse of demand during the crisis.

Then the next question is why should exporting SMEs be assisted with taxpayer money when at least half of them have been performing better since the devaluation of the baht in July 1997. It would be more sensible to select some promising domestic-oriented SMEs and envisage how they could start to expand overseas. It is recognized that the internationalization of SMEs has to face a number of management constraints, which are rather different from the experience of large firms.

Under S4, it also sounds unrealistic to recommend that some niche markets should be reserved to SMEs exclusively and that some SME products should be preferably purchased by the public sector. First, it would contradict fair and open competition principles. Second, such policies have failed even in heavily SME regulated economies such as South Korea. Thirdly, the feasibility of such a proposal is doubtful in a country like Thailand, which has a rather weak state tradition and is dominated by big corporate interest affiliations.

Strategy S5 (Improvement of Business Environment for SMEs) Here, there is some legitimate preoccupation regarding the challenge of the new information technologies and their networking potentials for Thai SMEs (Hall, 1995). But the creation of an additional body such as an industrial information centre within the DIP (MoI) seems a mere bureaucratic ploy when the MoI is not capable of providing credible, comprehensive and regularly up-dated national SME data.

Strategy S6 (Supporting Industries) During the current post-crisis recovery period, there is an obvious need for Thailand to attract foreign investment even more than in the past, and the Board of Investment (BOI) is putting some emphasis not only on transnational corporations' affiliates but also on their supporting industries. However, as already stated in Part I of this book, this strategy should not result in the neglect of local SMEs. So far, many local ones, even if active in the automotive or electrical/electronic sectors, have never heard of the BUILD program under the BOI, which is supposed to match SME supply and TNC demand.

A strongly foreign direct investment-dependent strategy may also imply that Thailand will not be able to climb up the technological ladder by autonomous–if not indigenous–means, and to develop highly integrated industries such as in Korea or Taiwan. This is perhaps inevitable in several sectors, but is debatable and should be discussed at least openly and democratically.

The rather exclusive promotion of supporting industries in the automotive and electronic sectors may shadow potentials in other sectors or market niches where the structural need for supporting industries is absent or much less apparent. As a matter of fact, Thailand has performed fairly well in agro-food, furniture and jewelry, and could boost skilled sub-sectors in machine-tooling, precision instruments, plastics, and others.

Notes

[1] Mainly supporting SMEs linked to the Japanese automotive industry are located there. According to Toyota (Thailand), about 3000 Japanese technicians lived and worked in this area at the end of 1999.
[2] National Economic and Social Development Board (1999), *Thai Economic Crisis and Direction of the Eighth Plan Revision*, Bangkok.
[3] Allal, M. (1999), *Business Development Services for Micro and Small Enterprises in Thailand*, ILO Office, Bangkok, p. 23.
[4] *Bangkok Post*, 17 December 1998.
[5] *Bangkok Post*, 21-22 December 1998.
[6] *Bangkok Post*, 17 September and 4 October 1999.
[7] *Bangkok Post*, 10 December 1998.
[8] *Asian Wall Street Journal* and *Bangkok Post*, 11 August 1999.
[9] *Bangkok Post*, 1 September 1999.
[10] *Bangkok Post*, 21 May 1999.
[11] Paul, H. and Tritos, L. (1999), *Implementation of ISO 9000 in Thai Manufacturing Industry: A Comparative Study of Large and Small-and-Medium Enterprises*, University Sains Malaysia, Penang, 28-30 September. See also: Mo and other authors (1997), 'Strategy for the Successful Implementation of ISO 9000 in Small and Medium Manufacturers', *The Total Quality Management Magazine*, 1997, vol. 9, no. 2, pp. 135-45.
[12] *Asian Wall Street Journal*, 'Japanese keiretsu supply system model in disarray', 20 October 1999.
[13] Until 1997, the DIP was used to divide manufacturing sectors into three groups. The priority group was composed of food and animal feeds, textile and garments, plastic products, electrical and electronic appliance, auto and auto parts.
[14] ILO (1999).
[15] UNIDO (1992).
[16] *Bangkok Post*, 21 September 1999.
[17] *Asian Wall Street Journal*, 22 June 1999.
[18] *Far Eastern Economic Review*, 20 May 1999, p. 44.
[19] *Bangkok Post*, 16 September 1999.
[20] *Bangkok Post*, 26 August 1999.

7 The Credibility of the New SME Policy

Beyond Political Rhetoric

The new concern for SMEs is a direct result of the crisis, not only in Thailand but all over the region. The Thai government can be praised for having recognized the problem, at least in principle. It remains to be seen how far this general commitment goes, and whether the business community and the existing or potential small entrepreneurs in particular can be convinced that the new SME policy will be implemented and produce tangible results.

Although the state gave the impression of sudden industrial activism in 1998-1999, the first criticism addresses the very concept of state intervention in the SME sphere. As shown in Chapter 6, it has not inspired a coherent and well-focused strategy in a few core fields where the government can effectively mobilize skilled competence and support, either alone or together with the private sector. Instead, the draft text of the SME Master Plan makes a piecemeal and sometimes unrealistic contribution.

As a result, and after the recent adoption of the SME Promotion Bill (January 2000), central administration and provincial bureaucrats could be tempted to implement short-term and even contradictory measures, without being even fully aware of possible counterproductive implications.

There is also a second potential scenario. If economic recovery is around the corner in 2000, and if exports and foreign direct investment resume at pre-crisis levels, another option would be to do nothing at all in favour of the SME sector. SMEs remained a marginal issue during the crisis and could be easily forgotten again during renewed times of growth, whether fragile or not.

The previous chapter has explained that not a single SME initiative was taken before the Japanese Miyazawa Plan pledged financial assistance to Thailand in December 1998. Then, hasty moves were initiated in all directions in order to design an SME strategy to comply with the short-term disbursement requirements of Japanese financial aid. Therefore, some proposed instruments were poorly conceived or did not even match the SME business culture of Thailand, such as the failed attempt to get SMEs listed on the stock exchange in March-April 1999.

In other words, the Thai authorities have not been motivated by a genuinely indigenous and spontaneous commitment towards an SME strategy. The big corporate sector has been tied up with huge debt management problems, while SME entrepreneurs have not been collectively organized to lobby the government. Only Japan, even if only for economic self-interest, was in a position to do so 18 months after the beginning of the Thai crisis. The Industry Minister has proven his ability to exploit not only economically but also politically this Japanese aid opportunity to give himself and his ministerial portfolio some high and popular visibility, while the Prime Minister and especially the Finance Minister have been fully involved in big scale and risky banking and corporate restructuring.

The initial credit policy mistakes combined with the relative neglect of the real economy have extensively contributed to the distress of SMEs becoming a rather prominent issue in the legislative elections due in 2000. Political pressure has even emerged from the New Aspiration Party led by former Prime Minister Chavalit, who, due to his previous record, finds it hard to convince anyone that he and his allies care much for small enterprises and small people in general.

A new opposition party established in July 1998, namely the Thai Rak Thai Party (literally Thai Loves Thai), is apparently more appealing. The concern for SMEs has been placed as one cornerstone of its political strategy, calling for a new competition policy supporting export-oriented SMEs and providing alternative financing options to sprout more home-grown entrepreneurs. Though it may be difficult to use the SME issue to political advantage, TRT's strategy is to bring up new issues, and present them in a new style closer to the preoccupations of the middle class and ordinary people. Nobody knows whether its leader would be truly an agent of change. Thaksin Shinawattra, 49, is not a small entrepreneur but one of the most influential tycoons in the Thai telecommunication industry. He is not a newcomer to Thai crony politics, as he was a former Deputy Prime Minister to Chavalit himself, and held Cabinet posts in three governments between 1994 and 1996 as the leader of the Palang Dharma Party. After prosperous development during ten years of government-protected monopoly, his own firm, Shinawatra Computer, Communication and Satellite Holding Co., suffered apparent stock losses of US$1.5 billion through the crisis. However, Thaksin had well anticipated most of its possible impacts and he then successfully changed the name of his business empire. His style and fresh ideas rank him in the shortlist of a few potential prime ministers belonging to the 'new generation'. But it remains to be seen if SME middle class entrepreneurs can identify themselves with his political constituency in the medium term.[1]

Equally positive but also troublesome for Prime Minister Chuan, the new SME policy has been cleverly used, among other calls for change and reform, as a political tool by Industry Minister Suwat Liptapanlop himself. As Secretary General of the Chart Pattana Party, he is a key element in the ruling coalition, but since 1999 he has been challenging more and more frequently the liberal market 'orthodoxy' of the Premier and some of his closest ministers from the Democratic Party. Born in a Northeast Thailand medium-sized construction business family, Suwat's economic interests have gained in size over the last ten years. The economic and political patronage he received from former MP and army commander Arthit Kamlang-ek, paved the way for his entrance into politics in 1988. Since he became Industry Minister in late 1997, it is widely believed that he has been using the symbolic SME issue and other media tools to meet his own agenda. At 44, he has become a prominent 'new generation' politician and a potential challenger to Thaksin. In late 1999, he sent a few political signals to Premier Chuan that his coalition loyalty may or may not last long after the King's sixth cycle birthday on December 5th. His irrepressible ambitions target the post of the current Chart Pattana Party's leader, Korn Dabaransi, which could then potentially propel him to PM candidacy.[2]

Facing controversies about the economic recovery and various corruption allegations in his close entourage, Prime Minister Chuan has been investing much energy in recent months to maintain the cohesion and integrity of his cabinet, especially in the face of a legislative censure motion in mid-December 1999. In a politically open and free-for-all competition up to the legislative elections in 2000, he has come to realize his own limits in being able to discipline his ministers and subordinates, while the whole economy is far from being fully back on track.

Bureaucratic Hazards

In addition to the loose commitments of both old and younger generation politicians, some bureaucratic hazards may also prevent the SME policy from taking off. This is of particular importance, considering that elected politicians' terms are normally limited, whereas senior civil servants tend to stay.

First, when the government decided at the end of 1998 to restore small business confidence as rapidly as possible, the new SME Promotion Bill was submitted through the normal but lengthy legislative process during 1999. The Bill was finally adopted on January 12th, 2000, but there is a long road to go before concrete action can be initiated and coordinated under the SME Promotion Office to be set up.

Second, Thai bureaucrats are well known for their propensity to reach consensus at the policy planning stage, but for their ineffective and poorly coordinated implementation efforts.

Thirdly, there have been some deadlocks and rivalries within the bureaucracy. This has been particularly true between the Ministry of Finance and the Ministry of Industry for control of the Miyazawa funds put at disposal for an SME strategy. This divide has overlapped with further divergences of views within the Cabinet regarding ways to deal with the crisis. It has poorly augured the ability to coordinate the new SME policy among a rather large number of ministries and state agencies in charge of various economic and social matters. Among them, some specialized financial agencies like SIFC and SICGC will be restructured in 2000-2001 and this could also complicate the SME policy prospects.

Other concerns can be traced such as the frequent struggle between the Ministry of Industry and the Ministry of Commerce, which are usually headed by different political parties. The MoI issues licenses for the creation or the expansion of factories while the MoC gives or denies approval for the importation of machinery. Some conflicts can also occur between ministries and the National Economic and Social Development Board (NESDB).

The matter can be further complicated because a special legislative act is often required for different ministries to share information or to work together on any specific project such as an SME-oriented one. The likely outcome is the over-fragmentation of policy, its lack of integration and focus, and the creation of illusive and face-saving coordinating bodies, often placed under the Prime Minister's Office (such as the newly created SME financial advisory centers). But, from another perspective, it can be argued that the fragmentation of public administration does not lead to one single political faction controlling access to crucial economic decision-making. The fact that the Ministry of Industry and the Ministry of Commerce are generally not controlled by the same political party guarantees that newcomers are not discouraged from entering business sectors and can obtain both factory licenses (MoI) and import permits (MoC).

Fourthly, there has been rising criticism during the second half of 1999 regarding the absence of SME expertise, understanding and good will in the ranks of the civil service, even at top levels and both in Bangkok and provincial capitals. The Ministry of Industry itself is hardly an exception, apart from the Department of Industrial Promotion (DIP). In October 1999, talented DIP Director General Manu Leopairote was promoted to the key post of Permanent Secretary of MoI. In January 2000, his highly competent former Deputy D.G and then acting D.G. Damri Sukhotanang was confirmed to the post of DIP Director General. This tandem of personalities should facilitate the implementation of the newly adopted SME legislation in 2000 and beyond. However, at lower levels within the Ministry and especially in its provincial offices, implementation will be a difficult task.

As stated above, planning can be excellent in Thailand, but concrete implementation is another matter. Then, also for cultural reasons, connections, influence and loyalty remain more important than competence and skills alone.

Fifthly, there is insufficient and especially ineffective decentralization of administrative bodies which tend to be unknown to most local entrepreneurs, even to those located across the street in provincial capital cities. Clear-cut mechanisms for policy implementation are lacking among ministries, provincial and local institutions, quasi-public bodies and commissioned or contracted third party organizations.[3] In many ways, the over-centralized state may have retarded the formation of an independent local capitalist class as well as counterbalancing private sector players able to influence public policy options and their implementation.[4] This further illustrates why SME entrepreneurs and starting-up newcomers do not rely on public inputs and do not expect any concrete support from governmental authorities (see also SME case studies in Chapters 9 and 10).

SMEs and the Real Economy: Facing the Limits of a Fragile Recovery (1999-2000)

As in Korea, Malaysia and Hong Kong, a number of macro-indicators have signaled emerging recovery in Thailand, though less clearly and primarily export-driven. However, the Thai government felt confident enough to announce on September 21st, 1999 that it would not tap the remaining US$3.7 billion of the US$17.2 billion bailout package put together by the IMF two years ago. This was officially confirmed by the IMF and the Thai government on February 8th, 2000.

Growth is expected to be positive again in 1999, between +3.5 and +4 per cent compared to -9.4 per cent in 1998, and overall demand has been improving (between +12 per cent and +14 per cent) after its tremendous collapse during the last two years.[5] Official sources have even stated that growth was close to +8 per cent in the third quarter of 1999, but such a large percentage rise may have been distorted by the low base in 1998. Furthermore, the Governor of the Bank of Thailand himself warns that a growth policy for the pure sake of growth fails to consider the components of growth, and as a result Thailand has plunged already once during the 1990s into the financial excesses that ignited the crisis.[6] The nascent recovery has so far been very uneven among companies and sectors (some have benefited from a stronger baht) and also across the differentiated segments of consumers.[7] Domestic demand remains extremely fragile, and the main concern will continue to focus on non-performing loans, which officially stood at 38.5 per cent of 1999 total credit. The public debt has increased to 48 per cent of GDP (against 15 per cent in 1996), and the budget deficit is already -4.5 per cent of GDP, with a further anticipated rise to -6 per cent in 2000.

On the external front, there are uncertainties in global markets due to shrinking GDP and massive debt in Japan and overheating of the US economy. Observers should not be too impressed by the spectacular growth of Thai exports in 1999. First, it should be compared with a very low base in 1998, and it has not yet come back to the high level of 1996-1997 just before the East Asian crisis. It can also be explained by low prices after the currency devaluation, and especially by price cuts at the expense of margins. Price cutting has been facilitated by the existence of surplus capacity (including inventories) facing collapsed demand, and only 60 per cent of industrial capacity has been used in 1999. This has little to do with efficiency gains, and many Thai exporters will find it more and more difficult to increase external sales once price cuts have been absorbed.

> There is going to be a trend towards higher export prices and declining volumes from the second half of 2000…This year may have lulled people into thinking we are going back to a period of 20 per cent export growth in Asia – that is not going to happen. [8]

This strategy cannot be sustained and is not helping to improve international competitiveness.

The Thai government is expected to keep public budget taps wide open to support recovery until the 2000 elections, but gears will have to be decisively switched at some point to avoid a debt blowout. At the beginning of the year 2000, the highly respected Deputy Prime Minister Supachai Panitchpakdi has declared that:

> It will be difficult to continue deficit spending to stimulate the economy after the September 30 end of the fiscal year because it would cause too much of an increase in public-sector debt. [9]

Weak consumption during the last quarter of 1999 has pushed tax collection below forecasts, and the Ministry of Finance does not quite know how to find money to support the BHT 860 billion in planned state spending over the next 12 months.[10] The burdens of the East Asian crisis will be felt at least until 2001-2002, provided that economic restructuring does not come to a standstill.[11] In February 2000, the IMF has praised the economic recovery but has warned that it is fragile and that reforms should not slow down but speed up.[12]

There are other worrying signals. Flows of hot money have started to come back attracted by the low price of local stocks, whereas longer-term investors are still looking at policy consistency and credibility. Commercial banks overloaded by non-performing loans and conflicts with large credit defaulters such as Thai Petrochemical Industry PCL (US$ 3.5 billion) do not inject new liquidities even in rather promising firms which have to invest to meet tough international competition and re-rising regional demand.

If the Thai government and the financial institutions continue to face some funding constraints in 2000-2001, fund managers will not wait long to pull out, as they did in mid-1997.[13] It is probably too early to celebrate together with Stanley Fischer, the first Deputy Managing Director of the International Monetary Fund, a structural rebound of Thailand and the other East Asian economies. World Bank Senior Vice-President, Joseph Stiglitz, stated in October 1999:

> Just because certain policies have led to recovery does not mean that they were the right remedies, and just because indicators suggest recovery is here does not mean the real economies have rebounded.[14]

As a matter of fact, Thailand and Malaysia have taken a different path of orthodox versus unorthodox policies, with short-term mixed but encouraging results, but very slow or little corporate and governance structural reforms so far. And even when some big or smaller corporations have swallowed the right restructuring medicines, business recovery remains slow as illustrated in the case of the well-known Thai furniture maker Modernform.[15]

In Thailand, there is a rather strong proposition that too much emphasis has been placed on financial restructuring as a prerequisite for economic recovery, considering for instance that Mexico's financial sector remains in a mess five years after the crisis there. In both cases, the stabilization of the national currency and the export sector drive have been major factors in the apparent recovery, but the prevailing pure domestic part of the economy has remained very weak, including most segments of the existing SME population. Misguided policies leading to cutting the flow of credit by the large financial institutions of Thailand in 1997-1999 had and could continue to have negative repercussions on SMEs, the bulk of economic and social life.

The Bank of Thailand estimates that contraction in total domestic credit deepened by at least another - 15 per cent in 1999 despite the continued decline of interest rates, but the Ministry of Finance is still confident that trade surplus, new equity issues and budget deficit will provide enough liquidity to the private sector, which means essentially to large corporations.[16] New equity issues by the non-financial private sector have primarily concentrated on new debt instruments. And state stimulation of demand has been facing two key problems:

- How to revitalize consumption among the middle and working classes?
- How to continue to run a big budget deficit when government revenue is shrinking?

The continued reluctance of Thai commercial banks to extend new loans remains problematic in many ways.[17] According to Capital Nomura Securities in Bangkok, the fourth quarter of 1999 has been the worst for local banks.[18] The corporate sector can only be restructured if it is supported by a strongly liquid banking and capital market system, which has been handicapped by IMF-led restructuring of a cosmetic nature only. Both the government and the banking community try to restore capital ratios by using all kinds of creative debt-off accounting techniques and tricks to mask insolvency and hide the fact that most banks–the largest public one (Krung Thai Bank)–are bankrupt or close to it. The President of Thai Farmers Bank declared in November 1999:

> When we say that bad loans have stabilized, we are talking about net figures. But new bad loans continue to come in. We also have to ask about the quality of debt restructuring to date, and whether restructured loans will turn bad again. [19]

Instead of using credit still being extended in guise of restructuring or rescheduling debts that cannot be paid back anyway, restoring liquidity should be the priority concern to alleviate the 1997-1999 credit crunch that has crippled the corporate sector and killed many local SMEs. An early 2000 Merrill Lynch report analyzing cash flow says that about 60 per cent of indebted firms can be saved but will require BHT 1 trillion at least to stay afloat.[20] So far, lending on that scale is not forthcoming. The Bank of Thailand declared on January 24th, 2000 that the total liabilities of the Financial Institutions Development Fund stood at BHT 1.4 trillion, but that if still needs at least BHT 350 billion to offset FIDF losses. Funding should be given to outstanding or most promising small and large firms so that banks would not have to make new provisions and could count the interest paid as interest earned.[21]

The non-payment culture is quite common and should change. There are many firms operating normally, having revenue, paying expenses and salaries. But they won't pay their creditors a single baht! It is even estimated that 15 to 20 per cent of restructured loans have gone sour again. It is also estimated that many Sino-Thai conglomerates are finished as pure family businesses. A number of them, even when they are able to keep their family business name as under their previous shareholding control, are being forced to turn to more focused activities and to sell non-core assets, primarily to foreigners. Many more have to rebuild their operations from severely diminished levels, and they may have to re-experience business life as small or medium-sized enterprises (Chaipravat and Hoontrakul, 1999). This trend is also related to the frequently raised issue whether the family-based SMEs, their 'minimal' structures, and their personal management and networks are the problem rather than the solution.

The whole problem is therefore far more political than either the government or the current opposition are ready to recognize. The attempts to restructure the non-performing loans, to reschedule debts, eventually to set up asset management instruments and to possibly merge some rotten banks are simply buying time to protect those at top banking and big corporate levels who bore heavy responsibilities before, during and possibly beyond the financial crisis.

There are certainly signals of economic recovery but the central question is how far it is real and sustainable. The American economist Paul Krugman indicates that the fundamentals of the Thai economy have not really improved since 1997. Independent research by the Thailand Development and Research Institute (TDRI) and several state universities tend to confirm this view quite different from the official discourse.[22] The obvious corollary is that it will be difficult for the Thai economy to achieve sustainable growth. The Institute of International Finance (IIF, Washington D.C.) states that 'neither Thailand nor any of the other Asian-crisis victims do a good job of reporting how their external debt is being amortized.' Standard & Poor's Ratings Group adds:

> The test will come in the next crisis where there's bound to be some differentiation between countries whose numbers you believe and those whose numbers you disbelieve. [23]

In its edition of January 26th, 2000, the business section of the Bangkok Post titled 'Many Lessons Remain Unlearned'. It is enough to mention that while a majority of SMEs and households continue to struggle, the gap between national saving and spending is once again starting to widen. By the end of 1999, luxury goods accounted for about 40 per cent of total imports. Looking only at the number of new luxurious cars in the streets of Bangkok, the irony is that there are most probably credit defaulters among their owners!

SME Policy Credibility among the Small Business Community

Though SME policy has been in existence for quite some time in some emerging economies like Korea or Malaysia, local authorities have recognized in recent years that government programs have remained largely unknown to the vast majority of entrepreneurs and that they have not been easily accessible for those few potentially interested to benefit (Abdullah, 1997, 1999).

Considering the rather new character of SME policy in Thailand and also its rather low pre-implementation credibility (see Chapter 6), there is little wonder why most–if not all–SME entrepreneurs express distrust in the current state initiatives. Actually, among many small entrepreneurs interviewed in 1999 by the author, only one had been once approached by a state institution. Most of them have expressed little expectation vis-à-vis the government's ability and willingness to provide real support. Their most frequent answer is a reminder that politics has long been dominated by vested interests, and that SMEs have learnt from the first day of their creation to rely primarily on themselves. Chapter 1 has also shown that not only state agencies, but even private commercial banks are at best a second or third source of capital after family and other sources.

The private sector associations have not been an alternative in providing help or lobbying the public administration. In September 1999, the Federation of Thai Industries (FTI) organized a one-day business seminar titled 'SMEs Supporting Measures: Is the Dream Coming True', which was attended by 3000 participants, primarily unemployed people. FTI Vice-Chairman Kietipong Noichaiboon, who also chairs the FTI SME Development Committee, criticized the Ministry of Finance and the Bank of Thailand for being exclusively preoccupied with the SME non-performing loans, and for not being able to communicate and disseminate proper information about the new SME Master Plan in the making. He also underlined the lack of distinction between short-term and long-term policies, the inability to select the SMEs in real difficulties, and the paradox of using tax-payer money or foreign assistance to grant facilities to a reduced number of best performing SMEs classified as supporting industries. According to him, the state agencies should also reconsider the profile of their SME evaluators and monitoring personnel, who are not trained to understand the nature and characteristics of SMEs. But what he did not say was also interesting. He did not foresee any specific role for FTI, and did not make any comment on the existing and potential contributions of large firms vis-à-vis smaller ones (outsourcing, subcontracting, venturing, etc). FTI is essentially dominated by conglomerates and large corporations, does not represent the SME sector, and functions more like a business club than like a service-oriented organization.

Other associations such as the Thai Bankers Association are even worse. Commercial banks have never cared for real SMEs. SME credit publicity inserted for instance by Thai Farmers Bank on the front page of the Bangkok Post is just there to restore the image of commercial banking. Even at high senior level, local bankers have little knowledge and even commonsense about SME financial and management needs, globally considered as too risky. There is no in-house policy to capitalize on the SME experience and portfolio of corporate banking officers.

In the absence of any representative association of SMEs, the author visited in 1999 some foreign donor agencies in charge of SME promotion programs in Thailand. Though they welcomed, in principle, the government's new interest in the SME sector and the new SME Promotion Bill, they did not identify fresh and genuine ideas in the SME Master Plan. Many did not even have access to the full copy of the text drafted with Japanese assistance.

In brief, they consider that a few senior bureaucrats and politicians are sincere in their desire to assist SMEs in a concrete way. But they have little faith in the capacity to implement an effective and well-coordinated public policy, especially at the provincial level. One simple example: there is still today a delay of about 9 to 18 months to get administrative approval for recruiting a technical consultant supposed to assist a small firm locally on a precise task.

Finally, the multilateral agencies active in Thailand do not have much of an opinion. So far, the IMF, the Asian Development Bank (ADB) and the World Bank have focused all their attention on macro-financial policy and on the restructuring of bad loans. On February 8th, 2000, the IMF has confirmed the end of its task in Thailand, which can start now to pay back the borrowed funds.

As mentioned in Chapter 6, it is only since December 1999 that the ADB has been initiating a reform of the public specialized financial institutions including those in charge of SME credit assistance. It remains to be seen how far re-capitalization and restructuring will be able to go with full Thai political support, and whether all existing institutions will continue to exist in the medium term.

In 1998-1999, the International Labour Organization has also launched a modest UNDP-sponsored survey dealing with the employment contribution of micro- and small enterprises. Its attempt to draw the attention of the local authorities to the importance but current neglect of the so-called informal sector has been so far met with limited success.

Notes

[1] *Far Eastern Economic Review*, 17 June 1999 and 30 December 1999.
[2] *Far Eastern Economic Review*, 16 and 30 September 1999.
[3] White, S. (1999), *Small Business Environment in Thailand*, ILO Office, Working Paper no. 3, Bangkok, pp. 32-3.
[4] Siffin, W. (1966), *The Thai Bureaucracy, Institutional Change and Development*, East West Centre Press, Honolulu.
[5] *Bangkok Post*, 20 December 1999.
[6] Interview of Chatu Mongol Sonakul, *The Nation*, 11 January 2000.
[7] *Bangok Post*, 21 December 1999.

[8] Desmond Supple, Senior Economist (Barclays Capital, Singapore), quoted in *Bangkok Post*, 9 December 1999.
[9] *Asian Wall Street Journal*, 11 January 2000.
[10] *Bangkok Post*, 24 December 1999.
[11] *Far Eastern Economic Review*, 23 December 1999.
[12] *IMF Quarterly Review (Thailand)* and *Bangkok Post*, 12 February 2000.
[13] *Bangkok Post*, 19 November 1999.
[14] Singapore, World Economic Forum Annual Regional Meeting, 18-20 October 1999.
[15] *Far Eastern Economic Review*, 9 December 1999.
[16] *Asian Wall Street Journal*, 20 0ctober 1999 and *Bangkok Post*, 14 January 2000. In November 1999 and January 2000, The Thai Finance Ministry has issued savings bonds for a total amount of BHT 20 billion.
[17] 'In Thailand, high levels of NPLs cast doubt on the strength of the recovery. Market-led financial restructuring effort has been slower to show results than the government-led plans in South Korea and Malaysia. The jury is still out on which strategy will yield the stronger financial system in the long term. In the short term, Thailand's strategy is a drag on growth: Banks remain focused on repairing balance sheets instead of seeking out new lending opportunities.' *Far Eastern Economic Review*, 4 November 1999, p.70.
[18] *Bangkok Post*, 19 January 2000.
[19] Banthoon Lamsam, President of Thai Farmers Bank, *Bangkok Post*, 23 November 1999.
[20] *Far Eastern Economic Review*, 17 February 2000.
[21] *Far Eastern Economic Review*, 14 October 1999.
[22] *The Nation*, 11 January 2000.
[23] *Asian Wall Street Journal*, 10 January 2000.

PART III

THE RESILIENCE OF SMEs LINKED TO FOREIGN FIRMS

8 Linking Local SMEs and Foreign Firms Operating in East Asia

Since the outbreak of the East Asian crisis, the necessity for increased internationalization of the Thai corporate sector, including SMEs, has been extensively discussed and largely recognized by the ruling coalition in order to explore new ways to meet market globalization challenges. The announcement in November 1999 of the forthcoming admission to the World Trade Organization of a giant competitor such as China has put even more pressure on Thai policy makers.

Part I of this book has demonstrated that the exclusively domestic market-oriented SMEs have been the worst hit in Thailand by the crisis, that the number of regionalized and internationalized SMEs is still limited, and that direct linkages between local SMEs and large firms (domestic and foreign) are absent or loose in most cases.

Part II has established that both government policy in the past and the newly envisaged SME Master Plan (2000-2004) have not primarily addressed the SME internationalization issue. It is not even certain that the public sector is well equipped to provide appropriate and effective instruments for this purpose. Data and literature dealing with the internationalization of Thai SMEs is nearly nil, especially in the English language, with the exception of a number of studies exploring the local outsourcing activities of Japanese transnational firms in automotive and electronics. Until 1999, no information had been collected to assess the possible resilience to the crisis of those internationalized SMEs.

This chapter is a first attempt to collect some data on the subject, while the effects of the crisis and the behavioural patterns of foreign firms are still fresh in the memory of small suppliers and subcontractors. The author has explored whether those SMEs linked directly or indirectly to foreign firms have been particularly resilient to the recent crisis. The survey was limited to the exploration of such linkages with OECD corporate affiliates operating in East Asia, including Thailand. It was assumed that they have not been too much affected by the recent crisis precisely because they are linked to global corporations. The survey has been conducted not only in Thailand but also in Korea and Malaysia, due to the fact that these three emerging economies aim to increase their foreign investment linkages in order to speed up their recovery. In addition to this objective, it is desirable for Thailand not only to collect data on the subject but also to be able to compare herself with the SME internationalization trend in competing economies such as Korea or Malaysia.

The Current Debate

As mentioned in its famous World Bank report (1993) on the so-called *'East Asian economic miracle'*, the internationalization of the East Asian emerging economies, including Thailand, was progressing in rather spectacular terms until 1996. However, the degree of global interdependence between such rapid growth and the inflows/outflows of foreign investment have become a very controversial issue since the outbreak of the East Asian financial crisis (UNCTAD, 1997, 1998).

In order to remedy some of the main causes of the crisis, structural corporate and financial reforms have been tentatively and gradually introduced in the most affected economies. They are targeting the necessary reforms of the domestic conglomerates and other big scale enterprises. Whether already widely or less opened to foreign investment before the crisis, those economies need to review the role of foreign direct investment (FDI) as a potentially important contributor to the ongoing restructuring process. In this approach, FDI is envisaged as a strong instrument for globalization of local firms, leading to the possible reduction of corporate and financial vulnerability vis-a-vis fluctuating domestic and regional markets.

The scale and degree of internationalization of the conglomerates and other big firms were widely studied before the crisis, particularly in the four Asian dragons (Korea, Hong Kong, Singapore, Taiwan) and neighbouring economies (such as Indonesia, Malaysia and Thailand). The restructuring contribution of FDI is already being envisaged for a number of large firms in countries such as Korea and Thailand.

On the contrary, in-depth knowledge of the East Asian SME sector remained extremely lacking (except in Japan, Taiwan and Korea) until the crisis. This is also true for the limited number of internationalized SMEs in the East Asian emerging economies (Fujita, 1998; UNCTAD, 1998).

As mentioned in previous sections of this book, existing knowledge on the relationship between local SMEs and foreign investment (FDI in particular) in Thailand and the other East Asian emerging economies remained very limited until the crisis. Even if the domestic and external market scene was primarily dominated by big scale indigeneous and foreign firms, it can be yet assumed that a segment of the existing SMEs were directly or indirectly internationalized, via (if indirectly) various forms of large and/or foreign firm affiliations, until the outbreak of the crisis. Therefore a distinction should be made between the few internationalized SMEs and the vast majority of them that work exclusively for the domestic market and through pure domestic channels. Focusing on the first category of SMEs, a few central questions can be addressed:

- Has foreign investment (FDI in particular) played a role in mitigating the impact of the crisis on Thai and other East Asian SMEs?
- Is it true that those local SMEs having a relationship with foreign affiliates (through subcontracting or other contractual arrangements) have been better able to survive the crisis than the pure domestic-oriented SMEs?

The hypothesis is that the more integrated the local SMEs were vis-a-vis foreign affiliates, the more resilient they were during the recent crisis. This observation, if demonstrated, could be of high value in order to learn from the 1997-1999 experience. In the future, it would encourage further SME internationalization accordingly, in order to improve the position of the SME sector when meeting new market competition, fluctuations and possible downturns. It would also mean that various forms of additional foreign investment would be locally welcomed by both the private and public sectors in order to promote more and more linkages between local SMEs and foreign firms.

Background of the 1999 Survey

The category of SMEs having linkages with foreign firms operating locally or from overseas includes those SMEs that have developed various forms of business links such as contracting or subcontracting (components, parts, intermediary products, etc), especially on the supply side (production and marketing of final products). Such links can go as far as including local SMEs having foreign equity in one form or another together with foreign partners.

This chapter is based on brief SME surveys conducted during the first half of 1999 in Korea, Malaysia and Thailand. As already underlined, there was almost no available data on the subject before those brief surveys were initiated locally.

Korea

In Korea, a sample survey was conducted with the help of Korea University, Seoul, in collaboration with the Korean Chamber of Commerce and Industry (KCCI). A questionnaire was sent to 300 SME members of KCCI. 33 SMEs returned the questionnaire, with most of them having answered all questions. Among the 33 responding SMEs, 16 have had a foreign affiliation of some kind (sub-contract, licensing, daughter company, etc), and 17 SMEs did not have any kind of foreign affiliation.

Malaysia

In Malaysia, the sample survey has been derived from two sources. The first one relies on three national surveys carried out in early and late 1998 and again during the first half of 1999 by the Association of Chinese Chambers of Commerce and Industry of Malaysia (ACCCIM). The second source is based on some direct surveys at SME sites conducted in 1999 with the help of a questionnaire (similar to the one used in Korea) and meant to verify some of the results derived from the ACCCIM surveys mentioned above.

In the ACCCIM surveys, the response was quite satisfactory. In the first two 1998 surveys, 130 and 113 enterprises replied out of a total of 600 questionnaires delivered nationally. In the 1999 survey, 293 replied out of 800 questionnaires. In all three surveys, over two thirds of the respondents were SMEs, defined as enterprises employing not more than 150 workers and having a maximum turnover of RM 25 million (US$ 1 = RM3.7).

Thailand

In Thailand, a sample survey was initially conducted using a similar questionnaire sent to 300 SMEs by the Faculty of Economics (Chulalongkorn University, Bangkok), with the help of the Ministry of Finance. But this first approach failed for several reasons already discussed at length in the first two parts of this book (unreliable ministerial data, inaccuracy of addresses, absence of small entrepreneur's trust in governmental sponsored surveys, etc).

Then, 20 SMEs in three distinct manufacturing sectors having a strong foreign market exposure (textile and garment, electrical and electronic products, automobile parts) were directly surveyed at the SME production site during the first and second quarters of 1999. Among the surveyed SMEs, 13 per cent of them practised some form of subcontracting with foreign affiliates, and a smaller proportion had some minority or majority direct foreign equity participation.

The Investigation

The three surveys were designed to elicit preliminary responses to three central questions, as follows:

- Q1: Have local SMEs with a relatively strong export orientation experienced a weaker decrease of production and sales than SMEs with an exclusive domestic orientation?
- Q2: Have local SMEs linked to foreign firms in various forms such as supplying and subcontracting (exclusive of direct investment and financial equity linkages) been more resilient to the crisis than the vast majority of local SMEs not linked to foreign firms?
- Q3: Have local SMEs linked to FDI and foreign investors' equity participation been particularly resilient to the crisis?

Current State of SME National Data

Local SMEs are expected to have been directly or indirectly affected by the financial crisis in itself and also, during a second phase, by the overall corporate sector restructuring taking place since 1998-1999 (in the cases of Korea and Thailand, but not Malaysia).

Direct channels possibly influencing SME recession can refer to: an overall slowdown of economic activity and consumer demand in particular, a severe financial crunch induced by foreign exchange and financial turbulence and/or a sharp but transitional depreciation of the national currency.

Indirect channels can refer to: business linkages with domestic conglomerates (especially the chaebols in the Korean case) and other large domestic firms, business and eventually financial linkages with foreign affiliates and companies established in the country or operating from overseas, and a favorable/neutral/or non-conducive SME government regulatory framework.

Korea

Compared to 11,589 SME bankruptcies in 1996 (against only 7 large firms), the figure sharply rose to 17,168 in 1997 (58 large firms) and to 22,828 in 1998 (39 large firms). Manufacturing SMEs suffered much more during the crisis than non-manufacturing SMEs. Manufacturing SMEs operating in light industries have been even more affected by the crisis than those involved in heavy and chemical production.

The very substantial contraction of SME manufacturing production and the double digit SME bankruptcy ratio have not been accompanied by a strong decrease in SME exports, which has even been much slower than total export contraction. SMEs have reacted more flexibly than large firms as far export performance is concerned. As a result, the share of SMEs in Korea' total trade has been expanding at least marginally from 41.8 per cent in 1996 to 42.6 per cent in 1998, and possibly to over 46 per cent in

1999. Even though national production seems to have recovered in the course of 1999, it has not yet been completely restored, and it is too early to measure its multiplier effect on SME manufacturing.

Malaysia

The financial crisis and the specific protective measures taken as a result (contrary to Korea and Thailand) have affected most enterprises. On the one hand, SMEs were no exception in the sense that they badly felt the contraction of the domestic market, the shrink in credit available and the devaluation of the ringgit (at least until its fixed rate pegging to the US dollar since autumn 1998). On the other hand, there were some other factors at play such as over dependence on the domestic market (for over two-thirds of SMEs), strong price dependence on raw material and component imports (affected by a devaluated ringgit and then the fixed peg), ineffectiveness of a new ten bank syndicated loan scheme initiated by the government and supposed to assist SMEs facing credit unavailability and high interest rates (Abdullah, 1998).

Since late 1998, the expansionary budget implemented by the government has produced an overall positive impact on the economy. However, its stimulating downstream effect on local SMEs still has been marginally felt, though business plans of SMEs have been less gloomy for 28.7 per cent of them against 14 per cent only in 1998. Yet, 60 per cent of all surveyed SMEs were still predicting worse business performance during the first half of 1999, against 53 per cent for the same period in 1998 and 81 per cent for the second half.

Thailand

The impact of the crisis on Thai SMEs has been discussed in Part I of the book.

Results of the Three Country Surveys

Based on each respective survey, this section presents tentative answers to the three central questions mentioned above. However, these answers cannot be considered conclusive for at least two reasons. First, available data dealing with the impact of the financial crisis on the real economy are still scarce, particularly in the case of Thailand, and not too reliable (Thailand and Malaysia). Information does not even exist when it comes to the direct and indirect effects on local SME linkages vis-à-vis large firms. Second, the three conducted surveys were very limited in scope in terms of the number of SMEs surveyed. Trends in SME resilience have been identified, but more detailed and precise data should be collected in the future to support policy decision making in this field.

Q1: Have local SMEs with a relatively strong export orientation experienced a weaker decrease of production and sales than exclusively domestic-oriented SMEs? The answer is positive in the three countries under study. Empirical data derived from the sample surveys tends to show that:

- the strong depreciation of the national currency had initially improved the international competitiveness of some but not all SME products; and
- the expansion of exports combined or not with preferential credit facilities (if and when put in place by government) had a positive impact on their sales and compensated for the decline of local demand, at least to a certain extent.

In the Korean sample, a trend has been identified: the stronger the export-orientation of the SME initially, the more positive the development in sales was in 1998. In a number of cases, it fully cushioned the downturn of domestic demand during the same period. In that respect, local exporting SMEs were relatively more efficient than big firms in adapting to new economic environments (such as drastic exchange rate fluctuations) so rapidly induced by the severity of the crisis.

In the Thai sample, it is interesting to note that most SMEs affiliated or not to foreign firms in the electric and electronic industry are export oriented, and that both categories experienced positive effects derived from the sharp favourable change in the exchange rate. But a distinction between the two categories has to be made in the textile and garment sector, where all non-foreign affiliated SMEs surveyed were less resilient to the crisis than the affiliated ones.

In the more specific Malaysian macro-economic context, both the ratios of SMEs exclusively export-oriented, and of SMEs working for export and domestic markets, have declined from 7 per cent to 4.6 per cent, and from 29 per cent to 20.4 per cent respectively. Due to the crisis but also to the protectionist financial regulations taken against foreign investors in September 1998, there was between early 1998 and early 1999 an 11 per cent increase in the number of SMEs working for the domestic market only.

In answering Question 1, the relative export performance of local SMEs during the crisis is not well enough documented to establish a strong correlation between the totality or a segment of the local exporting SMEs and their direct or indirect export channels. Those may be indirectly facilitated–at least in some cases–by the export channels of foreign TNCs and foreign trading houses.

Before the crisis, a number of limited empirical studies tend to show that most East Asian exporting SMEs relied primarily on direct export channels.[1] This is particularly true of most export performing SMEs in the region, such as the Taiwanese SMEs for instance.

Q2: Have local SMEs linked to foreign firms in various forms such as supplying and subcontracting (exclusive of direct investment and financial equity linkages) been more resilient to the crisis than the vast majority of local SMEs not linked to foreign firms? The answer is much less clear than to the previous question. There seems to be some rather positive but very indirect impact, which cannot be easily documented and precisely measured in either quantitative or qualitative terms, both from the SME and the foreign firm viewpoints. In addition, the survey has covered only a sample of SMEs, but not the large foreign firms concerned, which would require another necessary survey.

The Korean survey shows that a foreign affiliation did not materialize so much in the resilience of SME business performance during the crisis. It may have provided a certain degree of psychological security to some foreign-affiliated SMEs but not to all of them (depending on other variables such as the sector or sub-sector of activity, more or less affected by declining demand domestically and regionally). For example, an increase of sales during the crisis was experienced by a relatively similar proportion of foreign affiliated SMEs and non-foreign affiliated ones.

In the Thai survey, 12.9 per cent of the interviewed SMEs do practice subcontracting with foreign affiliates. The number one type of support received from foreign affiliates has been a relatively guaranteed and continued access to export markets.

Q3: Have local SMEs linked to FDI and some foreign investors' equity participation been particularly resilient to the crisis? First, some distinctions have to be made between the East Asian economies fairly open to FDI before the crisis (such as Malaysia and Thailand) and economies which have traditionally relied much less on FDI (such as Korea).

Second, even in the economies of the first category, data has shown that FDI has concentrated in certain sectors and primarily in large scale industry (in big domestic firms or in majority/wholly owned foreign enterprises). The number of local manufacturing SMEs linked to FDI is still very limited and no complete, systematic and up-dated information was available before the outbreak of the East Asian crisis.

Third, considering the rising importance of attracting more foreign investment to counterbalance the effects of the crisis and to help corporate restructuring, most locally surveyed SMEs welcome FDI and foreign ownership participation, but only in principle. Two factors militate exactly in the opposite direction. Due to the small size of their paid-in capital, most SME entrepreneurs–especially the numerous family-based ones–are rather reluctant to provide foreign investors with the possibility of controlling their own family-based management. In some cases, they may accept minority foreign equity participation, which may be unattractive to the foreign investor, or even resist the psychologically perceived 'selling out' of the SME to foreign interests.

In the Korean case, interestingly enough, most surveyed SME entrepreneurs are primarily interested in FDI for one single reason, which is to obtain transfer of advanced management skills. Supply of foreign exchange, transfer of advanced technology, linkage to foreign partners in international markets come a far distant second in their answers.

In the Malaysian survey, there is no clear correlation between SME export resilience and foreign firm affiliation: some SMEs fully affiliated to Japanese investors improved their export performance due to the weak ringgit, but at the same time they had to digest a sharp cost increase in the imports of raw materials and components (therefore, they are trying to outsource imports not from the USA any more but from neighbouring East Asian economies). Some other SMEs fully owned by US foreign investors– but working primarily for the domestic market–have faced such drastic cost rises in imports and such sales drop that they have closed some of their local production units and are trying to restructure and divest somehow, looking not for sole ownership anymore but for some form of joint venture with local partners. On the contrary, some 100 per cent Malaysian owned exporting SMEs (less than 4 per cent of total SMEs) have experienced only positive impacts from the crisis, thanks to a weakened Malaysian dollar. They have been increasing production at full steam, expanding factory size and recruiting additional employees.

There is some form of SME resistance to increased FDI ownership, which is specific to Malaysia in addition to the arguments presented in the above answer to Question 3. Pro-Bumiputra New Economic Policy affiliated SMEs tend to be more domestic market oriented and somehow protected from real market conditions, in comparison to local Chinese or Indian SMEs, which tend to be far more internationalized. The anti-foreign campaign led by the Prime Minister since the outbreak of the crisis may also have some impact on SME attitudes toward the supposed dangers of FDI.

In the Thai survey, the foreign affiliated SMEs (5.5 per cent of the total SMEs in manufacturing) tend to have survived the crisis better than the ones without such an affiliation. The more foreign equity participation involved in a local SME, the more likely it is that assistance has been already provided or is envisaged from the foreign partners (through access to export markets, technical assistance, loans and capital injection, etc...).

The surveyed foreign affiliated SMEs in the textile and garment industry are almost 100 per cent foreign owned and totally export oriented: these two characteristics alone may explain why they have been much more resilient than all the others (except one non-foreign-affiliated SME surveyed, which is also heavily export oriented).

In the electrical and electronic sector, only one SME surveyed that had a rather high foreign equity participation (49 per cent) has been particularly resilient, thanks not only to classical technology assistance for export market access, but also to even more capital injection and financial participation during the peak of the crisis. The other foreign affiliated SMEs surveyed have all experienced both positive and negative effects of the crisis, even though their foreign affiliation is different from case to case (one SME is a family Thai-Singaporean venture, one has a licensing agreement, one has a 10 per cent foreign equity).

In the automobile parts sector, only one surveyed SME, producing components of break wires for both export and domestic markets, has over 51 per cent of foreign equity. This SME had to reduce output and employment due to a sharp decrease in sales and profit, but the foreign partner has been providing some export market and cheap loan assistance. The other surveyed SMEs are non-foreign affiliated: all of them have mostly experienced negative impacts of the crisis, even though the majority of them are involved in both domestic and export markets.

Tentative Conclusions

First Conclusion

Combining the results to the three central questions raised at the beginning of this chapter, the country surveys tend to indicate that the export orientation of local SMEs had a stronger impact in terms of SME business resilience to the crisis, than the status of their foreign affiliation.

The more strongly linked local SMEs were to export markets before the crisis, the more resilient they have been so far, whereas local SMEs relying both on export and domestic markets have generally performed less well (but still better than those local SMEs working only for the domestic market). Considering the various types and degrees of foreign affiliation, SMEs having a high ratio of direct foreign equity participation (49 per cent and over) before the crisis tended to be the most resilient ones during the crisis due to various forms of assistance from the foreign partner, including additional capital injection and/or preferential loans in some cases. However, this rule is not true for all SMEs in this category, not even for those wholly or almost wholly foreign owned.

Second Conclusion

Local SMEs with no foreign participation welcome in principle some form of FDI-affiliation, but generally want to limit it to a minimum. Local SMEs with some foreign ownership do not want–despite the current crisis–any higher foreign contribution to their firm. In both situations, the fear of losing management control is central for financial and non-tangible reasons. This refers to the psychological and sociological profile of the vast majority of local SME entrepreneurs, who generally lead family-based SMEs and lack a proper long-term industrial, marketing and management strategy.

In addition, despite the short-term negative effects of the crisis, the financial situation of most local SMEs has not yet reached a desperate bottom line. Most of them are struggling with various downsizing constraints (and are directly responsible for the rapid rise in unemployment) but not to the extent of closing down; a good number of them even sound rather confident about their medium-term prospects in 1999-2001. The number of bankruptcies in 1998 more than doubled compared to 1996 (for example, in Thailand), but the direct and indirect real market fluctuations derived from the financial crisis may have primarily hit the most vulnerable domestic market-oriented SMEs.

Third Conclusion

The small FDI inflows attracted by the local SME sector developed gradually during the 1980s and 1990s until the outbreak of the 1997-1998 crisis. Though no precise data is available, it originated more from the Asian region (especially in terms of production de-localization from big and SME firms in Japan and some East Asian NIEs such as Korea and Taiwan) than from Western Europe and Northern America.

Newly established and wholly foreign owned SMEs were created locally in a majority of such FDI cases, and were assimilated to supporting industries in a number of examples. In other cases, FDI inflows (even before the crisis) targeted the most promising SMEs that were psychologically and financially ready to welcome some foreign participation.

Fourth Conclusion

It may be concluded that any sound anti-crisis policy targeting the domestic-oriented SMEs most greatly affected by the financial turbulence should know how to pick the winners or the most resilient ones. Such SMEs should be encouraged to meet foreign affiliates and partners, who are either ready or could be encouraged to join their up-grading efforts in business, management and internationalization. The development of sustainable linkages between these SMEs and foreign partners would certainly contribute to their long-term development, which has been extremely neglected so far. Directly and indirectly, such sustainable linkages would also contribute to the overall corporate reform and real market recovery in the East Asian economies most affected by the recent crisis. The external and structural vulnerability of these economies could then be reduced over time, at least in relative terms.

However, until now, SME government policy tends to go, especially in the case of Thailand, in all kinds of uncoordinated directions with very limited strategic planning and follow up implementation.

Fifth Conclusion

This chapter has focused on those SMEs linked to foreign affiliates operating locally and globally. The reader should keep in mind that they are still few in number. The vast majority of local SMEs remain primarily dependent on domestic market conditions and demand. This trivial but often neglected fact opens the debate whether domestic oriented SMEs are better suited than internationalized SMEs to local economic and social realities in the aftermath of the recent crisis. In other words, the sound and sustainable recovery of the affected economies, and their small and medium-sized corporate sector in particular, will primarily depend on the capacity to regenerate local demand to pre-crisis levels.

This chapter is therefore a small contribution to the open debate on globalization and the future of SMEs into the 21st century. Grassroots-level facts and realities may challenge the supposed 'wisdom' of promoting the globalization of a small segment of existing SMEs instead of concentrating on the bulk of domestic oriented ones. The two approaches are not contradictory and can be reconciled in many ways. What is more certain is that a majority of SMEs have neither the desire nor the capacity to venture overseas, and even less to go global.

Sixth Conclusion

Especially in the case of Thailand, whose economy plans to rely even more on FDI support, but also in the case of most other East Asian economies, the current and future pattern of outsourcing activities by foreign transnational corporations (TNCs) should be scrutinized in the aftermath of the recent crisis. On the one hand, TNCs could become global bridgeheads to enhance the domestic and international competitiveness of local SMEs (Bukley, 1997; Grunsven, 1998; Karagozulu and Lindell, 1998) at least those which are already active in external markets. But on the other hand, they could be tempted to benefit from the recent crisis and the more liberal

FDI policies adopted locally to invest directly into their own outsourcing facilities and related supporting networks. It would increase the competitive pressure on the pure local SMEs, at least in some key sectors such as electronics or automotive, and possibly in new IT sectors. The industrial base could deepen and widen, the local content of final exportable products could more rapidly increase, but the whole process could be detrimental to pure domestic market operators and benefit foreign global players–essentially American, European and Japanese ones.[2]

Recent studies tend to show that local conditions in host countries are important determinants of the size and significance of spillovers from FDI and TNCs in particular. However, measures to actively promote investment from abroad may not be sufficient to generate linkages and spillovers if most local SMEs are too far apart from the technologies and standards used by foreigners. Policies to ensure that foreign affiliates operate in a competitive environment appear to be essential, otherwise they may use their TNC specific advantages to capture the whole local market.[3] Thailand, among other emerging economies, should come up with policies to stimulate market environment conditions that support competitive local enterprises and simultaneously encourage FDI clusters with desirable spillover effects.

Notes

[1] A few studies were conducted on this subject in the late 1980s and 1990s by the International Trade Centre (UNCTAD/WTO), United Nations, Geneva.

[2] Blomstrom, M. and Kokko, A. (1998), 'Multinationals and Spillovers', *Journal of Economic Surveys*, vol.12, 247-78; Kokko, A. (1996), 'Productivity Spillovers from Competition between Local Firms and Foreign Affiliates', *Journal of International Development*, vol. 8, 517-30.

[3] Kokko, A. (1999), *Foreign Direct Investment and Technology Transfer*, Paper presented at the Asia-Europe Conference, Chulalongkorn University, 19-20 August, Bangkok, pp.14-15.

9 The Potential Resilience of Thai Subcontractors Linked to Foreign Firms: SME Case Studies

The SME case studies presented in Chapters 9 and 10 have been primarily elaborated to illustrate the main argument of Chapter 8. Therefore, it is recommended to read Chapter 8 first before going to the case studies. In other words, all the SMEs selected for the cases, chosen from various sectors of manufacturing, have been resilient to the crisis thanks to their differentiated links with foreign transnational corporations operating in Thailand or based overseas. This is even true for a few selected SMEs, which in 1997-1998 had to face a total collapse of orders from major foreign clients but have been able to overcome this business downturn in 1998-1999, thanks to their strong networks with transnational corporations.

Each case is presented in a concise briefing style to meet its purely illustrative purpose, and to stimulate the curiosity of readers who are not necessarily interested in the technicalities of detailed SME management case studies.

Those readers who happen to be small entrepreneurs or SME experts are kindly reminded of the purely illustrative objective of Chapters 9 and 10. The field research work behind these chapters was never conceived as a large SME sample survey. Such a survey would have required interviewing hundreds of SMEs active in different sectors and well distributed all over the country. This was far beyond the human and financial capacities of our small-sized research project conducted in Bangkok in 1999.

First Case Study
O.E.I. PARTS CO., LTD. (Automotive Sector)

The story of O.E.I. Parts Co., Ltd. illustrates the spreading dynamics of diversified and strong linkages established by young Thai entrepreneurs with Japanese transnational corporations. It can range from technological training to direct outsourcing of parts and components. In the automotive sector, such linkages grew so close during the booming early 1990s that the induced creation of a first local SME, Sang Charoen Tools Center Co., Ltd.

in this instance, led the same entrepreneur a few years later to start up a second SME: O.E.I. Parts Co., Ltd.

Even when a major business downturn occurs and some big-scale contractors suddenly stop their orders as they did in late 1997, formal and especially informal links and close interpersonal relationships can help a small firm to be resilient. In the six months between November 1997 and May 1998, O.E.I. was able to link up with new Japanese clients and to bring production back to full capacity during the last quarter of 1999.

Company Profile

Mr. Prasartsilp On-aht, who is 47 and fluent in Japanese, obtained a vocational degree in technical engineering in Bangkok in 1973, and joined the Japanese automotive giant Isuzu. In 1977 he was sent to Japan for further training in design and molding. After acquiring extensive on-the-job experience, he resigned from his entrepreneurial incubator, Isuzu. Sharing equity with his wife and their respective families, he set up Sang Charoen Tools Center Co. Ltd in May 1989, which is located in an industrial estate in Samutprakarn, 18 km. from Bangkok city center.

Sang Charoen specializes in stamping dies and stamping sheet metal parts for Japanese automobiles and also produces for the machine-tool industry and other sectors. With a registered capital of BHT 10 million in 1999 (about U$ 250, 000), it employs 95 full time workers.

In April 1993, the financial support of cousins and other relatives enabled the creation of O.E.I. Parts Co., Ltd., downstream the production activities of Sang Charoen Tools Center, with an initial capital of BHT 1 million. With the help of newly acquired CNC machinery, O.E.I. was set up to manufacture high-precision automotive parts. Located in the vicinity of Sang Charoen, O.E.I. has today a registered capital of BHT 25 million, fixed assets of 34 million, and employs 87 full time workers, 17 of them white-collar. The owner is in charge of all marketing and production activities at both companies, while his wife supervises administration, management and finance. Their key strategy is to produce good quality work which meets the needs of their Japanese customers.

The main reason for establishing Sang Charoen, and then O.E.I., is that Japanese buyers, both settled in Japan or having directly invested in Thailand, placed higher and higher outsourcing orders to local supporting SMEs during the 1980s and early 1990s. When O.E.I. started, it was the only local supplier of seven specific parts to a Japanese leading car and pick-up manufacturer. Within a few years of existence, it was able to maintain its privileged position, but also to diversify its deliveries.

From 1993-1997, parts supplied to the Japanese car manufacturer represented 80 per cent of total O.E.I. sales, the rest going to other clients. O.E.I. started with 6 M/C machines to manufacture 3,500 sets per month in

1993-1994. In June 1997, just before the crisis, it had acquired eight additional machines and was working at full capacity for the Japanese car manufacturer supplying 10,000 sets of parts. In 1995 and 1996, sales to this manufacturer sharply increased from BHT 9 million to 12 million respectively.

The strength of O.E.I. relies on its competitive advantage in product quality and sustainability. The owner has much knowledge and experience about the needs, standards and practices of the Japanese car manufacturer. The workforce is fairly specialized and the owner tries to set aside BHT 200,000 a year in order to send workers for up-grading skills training. Production costs are maintained at a moderate level compared to most other local manufacturers. 30 per cent of total costs are derived from the import of special steels via local brokers. Such steels meet the Japanese buyers' specifications and cannot be supplied from domestic producers in Thailand. Delivery-on-time used to be, at least until 1996-1997, another competitive edge.

Impact of the Crisis

The impact of the East Asian crisis has been tremendous on O.E.I. It started from a dramatic situation in late 1997 with an intensity that was not experienced by any other local SME presented in this book. O.E.I. was able to survive and recover, while many other SMEs facing a similar downturn simply ceased activity for some time or disappeared.

In November 1997, despite its close subcontracting links with O.E.I., the major Japanese automotive contractor decided to cancel its orders from nearly 9,000 sets a month to nil. Of course, due to its automotive segment specialization heavily dependent on local demand in developing Asia, the Japanese contractor was severely hit by the crisis in comparison with other Japanese auto makers.

This situation suddenly created a big cash flow problem, and the firm had to declare temporary unemployment for two thirds of the workforce. They were offered BHT 3,000 to go back to their families and provinces of origin until new orders could be secured. However, O.E.I. owners tried not to lay anyone off and to re-hire their former staff as soon as possible. Their aim was to keep their word in an atmosphere of mutual trust between employers and employees.

To make the situation worse, O.E.I.'s commercial banker imposed a credit crunch. O.E.I. could not service its original 1993 debt, which became a non-performing loan in 1997-1998. However, O.E.I. was successful in restructuring its debt. During about eight months, only the interest but not any principal was reimbursed to the bank.

In January-February 1998, the former Japanese contractor resumed orders but at a low level. It slowly increased to 4,000 sets in November 1999, 6,000 sets below the pre-crisis level of orders.

In such a dramatic context, the owners had to struggle to survive and used all their existing personal links and private relationships with Japanese companies and networks. It paid off within six months! New clients could be identified, mainly Japanese ones thanks to the above connections. From May 1998 onward, O.E.I. was gradually able to survive the business turbulence. In 1999, it was back on its feet and by the end of the year was not able to meet all orders despite working at full capacity.

The structure of production has been modified. Exports have increased and go mainly to a Kubota plant located in the USA, whereas Japanese auto-makers are directly supplied in Thailand. Automotive parts make up to 54 per cent of total sales and supply not only the initial Japanese contractor but also Honda, Mazda and Mitsubishi. Parts for small tractors, parts for motor bikes and miscellaneous parts represent 20 per cent, 5 per cent and 2 per cent respectively. Direct sales in the domestic market represent 60 per cent of the total, whereas 40 per cent are direct exports without using trading agents.

Financial relations have been also modified: O.E.I. has obtained a payment delay of 120-150 days (from suppliers) against 90 days before. Sales on credit have been reduced to 30 days instead of 60 days as before with most clients.

In such conditions, O.E.I. has been able to rehire most of its former employees and even new ones, bringing the total workforce up to 87 by the end of 1999. O.E.I. has so much work that delivery delays have to be extended for 55 per cent of all received orders.

SME Government Policy

During the period of the crisis, O.E.I. received no assistance from the government. In 1998-1999, O.E.I. was only asked by district officials not to fire any workers, if possible. When O.E.I. turned to public financial institutions, they asked for unreasonable collateral, such as letters of credit from O.E.I. buyers. The biggest surprise was that they would charge lending conditions above average market rates, most probably because they did not want to consider new clients and take risks. They might have been short of public funds at that time as well.

O.E.I. does not believe much in the new SME government policy announced in 1999. The only positive action is the creation of some SME training courses accessible at low cost. In October 1999, Mr. and Mrs. On-Aht themselves participated in a brief automotive training seminar sponsored by the Ministry of Industry (ISMED, Department of Industrial

Promotion, MoI) which took place at the Faculty of Engineering, Chulalongkorn University.

Business Perspectives

The major positive outcome from the whole crisis is that O.E.I. has been forced to drastically reduce its over-dependence on one single major automotive contractor. Even though local and regional demand for pick-up vans and light trucks sharply declined in 1998, this Japanese automotive contractor adopted a rather poor and very short-term strategy vis-à-vis its subcontractors, including close and reliable ones such as Sang Charoen Tools and O.E.I. O.E.I. 's business confidence has been also tremendously boosted because of its demonstrated capacity to find new customers within only six months. Furthermore, O.E.I. has been able not only to diversify its customers, but also the types of supplied parts.

On the more critical side, O.E.I. acknowledges that it has not concentrated so far on the design and implementation of a proper marketing system. As long as old and new Japanese clients could be cultivated through very personalized relationships and networking, the urgent need for such a system was disregarded or not considered a priority. O.E.I.'s business existence has historically been driven by its main client(s), and until the crisis at least, orders just came in without making a big effort to look for them.

A second and probably more important vulnerability of O.E.I. lies on the shoulders of Mr. On-aht himself. Despite his high entrepreneurial, technical and public relation talents, and his relatively young age, it is not very healthy for the future of both O.E.I. and Sang Charoen to rely exclusively on him both for securing clients and for supervising production operations. In a not too remote future, business succession might also become a problem, as in most family-owned SMEs. On the one hand, he and his wife seem to have confidence that their 18 year-old daughter, starting her studies in engineering, will gradually take over. But on the other hand, they may overestimate her ability to look after two companies, both internally and externally.

However, in the short- and medium-term, both owners are rather confident about business prospects. O.E.I. is already working at over-capacity, which is an impressive result in the context of the slow recovery of the Thai economy at the end of 1999. For 2000-2001, they have decided to remain cautious until sustainable growth is achieved and Japan has completely recovered. Therefore, O.E.I. investment will be devoted mainly to training or retraining staff, to attending a few highly specialized fairs and possibly to acquiring new machinery. All the production equipment used to be Japanese but the first German machine was purchased in November 1999. In 2001-2002, the physical expansion of the O.E.I. factory is envisaged on its existing premises. Overall business prospects sound rather bright.

In the medium-term, O.E.I. will have to continue the up-grading of products to remain competitive in a tougher and tougher marketplace. To do so, O.E.I. owners say that they are yet undecided whether to look for a partner or go ahead on their own.

Second Case Study
SATHIEN PLASTIC & FIBER CO., LTD. (Plastic Sector)

It is hard to believe that a former employee of Toyota (Thailand) has been capable of becoming one of the only two Toyota pick-up trucks' parts suppliers in Thailand. Toyota's benevolence enabled this former worker, navigating his tiny realm, to successfully weather the economic crisis. However, the likely dissolution in January 2000 of the required local content percentage in automobile manufacturing imposed by the Thai government has become a pre-eminent concern.

Company Profile

Sathien Shompoosri had been working in the area of technical planning for Toyota (Thailand) for ten years before quitting to help his father-in-law run his local business for a few years. His vision of becoming an entrepreneur, coupled with his technical experience acquired during his employment at Toyota, inspired him to start an automobile parts business. His dream finally materialized on March 21st, 1989 when Sathien Plastic & Fiber Co., Ltd. was established with a capital of BHT 1 million. The capital came from selling some land and from relatives' financial support. In May 1994, the capital was increased to BHT 10 million. The 11-rai factory (approximately 4.4 acres) is located in Pathumtani, a province adjacent to the northern part of Bangkok, and covers a manufacturing area of 1,250 square meters. The company has a sales office in Bangkok, situated close to Donmuang International Airport. Sathien Plastic & Fiber currently employs 65 workers (51 males and 14 females) who work 6 days/week. The Executive Committee of the company consists of Sathien himself, Vatsharee (his wife), Pravit Jiamburaset (his father-in-law), and Ampawan Jiamburaset. Sathien is also the Managing Director.

Sathien Plastic & Fiber's major products are classified as follows:

1. By extrusion process: plastic sheet of HDPE, LDPE, PP, ABS, EVA.
2. By vacuum thermoforming process: fender liner, wheelhouse liner, engine undercover.
3. By injection process (small parts): battery clamp, splash guard.

At the outset, Sathien Plastic & Fiber focused on the low-end market by selling splashguards to automobile accessories shops. Then the firm was able to penetrate the automobile manufacturing sector itself. As a result, the profile of its customers changed as follows:

- Toyota pick-up trucks: 50 per cent;
- automobile accessories shops: 30 per cent;
- Isuzu: 10 per cent;
- Volvo, Chrysler, and others: 10 per cent.

Sathien's previous 10-year employment at Toyota started to pay back not only in the form of accumulated technical experience but also in terms of value-chain partnership. His good relationship with Toyota's management enabled Sathien Plastic & Fiber to serve as one of the only two Toyota pick-up truck's plastic parts suppliers. Sathien prided himself on being chosen shoulder to shoulder with NSK, another formidable parts supplier. NSK is a large Thai-Japanese joint-venture manufacturer. Although NSK was physically and financially stronger, the prices of its products were less competitive than Sathien Plastic & Fiber. The sheer size of NSK resulted in high overhead costs, thus preventing the company from pricing its products as competitively as Sathien Plastic & Fiber. Toyota's policy of avoiding the risk of depending on only one supplier allowed both NSK and fortunately Sathien Plastic & Fiber to maintain value-chain partnership with Toyota in spite of the price differences between the two suppliers.

In addition, Sathien Plastic & Fiber's affiliation with Toyota brought about a valuable opportunity to export its products to India. Toyota (India), on the recommendation of its counterpart in Thailand, ordered some parts from Sathien Plastic & Fiber. Although the size of the order was not substantial, such internationalization of his SME firm brought encouragement and pride to the owner. However, his cooperative character led him to allow his Indian customers to visit the Sathien Plastic & Fiber manufacturing site in Thailand. He naively provided them with valuable advice and technical expertise. This backfired on him. Equipped with Sathien's know how, the Indian customers decided to produce their own parts locally in India rather than importing them from Sathien Plastic & Fiber.

Local plastic constitutes most of the input needed upstream of production. However, extruders are imported from Japan and injectors come from Japan as well as Taiwan. Sathien claims that his former experience at Toyota has contributed to his ability to self-develop the appropriate technology used in manufacturing the products. His major concern focuses on his somewhat outdated proprietary technology, resulting in low productivity. Although methods to improve the productivity have been conceived, investment in new machinery would require substantial financial resources.

Impact of the Crisis

With insufficient funds to invest in more productive machinery, Sathien Plastic & Fiber's situation was exacerbated by the recent economic crisis. Revenue generated from Toyota, worth 50 per cent of total sales, drastically decreased by 70 per cent, whereas that emanating from the low-end market such as automobile accessories fell by 40 per cent-60 per cent. Moreover, there was no contribution from export activities since the Indian customers ended up producing their own parts.

Since Sathien Plastic & Fiber obtained a bank loan in 1992 to finance its operations, the sharp decline in sales affected its ability to pay back the principal and interest periodically. Fortunately, Sathien was able to reach a new term payment compromise with the bank allowing his firm to pay back only the interest for a certain period. This act of mercy eased the company's financial burden temporarily.

Additionally, Sathien Plastic & Fiber received assistance from its only major customer, Toyota. Early 1998, Toyota offered a loan with an attractive interest. This type of assistance was extended not only to Sathien Plastic & Fiber but also to all Toyota's close suppliers who were in financial distress. On the contrary, Isuzu did not offer any help since Sathien Plastic & Fiber had just become its supplier and Isuzu was financially incomparable to Toyota. Among all large Japanese automotive contractors established in Thailand, Toyota was the only one that took care of its local suppliers and subcontractors throughout the crisis. In many cases, it was a deliberate strategy to further increase linkages and trust relationship with them. This long term strategy may pay back, as Toyota announced in mid-1999 that Thailand would become its major production hub in Asia outside Japan.

Besides Toyota's support, Sathien received help from his wife's relatives in the form of a bank overdraft.

SME Government Policy

Sathien has been a member of the association of automobile parts suppliers, and he was advised to seek financial aid from IFCT (Industrial Finance Corporation of Thailand) and SIFC (Small Industry Finance Corporation). But to his surprise, Sathien discovered that SIFC wanted to charge an interest rate higher than the one offered by his usual commercial banker at the time. This was proof that obtaining government assistance was more expensive than going to the private financial market.

Another measure that Sathien Plastic & Fiber implemented to reduce cost was the downsizing of its workforce from 170 to 40 employees during the worst period of the crisis.

Sathien acknowledges the existence of SME government policies implemented by various agencies. He knows about some of their activities from newspapers and considers that active government involvement is indispensable since SMEs play a predominant role in the Thai economy. However, time constraints and the low attractiveness of public assistance have prevented him from seeking more information that could be beneficial to his company. Moreover, he believes that a small business owner like himself would be somehow discriminated against by senior civil servants who tend to have more consideration for VIPs from larger enterprises.

His main recommendation to the government is to convince and/or influence the banking institutions to exonerate some non-performing loan SME customers so that they could have some access to fresh capital. Thereby, commercial transactions, new investment, and higher purchasing power could be restored.

Business Perspectives

Since local content requirement will be abolished for the automobile industry in 2000, Sathien is quite concerned about the future of his company.

Currently, parts from Taiwan, China, and Vietnam are more price competitive than those produced by Sathien Plastic & Fiber. The major component of the cost is plastic, and Thai plastic is more expensive than imported plastic. However, the government helps local producers by placing high tariffs on imports. Faced with such change in regional competition, Sathien is currently looking for a strategy to survive. He sees an opportunity to diversify his business into the production of freezers. In addition, Sathien plans to organize current operations in such a way that a standardized control system could be established. Unfortunately, Sathien is too pressured by daily operations and by the direct/indirect consequences of the crisis and newly emerging competition.

So far, he has not sufficient time to think about any family business succession plan either.

Third Case Study
A & V PLASTIC GROUP CO., LTD. (Plastic Molding Sector)

A visionary entrepreneur strategically expanded his mold manufacturing enterprise by forward integrating into another company producing plastic parts, A & V Plastic Group Co., Ltd. The economic crisis in Thailand compelled this second entity to reduce its labour costs in order to improve its cash flow. Beneficial relationships between the entrepreneur and his customers have enabled A & V Plastic to proudly enjoy supplying parts for export products to Swiss, Dutch, and Japanese joint ventures in Thailand, representing its major customers.

Company Profile

Established in 1991 with a registered capital of BHT 1 million, IPM Co., Ltd., a manufacturer of injection molds, blow mold forging, die-casting, extrusion and design mold, is located in Khet Tungkhru of Bangkok, not far from A & V Plastic Group Co., Ltd. IPM is jointly owned by Mr. Wichai Piyawatthanawirot's family, relatives and friends. He is currently the Managing Director of this 36-employee company. Wichai's expansionary vision inspired him to grab an opportunity of forward business integration by producing plastic parts for IPM's customers. However, to facilitate strategic flexibility, a separate entity had to be established. In fact, before legal establishment as a limited company, the plastic parts business had already been in operation within IPM. But this kind of operation did not facilitate professional relationships with stakeholders.

In 1994, Wichai finally decided to set up A & V Plastic Group Co., Ltd. owned solely by his family with a registered capital of BHT 1 million to manufacture plastic parts. It is located in Phrapradaeng District of Samutprakarn Province, adjacent to the southwestern part of Bangkok. His wife, Amphorn Wongjittapoke, became the Managing Director, currently in charge of a full-time workforce of 32. IPM's beneficial relationships with its customers facilitated the introduction of its newly established sister firm. A & V Plastic emanated from reliable in-house technology, allowing IPM to achieve competitive advantages in terms of on-time delivery and quality. Wichai's experience has been acquired from his studies in high school and vocational school as well as from study tours in Germany and Japan. In addition, he has received advice from a Thai friend, a professor at King Mongkut Institute of Technology.

The major customers introduced by IPM include:

- Driessen, a Thai-Dutch company, located in Lampoon Province, northern Thailand, manufacturing carts on aircraft, has been A & V Plastic's loyal customer since the inception;
- Bandai, a Thai-Japanese toy company, located in Chachoengsao Province, eastern Thailand, has been A & V Plastic's customer since the early times as well;

- Bernina, a Thai-Swiss joint venture, located in Lampoon Province, northern Thailand, producing sewing machines, became a new customer in late 1997;
- Schaffner EMC, a Thai-Swiss electronics company, located in Lampoon Province, northern Thailand, also became a new customer during the East Asian crisis.

Representing 80 per cent of total sales volume, their purchases as input for final export products have enabled A & V Plastic to be linked to global markets, since this SME does not export its parts directly. Therefore, merely 20 per cent of the sales volume is derived from domestic sales. Beneficial linkages and relationships between A & V Plastic and these four clients have been evidenced by the fact that they have allowed A & V Plastic personnel to visit their plants in order to better understand their needs and be capable of producing parts according to their specifications. In addition, the four firms can provide technical support whenever A & V Plastic needs it.

A & V Plastic's major products consist of parts for:

- electronics
- cars
- sanitary ware
- toys

Domestic customers include Karat and Siam Cement Public Co., Ltd., which is the largest Thai conglomerate. Siam Cement not only specializes in construction materials and industrial estate development, but has also diversified in many other sectors such as electrical products and air-conditioning compressors, machinery and metal products, tire and auto accessories, petrochemicals, paper and packaging, etc.

Although A & V Plastic has a close tie with the four foreign joint ventures mentioned above, it has still to face competition from large local and foreign firms (Singaporean, Japanese, and Taiwanese) as well as approximately ten Thai SMEs. Despite such challenge, A & V Plastic claims two competitive advantages: high flexibility in management and fast decision-making through full ownership and short chain of command; low overhead due to low administrative costs, machinery supplied by IPM, and a small number of workers.

Its limited physical facilities such as space prevent it from being fully qualified for ISO standards. But the implementation of strict quality control allows its products to be competitive with others. This claim is supported by the supplying linkages established with reputable foreign joint ventures operating in Thailand.

The Managing Director confesses that A & V Plastic has an apparent weakness in the area of marketing. Since most customers have been introduced by IPM, this functional dependence on IPM has deterred A & V from being proactive in marketing its own products. The genuine need to recruit a marketing expert has been recognized. However, the low profile of the company and its location in a shop house-like building have so far made it difficult to attract a capable person. Most potential candidates would prefer to work for a more prestigious enterprise, rendering their résumé more attractive.

Impact of the Crisis

Although plastic outsourced locally is cheaper, A & V Plastic has been forced by its customers to rely on foreign plastic for 90 per cent of total inputs. It does not import plastic directly but through trading agents. Of course, the devaluation of the baht led to an increase in input cost, but price volatility has remained minimal in regional and world markets. Therefore, total input cost has not increased too much. A & V Plastic has not been able to raise its selling prices accordingly because each time it was committed to an advance-order agreement. Revenue has consequently declined on those sales based on formerly agreed prices.

In 1997-1998, the reduction in domestic demand accounted for 80 per cent of total sales. The decrease was due to low purchasing power rather than to price increase, which was on average not significant for the reason just mentioned. Despite the slump in demand, there were no insolvent customers. On the financial front, the company had obtained a bank loan for its original start-up and the owner had provided land as collateral for the leasing of machinery. Apparently, the temporary decrease in total sales did not affect the ability to pay back the loan installments during the crisis.

However, the detrimental effects of shrinking revenue and profitability led the company to look for ways to reduce costs. The lean organization of such a small firm did not leave many choices as compared to larger ones. Cost reduction was applied to salaries in several ways. The elimination of overtime and the reduction in the number of daily shifts became the prime targets. The company used to allocate eight hours for regular working periods, while four extra hours were allowed for overtime work. There used to be three shifts per day. The reduction in orders led to a reduction in the number of shifts to only two. Overtime work was also eliminated resulting in a significant reduction in wages. The employees were offered free housing as compensation, but it was not attractive enough to induce some of them to stay with the company. The workforce was thus reduced from 60 to 32.

Nevertheless, on the positive side, the proportion of exported products was boosted by the currency devaluation. In addition, Bernina and

Schaffner, two new foreign clients operating in Thailand, were fortunately introduced by IPM at the outbreak of the crisis. As a result, revenue started to improve gradually.

In 1999, the proportion of exports has been reversed compared to the pre-crisis figure. Domestic sales have dramatically decreased to only 20 per cent against 80 per cent before!

SME Government Policy

The crisis did not really affect A & V Plastic to the extent that it encountered losses. Hence, the company did not seek any help from its major customers or the government. The owners have heard of the existence of an SME government policy as well as the Small Industry Finance Corporation. However, they are not aware of their objectives and how such instruments could effectively help SMEs. An ardent complaint is that the government has not been pro-active abroad in informing potential customers of the capability of highly skilled Thai manufacturers. A list of those manufacturers, especially small and medium ones, portraying their specialization and including A & V Plastic, should have been compiled by the government and should have subsequently been sent to potential foreign buyers.

Business Perspectives

A & V Plastic's short- and medium-term goals focus on business sustainability and increasing the number of customers. There is a downstream opportunity in forward integration of plastic parts into final products, which could help the company to alleviate its dependence on external manufacturers. Thus, one long-term objective is envisioned as manufacturing some agricultural equipment using plastic parts for growing vegetables.

Regarding the family's business succession plan, the owners hope that their daughter, currently studying in Grade 11 and planning to major in engineering, will be able to carry out the operations, also taking into account that the best-trained employees always leave A & V Plastic for larger and more reputable firms. Improvements in technology and production costing can only be achieved through IPM's assistance, but the owners doubt that their daughter could acquire sufficient specialized skills to successfully run the combined operation at the two firms. Consequently, IPM would need a highly skilled manager like the present owner, as it seems unlikely that anyone among his relatives and close friends could succeed him in the future. Another option would be for A & V Plastic to rely progressively on machinery supplied not by IPM but by independent suppliers. In other words, this option would mean that any possible termination of IPM activity would not affect the survival of A & V Plastic in the long term.

Fourth Case Study
MIS THAILAND CO., LTD. (Electrical Sector)

The electrical and electronic components and parts sector can be compared in many ways to the automotive subcontracting sector in Thailand. When the crisis came, MIS Thailand was among those lucky SME suppliers who had already forged strong linkages with some of its major clients, especially Japanese ones. The effects of the crisis were essentially positive on two fronts: some big Japanese customers placed additional orders and provided substantial up-grading technological assistance when it became even clearer than before 1997 that the domestic market would not absorb MIS products.

Company Profile

Like many other manufacturers of electrical products in Bangkok and its periphery, Mr. J.B. Aung, Managing Director of MIS, has expressed a strong motivation in setting up his company producing electrical kits. A friendly but rather reserved man, he explains that both his educational background and the influence of close friends already active in this sector were behind his decision. In this context, he admits that there were a number of factors and potential difficulties that he might have underestimated from the beginning. These were revealed in particular during the sudden unexpected crisis of 1997-1998, and he can now better figure out the whole macro- and micro-business environment of the electrical sector. Many of his previous doubts and questions have got clearer answers, paving the way for more balanced decision making in the immediate future and in the long run.

Mr. J.B. Aung, who is of Burmese origin, obtained his Bachelor's degree in electrical engineering in Rangoon, Myanmar. During his student life, he was already wondering how to prepare himself to become an entrepreneur. In order to make his dream become reality, he decided to create MIS Thailand in 1993 together with some close Thai friends based in Bangkok. Though he is the Managing Director, the legal structure of the company is a Thai partnership, whose majority is held by the Thai partners involved.

The company is specialized in two rather simple electrical products: wire-harnesses and plastic electric cords. Many electrical appliances normally require wire-harnesses and/or plastic cords as electric connectors for tool operation. Wire-harnesses and plastic electric cords are also used as internal elements placed inside electronic kits. Wire-harness, which is one specific type of plastic electric cord, has a different design, especially a pin-jack fixed at one extremity of the cord. The more common plastic electric cord covers copper wires transporting electricity. The products are mainly exported but are also used by local assemblers of more sophisticated electric appliances.

MIS Thailand received promotion incentives from the Board of Investment due to its export orientation. In 1998, despite the recession, total sales still made some modest progress up to BHT 4 million. The firm can be classified as a really small enterprise still giving work to 50 full-time employees.

Japanese buyers represent the bulk of foreign customers both domestically and externally, considering that big Japanese brands dominate the whole East Asian market for electrical and electronic products, including Thailand. Domestically, National and Panasonic are also rather important clients.

MIS has to cope with several vulnerabilities. First it is highly dependent on two types of imported inputs, copper pin (assembled to wire cord) and plastic material (used as cover), for about 50 per cent of the total sale value of the finished wire-harness and plastic cord. Quality imports are needed to meet Japanese buyers' standards and to compete with lower quality East Asian competitors. According to Mr. Aung, the development of local procurement capacity for such inputs would be highly desirable in order to reduce total fixed costs and provide downstream manufacturers such as MIS with more sustainable competitive advantage.

Precisely, the second difficulty lies with tough foreign competitors located mainly in China, Indonesia, and Vietnam, which can offer cheaper production costs and bigger economies of scale than Thailand.

Despite such potential handicaps, the competitive strength of MIS Thailand is the emphasis on quality and punctual delivery. Japanese buyers in particular are more sensitive on such issues than on price.

Impact of the Crisis

After the collapse of the Thai economy in July 1997, the entire electrical and electronic sector was badly hit. MIS had to cut over half of its domestic deliveries, but remained confident that the depreciation of the baht would boost its export activities. As a matter of fact, MIS received increased export orders, especially from Japan and Europe, which today represent 80 per cent of total production compared to 40 per cent in 1996. However, this has been barely enough to absorb the decline in domestic demand. Total sales in value terms have increased just modestly due to both high content dependence and increased cost of imported inputs, especially in 1997-1998. There was no other choice than to increase selling prices. Japanese customers such as Hitachi and Mitsubishi have played a significant role in helping a reliable small supplier such as MIS. They provided considerable assistance with more order placements and the injection of further consistent product quality improvements.

Interestingly enough, the crisis had some other unexpected and positive effects. Reduced local demand, normally more sensitive to price than anything else, enabled MIS to concentrate on productivity, quality and delivery service. As also observed in the automotive sector of Thailand, some Japanese buyers sent their technicians from Japan to MIS in order to upgrade quality and training of local workers. This resulted in an increase of export orders, concurrently facilitated by the devaluation of the baht. Among other improvements, a system of quality check-up in the production line was built up and the so-called Japanese concept of Just-In-Time (JIT) production and delivery was introduced.

In brief, it can be asserted that the introduction of standards matching the purchasing norms of the Japanese buyers has produced a dynamic spillover effect, calling in additional Japanese orders and sometimes new customers. Another positive effect for MIS was that under the JIT system a smaller range of electrical cords and wires has been requested, and orders have focused more on items matching each Japanese order specifications. Indirectly, it also helped the Japanese buyers to deepen and expand their home market for final electrical and electronic products sold in Japan, Thailand and elsewhere overseas.

Compared to other Japanese firms such as Toyota in the automotive sector, the Japanese contractors did not seek to invest in MIS as an alternative to support their local supplier. Actually, the financial situation of MIS was not too weak during the crisis, thanks to the healthy export situation.

Secondly, MIS did not have much of a banking problem like most Thai SMEs at the time. Since its creation in 1993, MIS has been quite satisfied with the financial services rendered by the Industrial Financial Corporation of Thailand (IFCT), and facilitated by the BOI and its links with large Japanese corporate investors in the electric and electronic sector. Unlike Thai commercial banks, IFCT did not ask for collateral in fixed assets when MIS was launched. There was no working capital loan problem at any point during the crisis.

SME Government Policy

In short, the crisis did not really affect MIS, which has not faced heavy financial losses. However, Mr. Aung still remembers that no public or private assistance was made available from financial institutions, except IFCT, when MIS went shopping around asking for a small additional credit line in order to manage its business transition.

He is of the opinion that the public sector should provide SMEs with specific support in the crucial fields of preliminary studies and development of self-technology, skill training, and research & development. Though the experience of MIS has been rather favourable vis-à-vis the Board of Investment (BOI) and the Industrial Financial Corporation of Thailand (IFCT) from the beginning, he thinks that most civil servants do not understand SMEs and do not take responsibility for any policy setting. Therefore, though he has heard of the new SME policy advocated by the current cabinet, he challenges the validity of its objectives and especially the capacity to implement concrete measures.

Business Perspectives

In the short term, MIS will continue to focus on upgrading its production capacity to meet the best international standards, which does not mean however to go for the certification status and grading much in fashion today.

The long-term goals are to expand market coverage, skill training and technology development. If MIS can concentrate on these fronts, its managing director is relatively optimistic about future growth. He is also much encouraged by the recent commitment of new direct investments by large Japanese corporations in the electrical and electronic sector. He has little doubt that they will continue to de-localize entire segments of production, also due to the recent acceleration in Japanese industrial restructuring needs.

10 The Potential Resilience of Final Goods Producers Linked to Foreign Firms: SME Case Studies

First Case Study
CRP JEWELLERY (THAILAND) CO., LTD.
(Jewelry Manufacturing Sector)

Within only 8 years, the combined entrepreneurial talents of the CRP management team, together with its culture of extreme hard work and extraordinary sense of urgency, and right strategic-alliance move in the global environment, have pushed the company up to the second or third rank among all Thai jewelry manufacturers. Even during the 1997-1998 crisis, sales continued to grow significantly, boosted by high demand from the American market. This has been made possible thanks, externally, to a strong and sustainable relationship with a world-class retail customer in the USA, and domestically to a flexible and well-integrated subcontracting system most probably unique in this profession in Thailand.

Company Profile

Established since 1985 as a family business on the basis of a pawn shop and retail jeweler, CRP decided to enter into jewelry manufacturing in 1991 in close cooperation with the biggest American diamond and jewelry wholesaler in the world, M. Fabrikant & Sons, New York. It resulted in a 50/50 Thai-American partnership with initial registered capital of BHT 25 million (about US $ 660,000 at the 1999 exchange rate).

The 8-year alliance with this company has been phenomenal. The American counterpart, that has a remarkable network of alliances all over the world, has named the young Thai joint venture one of its best, competing nip-and-tuck with a long-time partner in Israel. It also outperforms most other partners in Japan, Singapore and Hong Kong, let alone those in China and India.

Through the gigantic business network of its American partner, CRP Jewellery has cultivated world-class retail customers, namely Wal-Mart,

Sears and JC Penney. In 1994, CRP Jewellery (Thailand) was one of the major players helping M. Fabrikant & Sons, New York, to be named Wal-Mart Vendor of the Year. It was the first time in Wal-Mart's history that a jewelry vendor had been selected Vendor of the Year. Furthermore, in 1998, CRP Jewellery itself was named Wal-Mart International Supplier of the Year, the only jewelry supplier in the world and the only Thai firm to receive this prestigious award.

From BHT 40 million in 1991, the first year of the partnership, total sales skyrocketed to over BHT 900 million in 1999. The total work force of 40 jumped to a total of 400 in-house and more than 1,200 subcontractors. CRP has become within a few years an upper medium-sized enterprise, with several characteristics of a larger firm in the making.

Though it started as a small family business, the CRP management team has been trying very hard to build a real corporation, putting heavy emphasis on international management standards. From the very beginning, excellence has been the strategy: first class reputation of CRP's suppliers and customers, top creativity and innovation of CRP production and management, top skills of the workforce (including subcontractors) and optimal working conditions.

CRP cultivates a double international linkage. Its development and survival are entirely dependent on exports, and are primarily linked to one giant customer, Wal-Mart, which is expanding internationally, most recently to Europe. The over-dependency on one single customer and only one market is perceived more as a strength than a weakness for several reasons. In addition to the size of the American market, Wal-Mart is healthy and expanding and the one-to-one relationship is now considered well established and sustainable. One key explanation is that CRP is very responsive to US market fluctuations and seasonal peaks. Moreover, CRP has realized that Wal-Mart as a wholesaler cannot pretend to have specialized knowledge of American jewelry consumers. Therefore, it has developed together with its local partner a rather sophisticated monitoring system of consumers' tastes and evolving attitudes, which is highly appreciated by Wal-Mart's purchasing and marketing agents. In this way, CRP can always be at the forefront of new market trends and can anticipate new designs of jewelry items suited for the next sales season.

The high quality level of both CRP delivery flexibility and reliability is based on a genuine manufacturing system. Unlike any other jewelry manufacturers in Thailand, CRP has developed its own concept of production.

Upstream, it can easily outsource certain jobs and tasks to a wide network of over 1200 subcontractors who run small jewelry workshops, 70 per cent of whom happen to be formerly trained employees of CRP. In other words, this system is a kind of family or paternalistic one, where subcontractors get orders according to the rhythms of US demand channeled through CRP, which can also support them technically and even financially during low periods.

Downstream, CRP has kept in-house all the final production and quality control activities, which are performed by highly trained staff working in good conditions. The employees use appropriate machinery, including high tech equipment for final gold alloys and stone surfacing and fixing control operations. They also enjoy high salaries above normal Thai standards. Therefore, staff turnover is very low, and employers, subcontractors and employees can rely on strong teamwork that can go day and night during 36 hours in case of a very urgent order.

Impact of the Crisis

CRP did not suffer from the 1997-1998 crisis due to healthy American demand and its exclusive export orientation. In both years, total sales continued to expand rapidly. Total sales of about BHT 500 million in 1996 increased to over BHT 900 million in 1999. It was not affected by the sharp devaluation of the national currency since all transactions were strategically kept in US dollars. CRP management was also aware in 1996-1997 of a possible attack on the baht.

However, CRP financial management had to face the dramatic rise in domestic interest rates and the overall credit crunch affecting all Thai banking institutions. A first move came from family, who put at transitory disposal more than BHT 100 million (US$ 2.5 million) in order to ease tensions in cash flow and working capital.

A later and more sustainable move was to obtain a working capital credit line from the highly respected Dutch ABN AMRO Bank, which in the course of 1999 participated in the restructuring of the local Bank of Asia. The credit line of US$ 5 million or about BHT 200 million with ABN AMRO was facilitated by M. Fabrikant & Sons, New York.

SME Government Policy

During the whole period of the crisis, there was absolutely no help from the government. To the contrary, the corporate income tax administration got more aggressive to bring in more revenue badly needed by the State. The value-added tax was also increased to 10 per cent before being reduced back to 7 per cent, but only in April 1999. On one occasion only, the state EX-IM Bank helped with credit risk guarantee service. There was neither any kind of help, nor any collective government lobbying from the Thai association of jewelry manufacturers, which has tried its utmost, but has never had any significant impact on the industry.

Today, CRP is facing two pending problems, which should be addressed by the public authorities. First, despite its rather high status in the profession, CRP has been waiting for several years for some assistance from the Board of Investment (BOI). BOI should provide bond-warehouse facilities outside limited assigned industrial zones for exporting firms, such as CRP. CRP should be allowed to import raw materials and components (gold, stones, fine jewelry chemicals, etc) without import duty and with fewer cumbersome bureaucratic procedures. Though jewelry brings substantial export revenue to Thailand, the Board of Investment seems more interested in promoting other sectors directly linked to foreign direct investment, such as the automotive and electronic sectors.

Second, CRP is entitled to VAT deduction and reimbursement on various imported materials to be used in the final exported jewelry products. But the claiming procedures are extremely bureaucratic and slow. The government should improve the quality and reliability of the civil servants concerned and drastically speed up the reimbursement delays in order to ease working capital conditions of SMEs.

Business Perspectives

All its success did not come like a windfall or just from sheer luck. Besides the right strategy and good management, CRP Jewellery has earned its reputation through its culture of hard work and sense of urgency. How many companies are there in Thailand or in the rest of the world where the entire management and staff are willing to work non-stop sometimes as long as 36 hours several times a year to fill customers' orders or prepare product presentations? One Wal-Mart manager said after the beginning of the East Asian crisis: 'If all companies in Thailand had worked like CRP, the country would not have been in this tragedy'. One M. Fabrikant & Sons Senior Executive also made this comment: 'The greatest place for us, the place where we can get the best things out of all our partners in the world, is Thailand. I am sorry! It is CRP, not Thailand.'

The current and future development of CRP sounds quite bright, and CRP management seems confident in its entrepreneurial and innovative talents. In the long term, they expect their business to expand internationally and possibly in other sectors in addition to jewelry. CRP could become, down the road, a holding group with only core competencies and financial control kept at the center. In 1999, it has started considering venturing in India and starting-up some export-oriented production activities there. The ambition is to gradually develop a worldwide network of suppliers and producers to meet the new challenges of business globalization, and to avoid an over-concentration of CRP business in Thailand.

CRP may also start investing in other countries such as China and in other sectors (shoes, home furniture, leather products, etc.). At some point, it was envisaged to produce specialized machinery and tools utilized by jewelry manufacturers, but the idea was dropped due to a too narrow market in Thailand and to strong competition from a few highly specialized foreign firms.

Interestingly enough, and contrary to the vast majority of SMEs in Thailand, CRP is not inclined to remain a family business. It has attracted from the best universities in the country some young and entrepreneurial talents, and it also aims at training and retraining its staff to match the best international practices. So far, two senior executives have been sent to top-ten MBA programs in the United States, namely the Sloan MIT MBA Manufacturing Management Track and Duke's Fuqua GEMBA, MBA in global business.

During the next four years, the company has planned to invest more than BHT 40 million to send ten more of its best global managers to the best MBA programs all over the world. This aggressive human resource investment will also involve the universities of those countries where the company plans to establish new production facilities. For instance, in the year 2000, the company will start recruiting students from the highly reputable Indian Institute of Technology.

Second Case Study
LOM THAI CO., LTD. (Textile Apparel Sector)

This case study is the only one describing the destiny of an alien SME, which could be defined as a foreign-owned SME operating in Thailand but considering itself more and more as a local firm. As underlined in Chapter 8, linkages between local SMEs and foreign affiliates can go up to the level of FDI and financial ventures of different types.

Even more original, the so-called foreign parent company of Lom Thai is not a manufacturer itself, but a trading firm having identified an interesting oversea production niche upstream of its existing clients' demand for trading services.

This case has been chosen to show that not all textile and clothing enterprises have been systematically affected by the crisis. To the contrary, such SMEs like Lom Thai, occupying a rather specialized export market niche and having benefited from strong linkages with a foreign buyer, have been particularly resilient to the business downturn and have eventually become more successful than before.

Company Profile

A four-story building situated in the suburbs of Bangkok is the manufacturing location of a locally named world leading brand of children's apparel. Lom Thai Co., Ltd has developed a niche to produce the finest children's clothes under foreign brand licensing. However, it has also established its own local brand name. This SME wants to operate on two legs in both international and domestic markets.

The first initiative came up from a French entrepreneur, who was running an import business in France specialized in children's attire. Children's clothes are normally quite expensive in Europe, and he witnessed French and other European consumers purchasing more and more cheaper imported items. This observation led him to conceive the creation of a factory in Thailand, namely Lom Thai Company Ltd, set up in 1991 with a registered capital of BHT 2 million. Legally, Lom Thai is almost 100 per cent French owned, and has therefore been considered as an alien SME. The enterprise currently employs 70 workers. The majority of them are high school graduates.

Lom Thai specializes in infant apparel, primarily exported to France. Designs and styles are provided by the parent importing company, under the prestigious Christian Dior brand name. This licensing production system includes very precise orders and does not imply the constitution of large stocks. Though local production is under the exclusive control of the French parent import company, Lom Thai can export similar products to a few other markets such as the USA which, however, represents so far only 1 per cent of total export sales.

Regarding other export market potentials, Lom Thai has started more recently to develop its own brand named 'Petit Ours Brun'. It covers infant apparel and accessories that meet the domestic demand both in design and style.

The only two specific inputs needed upstream of local production consist of button molding and the original brand name logo.

Lom Thai has been able to rely on several strong assets:

- the French parent firm provided production and management assistance at the start of the factory;
- the supply of world class materials is secure;
- the factory is able to retain highly skilled workers; and
- the high quality of the final products is well recognized by final customers.

Impact of the Crisis

The Asian crisis has not directly affected Lom Thai, unlike most other Thai apparel manufacturers. The devaluation of the baht should have boosted its export orders, but Lom Thai was not able to expand its production line. This is due to the fact that it cannot have investment credit access to any commercial bank in Thailand because of its alien firm status. Therefore, it was unable to take advantage of increased order placements due to limited production capability. A number of these orders might have eventually gone to other Thai manufacturers, which might have received banking back up to expand production.

But in many ways, thanks to its alien status, Lom Thai was protected from unexpected debt problems. About one hundred local SMEs or large firms producing children's clothing were badly hit by the crisis due to the collapse of the domestic market. Foreign markets were not an option because the poor quality of their products could not match international standards. These standards are rather strict in most importing OECD countries where children's health and safety regulations are given high priority and may be used for import protection.

Lom Thai has not faced any difficulty in its business transactions with its parent company in France, based on a regular made-to-order relationship and on a simple financial transfer of funds. The planning of orders by the parent company has been a strong asset for Lom Thai, which does not have to try to keep up with the short product life cycles due to changes in baby health standards and consumers' tastes in Europe. Therefore, it can concentrate on the evolution of Thai demand for 'Petit Ours Brun' apparel, which is becoming rather popular.

There were a few problems regarding the purchase of imported materials because French and other foreign bankers refused letters of credit for consideration of sovereign risk, at least during the peak of the crisis. Lom Thai tried to solve these difficulties in two ways. First, the parent company in France assisted in buying and delivering the required materials for its Thai affiliate. Second, in a few cases, some local suppliers could be identified that were able to replace some foreign ones, at least temporarily. Globally, Lom Thai was not affected by the crisis, except positively. The weak baht was definitely an asset in boosting export demand to France. The collapse of domestic consumption was insignificant for a nearly fully export-oriented SME like Lom Thai.

Secondly, many local medium-sized and large firms in the textile and clothing industry had to downsize their workforce, and a number of qualified and experienced workers became suddenly unemployed. They were an excellent source of newly hired employees for Lom Thai to expand production capacity to keep pace with the growth of export orders.

Business Perspectives

Throughout the crisis, the company has been able to identify its medium-term strategy together with its French parent firm. It should gradually become a production base exporting to the region and elsewhere. The combination of high quality products sold at very competitive prices is its best asset, as already shown in the Thai domestic market with 'Petit Ours Brun'.

Another strength is the ability to enlarge the product line in the entire region and to control it under its exclusive brand name. At present, Lom Thai is studying how to diversify its production into infant accessories such as gloves and shoes, which are now under design and production testing.

Lom Thai seems to have found the appropriate niche to survive and even prosper throughout the recent crisis. This is quite rare among the many textile SMEs and even larger firms that had a rather bleak outlook during the last two years.

Third Case Study
HESCO FOOD INDUSTRY CO., LTD. (Agro-Food Sector)

Like many other Thai enterprises, Hesco ventured with a Japanese partner at a rather early business stage. When the crisis hit, the decision was made, again like most other SMEs, to diminish production and dig into the accumulated stocks. However, Hesco was primarily export-oriented and not highly dependent on imports, and the crisis was not too harmful.

The linkage with a major Japanese financial counterpart provided unexpected back-up in terms of product diversification and technological up-grading. The very competitive export orientation of Hesco was further confirmed and gradual changes in Thai consumers attitudes led to new market prospects domestically, even though the company had no previous experience in the domestic market.

Hesco could thus continue to develop on two fronts. External markets and globalization remained the top priority until 1999 when Hesco took a new direction with its first direct investment overseas, namely a joint venture in the United States.

Company Profile

The food processing industry ranging from rice milling to seafood packing has long been regarded as one of the sunrise export sectors in which, globally, Thailand has a comparative advantage. Mr. Tritip Telan, Managing Director of Hesco, was educated in Switzerland and the United

States. Influenced by the model of Nestle, his basic strategy was to manufacture value-added food products for export using high quality local content.

Hesco was created in 1985 as a Thai partnership with an initial capital of about BHT 25 million raised by Mr. Telan, whose family is active in the hotel industry, running 5-star hotels, with the support of his close friends and relatives. The first step was to produce cheap semi-finished food products to be processed, flavoured and packed in the markets of final destination.

A few years later, in order to expand food processing capabilities and grab export opportunities by adopting appropriate technology, Mr. Telan felt the need to bring in foreign partners. At present, with 51 per cent personal equity, he is the majority shareholder, but 49 per cent belongs to Japanese venture partners. Of these, the main investor is Japan Asia Investment Corporation (JAIC), which came to Thailand under a Japanese public investment scheme fostering industrialization in the developing economies of East Asia. The foreign importers were initially identified with the support of a family-related trading arm located in Hong Kong and also through Japanese connections. JAIC decided to provide fresh capital in order to diversify its existing investment portfolio in Thailand. The agro-food sector was considered to be among the best performing ones, and Japanese demand for imported snacks was evaluated as expanding and sustainable.

In terms of size, Hesco can today be categorized as an upper medium-sized firm. It has expanded rapidly, with a registered capital of BHT 81 million, total assets of BHT 350 million and about 500 employees in December 1999. Hesco employs blue-collar workers with vocational training to run the new machinery, whereas white-collar workers in charge of quality control have undergraduate degrees in food science.

The product line includes a variety of snack food items made out of starch, wheat, pineapple, and rice. Hesco realized the need to differentiate its line from ordinary products such as rice cracker snacks and Western style mixed snacks. To overtake most of its domestic and regional competitors, Hesco decided to diversify its snacks by flavour, taste, aroma, appearance and colour to satisfy different types of consumers. Compared to most Thai competitors, Hesco has relied on extensive marketing research and studies of consumer behaviour in various parts of the world. As a result, it learned that its spicy mixed snacks (derived from sticky rice) are in high demand in the Middle East.

Interestingly, the medley of flavourings which accounts for about 20 per cent of total raw foodstuff inputs, is imported. Mr. Telan was puzzled as to why so few local manufacturers are capable of producing fine quality flavouring although demand for flavourings has been continuously on the rise, particularly from snack processing factories. In fact, most of the know-how is controlled by Japanese and Western firms, and production requires rather sophisticated equipment.

Hesco's production has been entirely export-oriented. During its initial start-up, almost 90 per cent of total sales went to Japan while the rest went to the United States and Europe. At that time, the snacks produced were limited in taste and appearance. In 1993-1994, the company had to reconsider its market risks due to the rising demand for quality food and the effects of non-tariff barriers. It also took into account rising consumer demand in the West and the Middle East.

As a result, within a couple of years, Hesco invested in new marketing research. In this way, it was able not only to diversify its export destinations but also to adapt flavour and taste to local customs and specificities. Accordingly, the Japanese market has been reduced from 90 per cent to 30 per cent, while the shares for North America, Europe, and the Middle East have expanded to 30 per cent, 20 per cent, and 10 per cent respectively. The rest has been spread elsewhere, with increasing sales in South America (Brazil and Mexico).

Impact of the Crisis

In July 1997, the sudden depreciation of the Thai baht did not squeeze Hesco too badly as most revenue was derived from exports paid for and retained in dollars. Three months before the crisis, Mr. Telan had also wisely repaid some loans in advance. However, after July, when Hesco was targeting new markets, it became extremely difficult to secure an investment loan with acceptable interest rates. In addition, severe cash flow problems emerged because foreign buyers lost confidence in the Thai banking system, and the usual means of payment via trade documents was no longer accepted. One customer even told Mr. Telan that although Hesco was not a risky company, Thailand as a country was considered a full risk.

One way to ease the financial situation was to negotiate preferential trading arrangements directly with those foreign importers well known to Hesco. In a number of cases, commercial bankers were not even called in to provide any financial service.

The stock of food snacks also helped to solve the cash flow problem. Hesco relied on a strategy called 'build-to-stock'. As the devaluation of the baht motivated a surge in foreign demand, Hesco decided temporarily to cut its production by half and to sell most of its existing stocks until the financial crisis cooled down.

Most of this business transition was used to re-orient the production and export objectives. With Japanese assistance, it was possible to identify and recruit some food experts. They provided valuable advice concerning market expansion, product differentiation and financial management at the very crucial time of the East Asian crisis. This included on-the-job training by Japanese technicians visiting the factory for blue-collar workers and the transfer of Japanese technology and know-how.

SME Government Policy

From the very beginning of the crisis, Mr. Telan thought that Hesco had only one option: to help itself. Primarily dependent on foreign exchange earnings, the firm was already in much better shape than most domestic-oriented SMEs.

There was absolutely no expectation of assistance from the Thai government as very little had ever come from the public sector. Mr Telan is extremely critical of both the government and the local banking community, which ignored the SME sector even at the peak of the crisis. The so-called SME policy came too late and had not yet been implemented at the end of 1999. Even statistics were distorted for pure short-term political gains such as when the government claimed that SMEs are responsible for more than half of total exports, when the real figure is– according to him–close to 25 per cent at best! Most SMEs face tremendous difficulties in obtaining international export certification because of the low quality of their products, but this problem has never been properly addressed. Mr. Telan has no faith in the public capacity to deliver concrete support to SMEs.

So far, state policy seems to have favoured specific sectors and especially specific entrepreneurs close to power circles. These sectors are not necessarily the driving engines for the future of Thailand. Political clientelism is so great that senior officials want to please everyone. Lacking in-depth knowledge of manufacturing activities, they are incapable of making painful decisions, which would divert funding and protection from non-performing industrialists. In Mr. Telan's view, public action should focus on providing a fair market environment and appropriate infrastructures to all business players. The rest should be left to each entrepreneur's performance, but some key sectors with obvious comparative advantage could be promoted at least during a transition period. For instance, Thailand could have a bright and uncontested future in agro-business, and the government should promote knowledge of industries upstream and downstream agriculture.

Business Perspectives

Hesco's management is confident. It survived the crisis with little damage and business continues to expand.

On the external front, the strategy is to get closer and closer to local consumers and there is a natural convergence of interests between Hesco and some local importers which can provide reliable marketing knowledge in terms of local tastes, packaging and distribution. Hesco aims to develop its own brand of snacks in each important market. In 1999, it opened its first factory in Las Vegas together with a local buyer. In 2001 or 2002, it plans to open a second factory in Europe, probably in Germany or the Netherlands. In the long term, similar plans could be envisaged in the Middle East, Brazil and Mexico.

On the domestic front, there are also some new developments, even though much more modest. The crisis has drastically reduced the capacity of the Thai middle class to buy expensive food and to dine out in restaurants. There is a new market for snack products, more and more considered as supplementary food items by local consumers. New behaviours and modes regarding nutrition are also developing rapidly, especially in urban areas, Bangkok, in particular, where people spend a lot of time at the work place and in commuting.

Mr. Telan has three sons finishing high school, and he is rather confident that Hesco will have significantly expanded by the time at least one of them takes an interest in helping his father.

Fourth Case Study
HUSAN INDUSTRIAL CO., LTD. (Electrical Sector)

A Taiwanese immigrant has contributed to the economic development of Thailand by establishing a small business manufacturing a variety of fans and air-conditioned motors. It was noteworthy that during the economic crisis this SME received more help from a Taiwanese bank operating in Thailand than from local commercial banks or public financial institutions.

Company Profile

Mr. Numsin Laisathit, slightly over 20 years old, emigrated from Taiwan to Thailand during the 1960s. Equipped with business knowledge acquired during his study in Japan, this entrepreneur decided to produce fans and fan motors under his own company called Husan Industrial Co., Ltd. which was started in 1969, using a loan from Bangkok Bank, and some technical assistance from a Taiwanese friend knowledgeable in fan and motor manufacturing.

The company is located in Nonthaburi province, northwest of Bangkok. Numsin's familiarity with Japan allowed him to dispatch some Husan workers to Japan for technical training. Thus, Numsin has been able to improve its manufacturing know-how. His growth vision subsequently inspired him to diversify the existing products into air-conditioned motors.

In 1975, another company producing air-conditioned motors, Yamabishi Electric Co., Ltd. was established. During 1997, Fasco Motor Group, an American company which was the second largest motor manufacturer in the world, already present in Australia, showed an interest in jointly investing in Thailand. Coincidentally, Yamabishi's growth strategy was matched by Fasco's intention to penetrate the Thai market. As a result, Yamabishi, which had been fully owned by Numsin's family since 1975, was transformed into a joint venture, in which Numsin held 51 per cent and Fasco held 49 per cent of the equity in 1997. The proportion of ownership reflects the maximum percentage of foreign ownership in joint ventures allowed by Thai law during that time. In fact, Numsin did not have to contribute any capital for the 51 per cent equity; instead, the existing factory including machinery was appraised to represent the contribution.

However, the happy marriage did not last long. Fasco solicited TC Group, Yamabishi's competitor founded by Yamabishi's former employee, to join this original joint venture. The problem was exacerbated by other incompatible policies between the two partners. Dissatisfied with the relationship, Numsin finally sold his share in the joint venture in 1999 while retaining the legal right to use the brand 'Yamabishi'.

Husan's major products include the following:

1. Fans (desk, ceiling, wall, stand, oscillation, ventilation, industrial), sold under two brands 'Husan' and 'Yamabishi', representing 80 per cent of the total sales.
2. Motors, representing 20 per cent of sales, used for stone cutting machines and blenders.

The proportion of domestic sales revenue to export sales revenue was 60:40 before the economic crisis; then, it shifted to 45:55. The export market consists of the United States and Europe. Husan has acted as OEM (Original Equipment Manufacturer) for its U.S. customers, which assemble different parts and sell their products under their own brands. European clients order motors and propellers.

In terms of domestic sales, ventilation fans account for 50 per cent, while ceiling fans hold 25 per cent-30 per cent. Husan contends that at least 20 ceiling fan manufacturers in Thailand have copied its steel ceiling fan models.

The Japanese giant Mitsubishi has been Husan's principal competitor in the ventilation fans market. However, as the first fan manufacturer in

Thailand, Husan has enjoyed competitive advantages in the following areas:

- cost, which is claimed to be 30 per cent lower than that of competitors; and
- quality of motors.

However, Husan admits that its weaknesses have emanated from the lower attractiveness of the design of its plastic models and lack of R&D and formal training. Since Husan has to outsource plastic molding and lacks R&D in product design, it was not capable of completely controlling the design of the models. The design of its plastic models seemed to be outmoded as compared with its competitors although its steel ceiling fans have been copied by many contenders.

The Impact of the Crisis

Since only 10 per cent-15 per cent of the inputs are imported, Husan's input cost was only slightly affected by the currency fluctuation after July 1997. However, the direct effects of the economic havoc can be seen in a reduction in sales volume of 20-30 per cent.

Inertia in the property development industry and halts in government construction projects in Thailand have negatively affected demand in the fan industry. Although Husan used a promotion strategy offering price discounts as well as free gifts to lure individual potential customers, depressed purchasing power restrained them from responding to Husan's marketing gimmicks. The domestic sales volume (not revenue) decreased by 50 per cent!

As for export activities, the gain from baht devaluation reflecting in export price decrease contributed to a minuscule 5 per cent gain in export volume (not in revenue), as there was fierce competition from lower priced products of lower quality manufactured in the People's Republic of China. Although the quality of Husan's products is much better, the nature of the product meant that price played a more vital role in consumers' purchase decision. Apparently, the trivial gain in sales volume from export could not offset the ostensible contraction of the local sales volume. In terms of revenue, the proportion of domestic sales to export sales shifted from 60:40 to 45:55.

Moreover, Husan's cash flow has been affected by the difficulty in collecting account receivables and cashing dud checks from a few bankrupted customers. There has also been some delay in cashing export notes and Husan had to face Bangkok Bank's limited credit allowance. Some customers were unable to honor the specified collection period of account receivables, resulting in a delay of expected cash in-flow in some cases and a debt settlement for half the amount in other cases. Both bad checks and bankrupted customers led to a reduction in income. The liquidity problem was exacerbated by the fact that Bangkok Bank extended the export notes cashing period from at most 3 days before the crisis to 17 days after July 1997. Moreover, the bank's branch was not allowed to perform the transaction as in the past; instead, this activity became centralized at the headquarters. The less favorable service offered by the bank triggered Husan to ingeniously switch its export-related transactions to the International Commercial Bank of China, a Taiwanese bank operating in Thailand. The usual cashing period of at most 3 days offered by the local bank could not even emulate the better term of at most 2 days tendered by this foreign bank. It is apparent that a foreign bank, rather than local private or government-owned banks, come to the rescue in Husan's case.

To cope with the reduction in the cash in-flow, Husan inevitably had to resort to cost trimming measures and the most evident area has focused on human resources. A hiring freeze was mandated for both new and vacated positions. Reductions in salary and dissolution of Saturday workdays were decreed. The IFCT (Industrial Finance Corporation of Thailand) and the Government Savings Bank did offer low-interest loans to Husan. However, the interest rates offered were not as favorable as the Taiwanese bank's. In addition, the Federation of Thai Industries and the Association of Consumer Electric Manufacturers sent newsletters to their members informing them of low-interest loans offered by government-owned banks and public agencies, and updated laws and regulations on VAT and tax refunds. As for the VAT refund policy, Husan was not content with the delay in VAT refunds. Before the crisis, the Revenue Department used to refund VAT within 2 months. However, Husan subsequently rarely received the refund on time. In this regard, Husan management wondered whether the delay was caused by a change in the Nonthaburi province tax refund policy or in the nationwide tax refund policy.

SME Government Policy

Husan's assessment of the SME government policy is that it has been neither sufficient nor timely. Although Husan's manager admits that he has not closely followed the development and exact content of the new SME policy, he believes that the government is not sincere in helping SMEs. Moreover, SME policy has not stood high on the agenda of the Democrat Party (the leading party in the current coalition government). In fact, the policies of both Chat Pattana Party (another party in the current coalition government) and Thai Rak Thai Party (a newly formed political party) emphasize to a higher degree the importance of SMEs and governmental assistance. The current government places more emphasis on solving financial institutions' problems more than assisting SMEs.

Husan would like to appeal for government assistance in the areas of more rapid VAT refund and productivity increase. VAT refund should also be timely, especially during a period of recession. Since Husan does not have research & development activities, government aid is needed, especially from the Productivity Institute, in terms of improving productivity through the acquisition of new technologies.

Business Perspectives

Both in the short-term and medium-term, Husan aspires to obtain ISO 9002 certification and improve its product design. It is believed that improvement in design and quality of its plastic models would enable Husan to increase its export market.

Faced with increasing price competition from Chinese and Vietnamese lower-cost manufacturers, Husan is also considering the possibility of related diversification in the long-term. Capitalizing on its knowledge of motor manufacturing, Husan continues to search for new products that could allow the company to achieve positive synergies.

Conclusive Chapter
SME Policy Alternatives

Part I of this book has evaluated the degree of distress among Thai SMEs during the East Asian crisis and through IMF-led structural adjustment policies. Various indicators about the resilience versus the vulnerability of SMEs have been identified and should be further explored to anticipate the potential effects of future economic and financial fluctuations.

Part II has underlined the absence or marginal role of the state until 1999. The state was not able to address market distortions and failures working against SME survival and development. Until today, it has not become an effective facilitator to promote a business environment conducive to entrepreneurship and SME dynamics. The author has expressed doubts about the fragmented and sometimes contradictory components of the newly drafted SME Master Plan. Even if the SME Promotion Bill adopted in January 2000 is a positive step, the effective implementation capability of the concerned public institutions must be questioned and tested.

Part III has tried to demonstrate that the impact of the crisis has been uneven on different categories of SMEs. The hypothesis has been substantially documented but is not yet fully verified that those local SMEs linked to foreign firms and their affiliates were particularly resilient to the crisis. However, this may not be true for all of them, and more research is obviously needed. This category of SMEs also represents a vibrant but small minority among all existing SMEs. Even if further research should illustrate this trend with more data, the SME internationalization linkage strategy cannot be applied to the entire SME sector. The vast majority of SMEs remain primarily domestic market-oriented and the facilitation of their local transactions should be first addressed.

Therefore, Part III does not go as far as suggesting that Thailand and possibly other emerging economies should adopt this strategy. Nevertheless, and due to the difficulties of designing and implementing a convincing SME government policy, this strategy could represent a concrete boost for a number of existing and newly created SMEs attracted by the dynamics of international demand. However, the East Asian crisis has shown that excessive reliance on external demand can be an easily reversible stimulus to economic growth.[1]

This Conclusive Chapter suggests SME policy options, which could work either autonomously or in combination with some of the SME promotion instruments reviewed in both Parts II and III.

SMEs Looking After Themselves

In developing countries and emerging economies in general, and with only a few exceptions, the vast majority of SMEs has been created and has operated autonomously, without any external support from public or private institutions apart from so-called informal sources of capital (Karlsson, 1993). This is also true of Thailand, which shows a dynamic SME contribution by Sino-Thai entrepreneurs in particular. They control extensive inland and overseas business networks, and their relational contracting behaviours (*guanxi*) can offset the relative absence of public support. However, even before the East Asian crisis, the question has often been raised whether family-based SMEs, their minimalist structures, their pluri-dimensional activities, their speculative attitudes, and their crony capitalist networks are the problem rather than the solution for their own expansion and the sustainable recovery of the Thai economy as a whole. This was underlined again by Mr Myoung-Ho Shin, Vice-President of the Asian Development Bank, during UNCTAD X in Bangkok on February 17th, 2000, who declared:

> The challenge for Asia is to get away from the traditional family-led business model. That model has bred practices that have severely limited transparency and disclosure. It is a model that cannot contribute the capital, technology, strategic vision and continuity of cutting-edge management that we need in Asia if we are to achieve world-class competition. The transition away from family-led business took place over a century ago in the United States. Now it must also happen in Asia. Let me take just one measure of wealth concentration: the share of market capitalization held by the top families... The top ten families in Indonesia and the Philippines each control more than half of the corporate sector. Control is also very concentrated in Thailand at 46 per cent, and Hong Kong at 32 per cent. And in Korea, Malaysia and Singapore the top ten families control a quarter of the corporate sector. Broadening ownership ... could help to modernize the business model while also improving the structure of the economy.

In essence, entrepreneurship is based on pure individual initiative within the opportunity limits of a potential market, where the entrepreneur can minimize risk and maximize trust to sustain production and input-output channels. The state cannot be a substitute except in a few strategic activities of general community interest. It is not there to subsidize businessmen or to replace their sense of creativity and risk-taking. However, it can play an important direct or indirect role in providing an institutional environment conducive to the reduction of SMEs' transaction costs domestically and externally.[2]

Until 1997, and despite the frequent changes of Cabinets, it can be argued that Thailand's monarchy and the military provided political stability conducive to entrepreneurship and business development. However, as described in Part I of this book, the nature of the regime and crony capitalist governance introduced all kinds of market distortions and big corporate malpractices not favourable to SME creation and development. The East Asian crisis has suddenly exacerbated domestic economic gaps and policy imbalances.

A top priority should be to restore a business environment with more equal, fair and transparent opportunities for all categories of economic players. Government policy, including the SME Promotion Bill and Draft Master Plan, should primarily target overall conditions more conducive to local entrepreneurship initiative, which should not be jeopardized by the current economic recovery primarily driven by external trade and foreign investment alliances. Otherwise, there is a danger that existing and new small entrepreneurs may continue to mistrust the public authorities and their big scale corporate supporters. The 2000 legislative elections will be a test in this regard, with its potential to start a new type of governance. If so, SME entrepreneurs and the middle class at large could start to identify themselves with state policy, contrary to the past. It is in this respect that the Introductory Chapter has underlined the possible contribution of SMEs to a pluralistic, if not fully democratic society in Thailand, especially on the economic and social fronts, as has happened elsewhere throughout the world.

The crisis has tested the adaptability, flexibility and innovation of Thai SMEs. The process is far from over, but this study has proven that a significant proportion of small entrepreneurs have revealed a capacity for resilience. Their stories are mostly unknown, undocumented and unfortunately not taught in the classroom. Most of them, but not all of them, tend also to prefer confidentiality and to keep a low profile due to limited trust in the formal institutional environment.

The crisis has produced two types of effects. It has destroyed a number of SMEs, but bankruptcies do not necessarily mean less competition and more business opportunities for those remaining in business. It has also simultaneously created new business opportunities at home and overseas for a number of well positioned and well managed SMEs. In the medium-term, this type of SME can attempt to consolidate unexpected new market shares. Those SMEs still in distress or just surviving may expect a positive spillover effect from the national and regional economic recovery, especially if it deepens in 2000-2001. However, it remains extremely fragile so far and could go either way after the next legislative elections due before November 2000. The sustainability of high growth in the USA and the pledge for better performance in Europe and especially Japan will also determine the level of OECD import demand, and the future patterns of foreign direct investment and local outsourcing operations led by transnational corporations.

The pushing capacity and dynamics of Thai SMEs can also produce other types of tangible results. The development of domestic and international small business networking can be left to Sino-Thai businessmen's multi-directional and multi-level activities. They have also been re-evaluated and somehow transformed under the drastic constraints of the recent crisis. Both public and private business facilitators could be possibly developed in the future to promote production system integrating schemes in key sectors of outsourcing and subcontracting and to minimize SME transaction costs.

Family business restructuring and its redeployment process are far from over both domestically and in the whole Asia-Pacific region. An in-depth understanding and smooth management of SME ownership will be important not only to grasp who the 'real' SMEs are, but also to anticipate and canalize the trajectory of industrial development, especially in the high and new tech sectors. The competitive and combined potentials of the Chinese economies (China, Taiwan, Singapore and beyond), also linked to the Sino-Thai entrepreneurs, could be further strengthened by the entries of China and Taiwan in the World Trade Organization.

From another perspective, the sound development of SMEs can also produce direct or indirect entrepreneurial multiplier effects.

Directly, SMEs can expand by themselves and create their own affiliates such as in the case of OEI Co., Ltd presented in Chapter 9. They can also feed micro-enterprises, workshops and household workers with more regular and substantial orders. Of course, this depends on the characteristics of each manufacturing sector, and on each SME owner's business strategy as to whether he wants to control all production aspects in-house or not.

Indirectly, an SME success story can motivate skilled in-house workers to set up their own small business, while keeping formal or informal linkages with their former boss (see the case of CRP Co., Ltd. in Chapter 10). This rather spontaneous phenomenon is far from rare in Thailand and would merit some attention, possibly some institutional support as well, in the future.

SME networking and eventual clustering remains a marginal phenomenon compared to the total number of SMEs (Sengenberger and Porter, 1998). It does not mean that a collective sense has significantly increased among small entrepreneurs, and the crisis may have even produced the opposite effect. Each employer has turned to the core fundamentals of his own business and has tried to keep it standing through the storm. Collective bargaining and lobbying have never been strong in the Thai private sector, not even among the big corporations, owing their existence to the monarchy and a limited number of families.

A major obstacle to the implementation of SME policy lies in the absence of business associations or non-governmental organizations representing SMEs and having a minimum critical mass. In one of its first report on this subject (ILO, 1993, p. 2), the International Labour Organization already mentioned 'the paucity of support to SMEs from the private sector and NGOs.'

Part of the explanation can be found in the Sino-Thai identity of the majority of SME entrepreneurs. Through their family and social organization, many have ownership and participation in several SMEs, and have extended their business interests across several sectors instead of concentrating their wealth in a single one. Such fragmentation and multiplicity of SME activities does not facilitate small enterprise collective action and is not conducive to specific lobbying on any common and well-focused objective. Furthermore, it has not produced so far a horizontal division of labour and high specialization among SMEs. Most existing SMEs have essentially prospered through versatility and low market costs.

It is rather illuminating to observe that the ATSME (Association of Thai Small and Medium Entrepreneurs) was recently initiated by civil servants and is located at the Ministry of Industry. It is not chaired by an SME entrepreneur but by Mrs Chutipa Obhasanond, a former Deputy Director General of the Department of Industrial Promotion (DIP). By the end of 1999, the ATSME can claim no more than 2,000 SME members. Even if we turn to the most powerful trio of private sector associations, namely FTI (Federation of Thai Industries), TBA (Thai Bankers Association) and TCC (Thai Chamber of Commerce), their major focus and membership have remained devoted to the representation of large corporate interests, as mentioned earlier. They are not yet much service-oriented to advise and support local SMEs, particularly outside the Greater Bangkok Region.

With or without external collaboration, let us remember that not all SMEs are equal when it comes to their contribution to growth. Even in the developed countries, the OECD underlines that over 60 to 70 per cent of economic dynamism and employment growth come from no more than 10 per cent of all SMEs, which can really be described as the 'entrepreneurial engine'. Perhaps 20 to 25 per cent of all SMEs are serious about seeking growth, but only 5 per cent are successful in actually achieving sustainable growth.

We should also remain aware that the definition of proper SMEs is becoming more and more difficult. Many so-called SMEs are increasingly part of larger alliances or companies, and some can even become a subsidiary of another SME or big firm (Nagamura, 1999). Many other SMEs are founded by entrepreneurs stepping out of large firms, who keep loose or close links with their previous employer,[3] as also observed in some case studies presented in Chapters 9 and 10.

Building Networks between the Private and Public Sectors

The new SME policy is supposed to rely on so-called private-public joint collaborations. Though not much experienced before in the Thai context, this proposal is consistent with the prevailing thinking nowadays among SME development experts, especially within the World Bank group of SME donors. Considering the dominant role of foreign and domestic private market forces, and the decline of public revenue and state investment capacity, it is far from clear whether the establishment of private-public collaborations is merely a catch-word strategy or can really match the business culture and politics of Thailand.

First, the number of business associations has gradually increased during the last two decades (Chenvidyakarn, 1979). Some of them take part at least formally in the planning process guided by the National Economic and Social Development Board (NESDB), but planning was never considered too seriously in a country like Thailand. At the sector-level, such consultations have centered on the automotive industry and on export promotion across targeted sectors. During the 1980s, the biggest associations representing large corporations such as the Federation of Thai Industries, the Thai Bankers Association, the Thai Chamber of Commerce, and the Joint Public-Private Consultative Committee (JPPCC) have gained fairly easy access to state officials and have gained policy influence (Laothamatas, 1992). But the provincial Chambers of Commerce represent less than 20 per cent of locally registered businesses, not to mention the unregistered ones.

Much more significant, the influence of big business carries on through informal and relational channels, and not so much through institutionalized associations or joint committees. For instance, the Ministry of Industry used to be under the control of the Chart Thai political party, which has had close ties with large textile corporations.

The lobbying role of the private sector may have amplified during the 1990s due to deregulation and increasing competition. However, it has led to closer cooperation among private firms and state agencies but has not provided public officials with the necessary information to formulate policies well adapted for each branch of industry as a whole. It is only since mid-1993 that the Provincial Development Committees (20 members) have invited two members to represent the private sector, meaning exclusively urban and large firms in practice. The real involvement of the private sector has also been minimum in the JPPCC mentioned above, especially in the provinces.

An other example refers to the textile associations such as TTMA (Thai Textile Manufacturers' Association) or the TGMA (Thai Garment Manufacturers' Association) which in 1995-1996 called for drastic adjustments in the textile industry due to the decrease of tariff protection and the increase in foreign competition, but they were not heard by the bureaucracy until the outbreak of the crisis. Similarly, since the late 1980s, they regularly called for the creation of a National Textile Training Institute, which was finally approved but only ten years later.[4]

The situation became more confused during and throughout the crisis. The Chuan democratic government has been facing two impediments: first, the need to re-establish private investors' confidence and to attract fresh capital, and simultaneously, the obligation to regulate and supervise as impartially as possible debt restructuring and corporate reform. Despite a few corruption allegations or rumours, the Chuan administration has been much cleaner than its predecessors, and this has been reflected in the continued support of public opinion and the failure of the censure motion introduced by the New Aspiration Party in mid-December 1999.

Until today, it must be deplored that Thai officials seldom reach decisions after consulting the most concerned. Contrary to Japan for example, the Thai state has never been able to consult at length with local industrialists and other social partners before launching industrial policies, which would then receive strong support from the most concerned enterprises. Due to weak formal channels linking business and state officials and due to the lack of interest-aggregating institutions and forged consensus before, new policies face all kinds of obstacles, which reduce their capacity for concrete implementation.

First, a striking feature of Thai politics is the ease with which a fairly large number of actors can force the reversal of state decisions.

Second, no political party, except perhaps the newly formed Thai Rak Thai Party, has a respected voice articulating the concerns and needs of the industrialists.

Thirdly, close consultation and cooperation between the private and public sectors can be hindered by a very clear societal divide. The ethnic Chinese or so-called Sino-Thai entrepreneurs dominate the economy with their specific pattern of social organization, while the ethnic Thais prevail in state agencies. The two spheres do not interact much, even if the ethnic divide is shrinking and if superficial relations are harmonious, contrary to the situation in some other Southeast Asian countries. The profile of the

Chinese business community involved in both large firms and SMEs may be associated with the fact that:

> Trust may be particularly high within social networks characterized by high degrees of closure and high entry barriers. [5]

The Thai elite and the Chinese business community have learned to co-exist and to exchange gifts and favours to achieve their goal of capital accumulation, but there is a relative absence of mutual obligations and of regularly constituted pluralistic groups.

In his recent book, Unger (1998, p.4), who has spent considerable time in both Japan and Thailand, argues that:

> Individuals and firms' capacity to bypass market failures (such as the recent crisis) depends in part on their ability to cooperate with one another, a skill that varies over time and populations.

He suggests that the organization of a nation's social capital conditions the ways in which individuals and firms respond (or not) to frameworks of material incentives put tentatively in place by state or non-governmental institutions. In other words, the desire and capacity of individuals and firms to work with those institutions command the outcome, whatever the objective.

In the case of Thailand, traditional state weakness is not only a cause of particular outcomes–absence of SME policy until 1999 for example–but also a result of specific patterns of societal organization, which can evolve only gradually overtime. According to Unger (1998, pp. 7-8), the nature of Thai social organization induces:

- a rather high number but diffused density of SMEs and micro-enterprises;
- a small number of large and privileged monopolies and oligopolies;
- few and ineffective pressure groups (such as labour unions, peasant cooperatives, consumer groups, NGOs, etc.);
- relatively weak organization among firms (including large ones);
- definitely weak public policy and coordination among state agencies; and
- a loose pattern of interest aggregation in which personal and patronage relations dominate over weak participatory institutions such as highly fragmented political parties.

On the one hand, state measures even during periods of military rule have often remained ineffective but have been conducive enough to attract private sector investment, and the scope for state intervention has been limited due to limited market failures during the last decades of rapid economic growth. On the other hand, state authority has been incapable of imposing consensual solutions to collective problems. It seems that costs and benefits were hardly divisible or could not be balanced among well-organized private sector and non-governmental players, which were not as yet well structured.

Until the mid-1990s, Thailand was able to achieve a rather stable and effective macro-economic policy controlled by a small group of institutions (Ministry of Finance, Bank of Thailand, Budget Bureau, NESDB, and a few public and private commercial banks), and there is a reasonable chance that it can perform again reasonably well beyond the East Asian crisis.

Micro-economic policy has been much less successful when it has tried to target certain actors and sectors, and there are doubts that the new SME strategy objectives can be rapidly achieved through effective and smooth public-private collaboration. However, under increased internationalization pressures, Thai SMEs will have to rely on external linkages more and more for buying inputs and selling outputs. In order to meet this challenge, they will need more supportive public policies and will also have to demonstrate a capacity to cooperate among themselves and vis-à-vis large firms.[6]

Despite the existence of the Federation of Thai Industries (FTI), the Thai Chamber of Commerce (TCC) seems to be the only major private sector organization providing in principle a range of business development services, supposed to be accessible to all categories of firms. But even there, SME membership remains unimpressive and no evaluation of existing services is available. Although some other organizations charge fees for their services, most of them are far from reaching a sufficient level of financial sustainability. There could be only a few possible exceptions in some not too distant future such as the Foundation for the Thailand Productivity Institute (FTPI), the Thai-German Institute (TGI) and the Industrial Estate Authority of Thailand (IEAT). Very recently, the US Agency for International Development has also decided to fund an SME advisory centre in Thailand. The centre is supposed to screen SME applicants and select only firms with a genuine intent to improve their business that are ready to pay a fee of about BHT 3,000 a day.[7]

Thailand has still a long way to go in the direction of mentoring an SME incubation system, where business development services can be provided by government, private consultants or large enterprises, depending on their respective core competencies.

Development of Intra-private Sector Collaborations and Linkages

The recent crisis has revealed the limits of foreign investment-based and export-driven industrialization as a model vulnerable to structural weaknesses and to sudden external shocks. The desirable development of competitive local firms and resilient SMEs may have to follow different but not necessarily contradictory avenues. As mentioned in the first section of this chapter, spontaneous clustering and networking among SMEs can be seen as one option but is difficult to implement effectively at the grassroots. Important clusters have to be selected based on geographical concentration, sectoral specialization, ancillary relationships, and value-added and supplier-vendor value chain contributions.

Among hundreds or thousands of firms in one specific sector of industry, most SMEs tend to be confined to a single or a few low specialized sub-sectors, whereas the large firms dominate all the others. Among the big family-based industrial groups, the typical Sino-Thai pattern of chain ownership means that the various members of the family have shares in a wide range of companies, both large and medium (if not small). This pattern tends to produce a high degree of vertical integration, unlike the possible horizontal clustering among truly autonomous, innovative and neighbouring SMEs.[8]

A second option would be to rely on private sector associations to contribute to industrial development and SMEs in particular, and to help firms to cooperate with one another. But, as noted earlier, this has not happened much until today, despite clear evidence of increased activism on the part of the associations during the 1990s, at least until the crisis.

Perhaps more significant than the associations, some big commercial banks and service-oriented groups have occasionally induced collaborations among local manufacturers. Since the crisis, they have naturally focused on more urgent priorities. But, in the near future, they could possibly expand into new areas such as investment banking, factory monitoring, management consulting, and federate fragmented business interests in various sub-sectors or sectors of industrial activity. Their recently established or forthcoming partnerships with foreign firms could also help in this direction. However, it is far from sure that large commercial banks will find profit enough in implementing a corporate credit strategy matching the real needs of SMEs.

Alternative financial instruments will have to be gradually developed such as: a flexible second board for SME stocks, apparently rather successful in the case of South Korean SMEs; accessible venture capital and business start-up funds like in Hong Kong; specialized small capital funds like in Singapore.[9] Various interesting experiences can be derived from the OECD economies in this respect, and locally adapted. The Vice-President of the Asian Development Bank also declared during UNCTAD X on February 17th, 2000:

> Asia's model of extensive growth, based on very high savings and investment rates, may also need change. Asia needs to invest smarter, not invest more. It needs to develop an intensive growth

model, that creates more, with less, and allows more for consumption.

We know that competition between local firms and foreign affiliates can be strong in some sectors and sometimes destructive for a number of domestic entrepreneurs (Kokko, 1996). A third option, already underlined in Part I of this book, is to use and further promote the supply and export linkages between local SMEs and large firms, particularly but not exclusively through foreign affiliates of transnational corporations (TNCs) operating in Thailand and the region. However, this strategy shows that local procurement and outsourcing policies, whether proposed by host governments and/or TNCs themselves, do not automatically lead to further development, diversification and up-grading of existing SMEs (Bruch and Hiemenz, 1984; Chareanwongsak, 1999).

In recent years, the internationalization–if not globalization–of the leading SMEs from the OECD countries has also accelerated, and some have started to settle in Thailand and elsewhere in Southeast Asia (Fujita, 1998; Milton-Smith, 1998; UNCTAD, 1998, 1999).

Looking at the more liberal FDI and foreign ownership legislation adopted in Thailand in 1998-1999, and at the fifth strategy of the draft SME Master Plan in particular (Chapter 6), the authorities may prefer to use the recent crisis as an opportunity to attract even more relocation of TNCs' activities. TNCs are encouraged to relocate additional segments of production, but also to invest capital in local firms and to bring along some of their suppliers and subcontractors (so-called supporting industries). This strategy seems to pay off. Thailand has been among the first FDI world destinations in 1998, together with Brazil, China, Korea and Venezuela. New flows of FDI in 1998-1999 represent about one third of total cumulative FDI in Thailand since 1980 (UNCTAD World Investment Report, 1999). Although FDI flows to Thailand dropped in 1999 to about US$5.8 billion, this was in part due to the flattening wave of massive re-capitalization in the banking sector. Nevertheless, FDI surpassed the historically high level Thailand had achieved in 1997, particularly in manufacturing activities.[10]

For instance, automotive production could soon become the fastest-growing export sector together with the three traditional leaders: electronics, jewelry and canned food. In mid-1999, Toyota announced that Thailand would become its major Asian production hub outside Japan. Several other automakers such as BMW, Ford, General Motors, and Mazda have also committed some direct investments in order to gain at least modest market shares, both domestically and in the region.[11]

There is little reason not to believe that such new flows of FDI will continue to materialize, taking into account post-crisis deflated investment costs and long-term attractive market opportunities in the most populated region of the world. In 1998, FDI jumped to US$7 billion compared to 3.7

billion in 1997. Despite a slowdown in 1999, both the Thai government and business circles could be inclined to maintain their strong commitment to laissez-faire and liberal export-driven policies.[12]

This likely trend will also mean additional foreign competition domestically, with the risk of confronting the non-internationalized local firms, and particularly the less productive SMEs. It could modify the local features of existing entrepreneurship and the modalities of creating new SMEs in several ways.

Therefore, the government should play a limited but effective role in addressing the barriers to business entry of local SMEs and local firms in general. It should target its efforts at two ends:

- on the demand side, foreign affiliates should be encouraged to consume locally produced intermediate goods;
- on the supply side, local enterprises and SMEs in particular can be envisaged as potential producers of intermediate goods.

In this context, SME development would be spurred predominantly from above by large domestic groups, foreign TNCs and joint ventures. This pattern would not be fundamentally different from the typology of SME evolution observed during the last twenty years, and recalled in Chapters 1 and 3. The process could simply accelerate in the Greater Bangkok Region, and also produce more and more business linkages and multiplying effects at the provincial and district levels.

However, as mentioned above, specific attention and measures will have to be devoted to tackle the problem. As indicated by Bello (1998, p.55):

> Economic growth has not been accompanied by industrial and technological deepening...A great part of the problem has resided in the practices of multinational corporations, which have spearheaded the industrialization drive in Thailand.

So far, with most intermediate components and parts been imported, the development of export-oriented industries has not been much sourced locally and has therefore failed to stimulate the start-up of new domestic SME suppliers, at least in big numbers. In Thailand today, linkages between transnational corporations and local companies in general, not to mention true SMEs, are still few.

The model experience of Japan and Taiwan indicates that SMEs have played a foundation for industrialization and improved competitiveness. However, the so-called keiretsu system linking large companies and their suppliers in Japan is perceived negatively in the USA and the West in general. It is perceived not only as the manifestation of the closed nature of the Japanese market, but also as one mode of production responsible for the current slowdown in Japanese economic performance. Therefore, it remains to be seen how Thailand can develop its SME sector under specific guidance of large corporations but without necessarily copying everything from Japan.

As already suggested by the BUILD program under the Board of Investment, the setting-up of linkages between SMEs and large firms, especially foreign ones, could enhance:

1. The transfer of technology and know how;
2. The substitution of costly imports by local supply;
3. The deepening and widening of the local industrial base;
4. The resilience and productivity of local enterprises.

There is certainly scope for BOI acting as a matchmaker between local industry (possibly including SMEs) and foreign investors. Yet, BOI has to coordinate with no less than a dozen of other institutions to provide effective information and service to the local supporting industry (Kawabe, 1996, pp. 129-30). Despite renewed efforts, the 200 auto-parts producers, most of them Thai and coordinated by the BOI, still lack the capability of producing the really critical parts.

Probably, the central problem lies elsewhere following the fast trade liberalization imposed on Thailand under the GATT Uruguay Round of Multilateral Trade Negotiations. All local content rules for passenger-car manufacturing are supposed to be lifted in January 2000. This has already meant bankruptcy or tough survival for many Thai-owned component and part SMEs that had grown up under the 25-year old local content policy.[13] The result is that the only survivors will be those few supporting firms and joint venture subsidiaries controlled, directly or indirectly, by the large car manufacturers which are essentially Japanese. For instance, it is little problem for Toyota to announce that its local content is already close to 70-75 per cent for the production of pick-up trucks. It plans to further increase local manufacturing, and to continue financial and technical assistance to its cash-trapped joint ventures and supporting SMEs as initiated during the crisis.[14] Thailand's free trade reorientation brings the Japanese, who have already a virtual monopoly of the domestic market, to transform it into a main production base in order to benefit from low labour costs and loose business environment regulations (Bello, 1998, pp.67-8).

Furthermore, the breakup of large firms should be envisaged as a major trend of today's industrial evolution. Such breakup is the result of business decentralization, vertical disintegration and downsizing. It is induced by the arrival of new technologies, which permit the manufacture of more differentiated products, and by increasingly sophisticated consumer demand. Therefore, large firms are following fragmentation strategies at the global level, focusing on product differentiation. This creates new opportunities for middle-income countries such as Thailand to create inter-firm linkages through subcontracting with the advent of niche marketing, that can allow SMEs to specialize production at low overhead cost.

Finally, the preliminary implementation of the ASEAN Free Trade Area (AFTA) is supposed to start in January 2000, and the recent ASEAN Summit in Manila has indicated that it is expected to proceed despite some reservations by a few member-states. AFTA will not discriminate against the regional operations led by transnational corporations. To the contrary, the promotion of brand-to-brand complementation is supposed to encourage the outsourcing of different industrial components and parts in various member-states. The groundwork for such supporting industry or SME specialization is thus being laid at least in a few key sectors. For instance, it is already the case in the electrical industry: Thailand manufactures so-called white goods (refrigerators, washing machines), Malaysia supplies air conditioners and audio equipment, and Singapore has become the focal manufacturer of high value-added goods and the center of regional distribution networks.

Business transactions and de facto economic integration will also expand between Thailand/ASEAN and other regional partners like China, Japan, Korea and Taiwan. In other words, East Asian intra-regional specialization among foreign firms and local partners will increase and put additional competition pressure on local SMEs in each individual ASEAN economy, including Thailand of course.

Prospects

Since the outbreak of the East Asian crisis, the central concern has been to prevent worldwide spillover effects and to protect domestic and foreign creditors. Structural adjustment policy has focused on debt restructuring and corporate reform among the large institutions and firms concerned. The heavy and often overpriced burden of such policy on local SMEs has not been addressed. The distress of the SME sector has been totally neglected by international donors and national governments, despite its important contribution to economic and social development.

Although the literature dealing with the East Asian crisis and produced since 1997 is vast, it has interestingly not addressed the SME issue. Among the few potential merits of this book, its key message is to bring up new ground: the analysis of structural adjustment policy should not stop at the door of micro-, small- and medium-scale enterprises, which represent the bulk of business and employment creation. There is no contest that Thailand and the other affected economies of the region had first to address financial stabilization in late 1997 and early 1998. But it did not necessarily imply that structural adjustment had to be continued in 1998-2000 for the sole salvation of large banks and corporations and without any concrete support to SMEs.

A number of lessons can be derived from the SME experience of Thailand before, during and possibly beyond the recent crisis:

- a rather high number of low-cost and non-specialized SMEs developed along the path of rapid growth during the two decades preceding the crisis, but the core industrialization strategy relied on large export-oriented firms and on foreign direct investment by transnational corporations. In other words 'SME opportunities arose from the groundwork laid at the national government/big business level' (McVey, 1992, p. 9);
- both public and private interest for local entrepreneurial capacity and SME development remained very scarce and many existing SMEs were related to top business families and large firms in various ways; therefore, the alarming distress of SMEs during the crisis was disregarded primarily due to lack of proper awareness, information channels and in-depth knowledge;
- contrary to initial assumptions in 1997-1998, SMEs suffered much more than large firms and primarily from the collapse of domestic demand. The credit crunch hit them at a later stage and as a second constraint at least for those SMEs relying on institutional banking as a source of finance. It resulted in further decline of trust and transactions between commercial banks and SMEs;
- SME data and sources of information remained too limited to obtain an estimation of the real effects of the crisis and there is no indication that this major problem will be solved in the near future. Yet, this book together with the few industrial surveys conducted by the World Bank and the Japanese cooperation tend to suggest a series of SME performance indicators which could contribute to the regular publication of a national SME index able to anticipate and possibly contain the most negative aspects of future market fluctuations;
- there is a missing middle between large firms (domestic and foreign ones) and local SMEs; the vast majority of SMEs tend to be too localized and not prepared to respond to the outsourcing and subcontracting standards of larger firms producing for both external and domestic markets; well-focused policies and instruments should be developed to facilitate wider and deeper mutually supporting linkages between these two categories of firms;
- empirical research tends to prove that a minority of SMEs already linked to foreign firms operating in Thailand have been rather resilient to the crisis in comparison with most purely domestic-oriented SMEs;

however, the internationalization and globalization of a significant segment of SMEs can be envisaged only as a long-term objective;
- the fragile economic recovery and the inflow of new foreign direct investment alone do not guarantee direct and positive spillover effects on the real situation of SMEs; if the ongoing credit crunch and the paralysis of commercial banks are not rapidly inverted, more innovative sources of cash flow assistance and investment capital will have to be explored to match the real needs of the SME business community;
- public governance and private sector citizenship will have to include the horizontal and vertical contributions of SMEs in the overall production process to avoid holes and gaps in the 21st century modalities of Thai industrialization; SMEs should be envisaged as an important agent of sustainable development both in economic and social terms; SMEs will also play a dynamic and innovative role in new industries and services.

Part III of this book brings additional material to the current international debate preaching for the multiplication of linkages between SMEs and large firms, big and small-scale transnational corporations in particular. If SME resilience will be more and more dependent on various forms of contractual and relational linkages vis-à-vis foreign direct investors having direct access to global markets, what should be the role left to the Thai government? This would lead to a local enterprise promotion policy producing a kind of subsidiary capitalism or so-called 'ersatz' capitalism (Kunio, 1988).

But, even if Thailand was able to internalize a majority of components and parts going into high tech manufacturing, the cost of capital goods (machinery) and other related costs (licenses, royalties) would be enormous in addition to the investment to be made in educational and training facilities at a different scale and quality than today.

There is no doubt that more systematic and competitive outsourcing by large firms would positively boost a certain category of SMEs able to come up with high production standards, intra- and inter-industry networking interactions and clear commitments vis-a-vis the major players. However, this strategy would put further emphasis on supporting SMEs whose autonomy would be limited by formal and informal agreements with foreign parent companies dictating modalities of production in accordance with their own global sourcing interests. The risk here would be to minimize SMEs' exposure to market driven demand for more sophisticated products and to subordinate it to single large corporation demand. This strategy could also delay or reduce local entrepreneurship development as supporting SMEs may end up being those partly or wholly owned by foreign investors and, in some cases, directly by large contractors themselves.

In some sectors like agro-food, automotive, electrical products, electronics, telecommunications, there is already a clear trend in Thailand showing that transnational corporations cultivate both their hard core business interest and corporate citizenship profile in supporting not only their existing SME suppliers and subcontractors but also in promoting some SME newcomers, clusters, cooperatives and business associations through educational, vocational training, technical and financial facilities. In the case of foreign affiliates established in Thailand for decades and nearly considered as local companies, they tend to supply financial assistance and become a substitute to commercial banks which usually consider SMEs as too risky, not profitable, and are now paralyzed by large corporate non-performing loans.

This type of SME internationalization or globalization opens up three questions:

- can Thailand mobilize and combine public and private resources to boost a diverse and strong SME sector to catch up with newly industrialized economies (NIEs) like Korea or Taiwan? In 1999, some of the most eminent Thai economists, such as Senator N. Akrasanee, openly declared their pessimism and their doubts about the validity of catching up with industrialization as pursued since the 1960s. On the occasion of his 72nd birthday (December 5th, 1999), His Majesty the King suggested more modest growth objectives based on self-contentment and absence of greed. After the recent crisis, matching the development of the NIEs and OECD countries is perhaps more out of reach than ever; national priorities may be elsewhere;
- can Thailand produce enough wealth and jobs domestically by adopting –like in the past– an industrial strategy solely linked to big foreign investors and large export-oriented corporate interests? There is an obvious need for more and more outsourcing locally and Thailand may become a base for upstream support to mass production and export activities. But what is going to happen to those sectors producing only for the domestic market and local consumers?
- can Thailand anticipate and avoid possible economic and even social backlashes if too many SMEs are left out of the main competition stream and are pushed at best to focus on second-class domestic market segments? This may lead to a heavily polarized economy and dual social system, which can hardly be sustained without government intervention and welfare redistribution.

Epilogue

The manuscript of this book was completed during the UNCTAD X Conference held in Bangkok on February 12-19, 2000.

Let us conclude here with this declaration of Mr. Rubens Ricupero, Secretary-General of UNCTAD, on February 15th:

> Though transnational firms have investment and technology transfers in developing nations, most have only channeled them through their subsidiaries and not through local SMEs...It is necessary to encourage the transnational corporations (TNCs) to work with local SMEs...Local SMEs in developing countries are likely to face more hardships amid a World Trade Organization drive for a rapid change in international trade in the future... TNCs should try to make SMEs stronger to ensure their survival as the WTO will in the future wipe out current rules such as local content requirements proposed by developing countries... National governments should treat SMEs and TNCs differently.

Notes

[1] Islam, A. (2000), *Comments as a Panelist*, Symposium on Economic and Financial Recovery in Asia, UNCTAD X, Bangkok, 17 February 2000.

[2] Nooteboom, B. (1993), 'Firm Size Effects on Transaction Costs', *Small Business Economics*, vol. 5, no. 4, pp. 283-95.

[3] Hall, C. (1999), *The Challenges and the Opportunities of E-Commerce and International SMEs: Implications of Human Resource Management in APEC*, Sun Yat-sen University and SME Administration of the Ministry of Economic Affairs, APEC Symposium on Human Resource Management Symposium on SMEs, Paper, Kaoshiung, 29-30 October.

[4] *Bangkok Post*, 14 October 1995 and 15 February 1996.

[5] Coleman, J. (1994), 'Social Capital in the Creation of Human Capital', *American Journal of Sociology*, pp. 105-08.

[6] Lazonick, W. (1991), *Business Organization and the Myth of the Market Economy*, Cambridge University Press, Cambridge, pp. 6-13.

[7] *Bangkok Post*, 4 December 1999.

[8] Somsak, T. and Yamazawa, I. (1981), *Manufactured Exports and Direct Foreign Investment*, Thammasat University Press, Bangkok, p. 5.

[9] *Far Eastern Economic Review*, 3 February 2000.

[10] UNCTAD, *FDI Holds Steady in Developing Asia as a Whole in 1999*, Press Release, 25 January 2000, TAD/INF/2834, Geneva.

[11] *The Nation*, 20 October 1999; *Asian Wall Street Journal*, 2 November 1999.

[12] *Bangkok Post*, 16 December 1999.

[13] *Bangkok Post*, 31 May 1996.

[14] *The Nation*, 27 October 1999.

Bibliography

Sources

APEC (1994), *The APEC Survey on Small and Medium Enterprises*, APEC Committee on Trade and Investment, Singapore.

Asian Productivity Organization (1996), *Developing Supporting Industries In Asia-Pacific*, Tokyo.

Bank of Thailand (1998-99), *Quarterly Bulletin*.

Board of Investment (1998-99), *BOI Investment Review*, Bangkok. Department of Industrial Promotion (1987), *The Development Strategies for the SMIs in Thailand*, by K. Akira and S. Kasajima, SMI Promotion and Finance Project, Ministry of Industry, Bangkok.

DIP (1988), *Small and Medium Industries Modernization Policy by Sector in Thailand*, Ministry of Industry and JICA, Bangkok.

DIP (1999), *SMEs*, Ministry of Industry, Bangkok.

DIP (1999), 'The Direction for SME Promotion in Thailand and Supporting Industry', *Journal of Business Administration*, Thammasat University, Faculty of Business Administration and Accountancy, March 2, Special Issue, Bangkok, pp. 66-90 and 140-76 *(in Thai language)*.

ESCAP (1995), *Expansion of Manufactured Export by SMEs in the ESCAP Region*, United Nations, ESCAP Studies in Trade and Investment, Bangkok.

ESCAP (1997), *Small Industry Bulletin for Asia and the Pacific*, United Nations, Economic and Social Commission for Asia and the Pacific, no. 30, Bangkok.

Industrial Finance Corporation (1998), *SMEs Support and Promotion*, A Report to the Ministry of Finance, Bangkok *(in Thai language)*.

Industrial Information Center (1999), *Industrial Statistics*, Office of Industrial Economics, Ministry of Industry, Semi-annual Report, Bangkok.

ILO (1993), *Development of Provincial SMEs, with the Involvement of the Private Sector and NGOs*, International Labour Office, Regional Office for Asia and the Pacific, Bangkok.

ILO (1995), *Creating an Enabling Environment for SMEs Development*, by S. White, Geneva.

ILO (1998), *The Social Impact of the Asian Financial Crisis*, ILO Regional Office, Bangkok.

ILO (1999), *Towards Full Employment, Prospects and Problems in Asia and the Pacific*, ILO Regional Office, Bangkok.

ILO (1999), *Micro and Small Enterprise Development and Poverty Alleviation in Thailand*, A Series of Working Papers edited by G. Finnegan, ILO Regional Office and UNDP, Bangkok (6 Working Papers).

ILO (1999), *Micro and Small Enterprises: Giants in Employment and Development*, Seminar, Conference Package Paper, Project on Micro and Small Enterprise Development and the Potential for Alleviating Poverty in Thailand, with Particular Reference to Urban Areas, ILO Regional Office and UNDP, 26-27 October, Bangkok.

Ministry of Industry (1998), *Strategies for Incubation and Strengthening of SMEs under the Five-Year Industrial Restructuring Plan 1998-2002*, Industrial Restructuring Plan Working Group, Bangkok *(in Thai language)*.

Ministry of Industry (1999), *Institute for SME Development Foundation Project*, MoI and Thammasat University, Bangkok *(in Thai language)*.

Ministry of Labour and Social Welfare (1999), *Yearbook of Labour Statistics 1998*.

Mizutani, S. (1999), *Master Plan for SMEs Promotion Policy (Draft)*, An Advisory Report to Minister of Industry/Minister of Finance, Bangkok.

National Economic and Social Development Board (1997), *The Eighth National Economic and Social Development Plan (1997-2001)*, Bangkok.

National Statistics Office (1998), *The Impact of the Economic Crisis on Employment, Unemployment and Labour Migration*, Bangkok.

NSO (1998), *Report of the Labor Force Survey (Whole Kingdom)*, Bangkok.

NSO (1998), *Report of the 1996 Listing of Industrial and Business Establishments (Whole Kingdom)*, Bangkok.

NSO (1999), *Report of the 1997 Industrial Census (Whole Kingdom)*, Bangkok.

NSO (1999), *Report of the 1997 Listing of Manufacturing Industry Establishments (Whole Kingdom)*, Bangkok.

National Economic and Social Development Board (1997), *The Eighth National Economic and Social Development Plan (1997-2001)*, Bangkok.

OECD (1997), *Globalisation and SMEs*, Synthesis Report, Paris.

OECD (1999), *Industrial Restructuring in the Asian Economies*, DSTI/IND (99/2), Paris.

Small and Medium Enterprise Administration (1999), *The Experience and Achievements in Providing Guidance and Assistance to SMEs*, Ministry of Economic Affairs, Taipei.

Small and Medium Enterprise Agency of Japan (1999), *SMEs White Paper*, Ministry of International Trade and Industry, Tokyo.

Stock Exchange of Thailand (1999), *The Guideline for Debt Restructuring for SMEs*, SET and Board of Debt-Restructuring Promotion (Bank of Thailand), Bangkok.

Thai Rak Thai Party (1999), *SMEs Management and Policy Report*, Bangkok.

UNCTAD (1998) (1999) *World Investment Report*, United Nations, Geneva.

UNCTAD (1998), *A Handbook on Foreign Direct Investment by Small and Medium-sized Enterprises: Lessons from Asia*, United Nations, Geneva.

UNDP (1998), *Responding to the Thai Economic Crisis*, United Nations, New York/Bangkok.

UNICO International Corporation (1995), *The Study on Industrial Sector Development, Supporting Industries in the Kingdom of Thailand*, Draft Final Report, Tokyo/Bangkok.

UNICO and International Development Center of Japan (1999), *The Follow-Up Study on Supporting Industries Development in the Kingdom of Thailand*, Draft Final Report and Summary, Tokyo/Bangkok, 2 volumes.

UNIDO (1990), *Industrial Development in Thailand in the 1990s: Prospects, Constraints, and Priority Areas for Technical Assistance*, United Nations, Vienna/Bangkok.

UNIDO (1992), *Thailand: Coping with the Strains of Success*, Blackwell Publishers, Vienna.

UNIDO (1999), *Industrial Reform to Enhance Industrial Competitiveness: Implications and Strategies for SME Development*, by M. Leopairote, Department of Industrial Promotion, Ministry of Industry, UNIDO Asia-Pacific Forum, Vision and Challenges for Sustainable Industrial Development: Lessons from Asian Crisis, Bangkok, 23-24 September.

World Bank (1993), *The East Asian Economic Miracle*, Oxford University Press, Washington D.C.

World Bank (1994), *Industrial Structures and the Development of SME Linkages: Examples from East Asia*, edited by S.D. Meyanathan, Economic Development Institute of the World Bank, Washington D.C.

World Bank (1998), *East Asia: The Road to Recovery*, Washington D.C.

World Bank (1998), *Competitiveness and Sustainable Economic Recovery in Thailand*, NESDB and World Bank, Bangkok, vol. I and II.

World Bank (1999), *Asian Corporate Recovery: Corporate Governance, Government Policy*, Regional Conference Papers Based on Firm-level Surveys in Indonesia, Korea, Malaysia, the Philippines and Thailand, Bangkok, March 31-April 2.

Books and Works

Abdullah, M. A. (1998), *SMEs in Malaysia, Policy Issues and Challenges*, Ashgate Publishing Co., Aldershot.

Acs, Z., Carlsson, B. and Karlsson, C. (eds) (1999), *Entrepreneurship, SMEs, and the Macro-economy*, Cambridge University Press, Cambridge.

Akrasanee, N. (1999), *Walking the Lost Path*, Informedia, Bangkok *(in Thai language)*.

Akrasanee, N. and other authors (1982), Small and Medium Scale Industries in Thailand, World Bank Office, Monograph, Bangkok.

Bell, P. (1968), *The Role of the Entrepreneur in Economic Development: A Case Study of Thailand*, University of Wisconsin, Ph.D. diss., Madison.

Bello, W. and other authors (1998), *A Siamese Tragedy, Development and Disintegration in Modern Thailand*, Zed Books, Bangkok/London.

Bowie, A. and Unger, D. (1997), *The Politics of Open Economies: Indonesia, Malaysia, the Philippines and Thailand*, Cambridge University Press, Cambridge.

Bridge, S. and other authors (1998), *Understanding Enterprise, Entrepreneurship and Small Business*, Macmillan, London.

Bruch, M. and Hiemenz, U. (1984), *SMIs in the ASEAN Countries: Agents or Victims of Economic Development?*, Westview Press, Oulder and London.

Brusco, S. (1995), *Global Systems and Local Systems of Small Firms*, OECD, International Seminar on Local Systems of Small Firms and Job Creation, Paper, Paris, 1-2 June.

Bualek, P. (1987), *The Chinese: Two Hundred Years Under Royal Patronage*, Chulalongkorn University, Economic Outlook Special Issue, Bangkok, vols I and II.

Bukley, P. and other authors (eds) (1997), *International Technology Transfer by SMEs*, Macmillan, London.

Bunjongjit, N. and Oudin, X. (1992), *Small-Scale Industries and Institutional Framework in Thailand*, Chulalongkorn University and ORSTOM, Technical Paper for the OECD Development Centre, Bangkok/Paris, no. 81 & 81a.

Bunmark, J. (1999), *HRM Practices and Strategies of SMEs in Thailand to Fight with Asian Economic Crisis*, Sun Yat-sen University and SME Administration of the Ministry of Economic Affairs, APEC Human Resource Management Symposium on SMEs, Paper, Kaoshiung, 29-30 October.

Chaipravat, O. and Hoontrakul, P. (1999), *Market Failure in Credit Extension: Thailand Case*, Siam Commercial Bank and SASIN Graduate Institute of Business Administration, Chulalongkorn University, Discussion Paper, Bangkok, July.

Chaisakul, S. and Yoshida, M. (eds) (1990), *The Thai Economy in the Changing Decade and Industrial Promotion Policy*, Institute of Developing Economies, Tokyo.

Chamonman, W. and other authors (1986), *Characteristics of the Thai Small-Scale Industries: Annotated Bibliography*, Faculty of Commerce and Accountancy, Thammasat University, Bangkok.

Chareanwongsak, K. (1999), *SMEs or SLEs? Thai Business for the Next Century*, Success Media Publishers, Bangkok *(in Thai language)*.

Chenvidyakarn, M. (1979), *Political Control and Economic Influence: A Study of Trade Associations in Thailand*, University of Chicago, Ph.D.

Chiasakul, S. and Koike, K. (1998), *Financial Crisis in Thailand: Adjustment of Local Companies*, Institute of Developing Economies, Tokyo.

Chiasakul, S. and Yoshida, M. (eds) (1990), *The Thai Economy in the Changing Decade and Industrial Promotion Policy*, Institute of Developing Economies, Tokyo.

Christensen, S. and other authors (1993), *The Lessons of East Asia: Thailand – The Institutional and Political Underpinnings of Growth*, World Bank, Washington D.C.

Chunhaphanthantharuck, C. (1998), *Small Business Management*, Rajabhat Institute Suandusit, Bangkok *(in Thai language)*.

Clapham, R. (1985), *Small and Medium Entrepreneurs in Southeast Asia*, Institute of Southeast Asian Studies, Singapore.

Deakins, D. (1996), *Entrepreneurship and Small Firms*, McGraw-Hill, London.

Dierman, P. (van) and other authors (1998), *The IMF Reform Agreements: Evaluating the Likely Impact on SMEs*, The Asia Foundation, Jakarta, June.

Dieter, E. and other authors (1998), *Technological Capabilities and Export Success in Asia*, UNCTAD and Routledge, London/New York.

Dijk, M.P. and Marcussen, H.S. (1990), *Industrialization in the Third World: The Need for Alternative Strategies*, Frank Cass, London.

Fujita, M. (1998), *The Transnational Activities of SMEs*, Kluwer Academic Publishers, New York/Dordrecht.

Girling, J. (1996), *Interpreting Development: Capitalism, Democracy and the Middle Class in Thailand*, Cornell University Press, Ithaca.

Gohlert, E. W. (1991), *Power and Culture: The Struggle against Poverty in Thailand*, White Lotus, Bangkok.

Gough, J.W. (1969), *The Rise of the Entrepreneur*, Oriel College, Batsford Co. Publishers, Oxford.

Grunsven, L. (van) (ed.) (1998), *Regional Change in Industrializing Asia: Regional and Local Responses to Changing Competitiveness*, Avebury, Aldershot.

Grunsven, L. (van) (ed.) (1999), *Development of Local SMEs through Supply Linkages with MNC Transplants: Opportunities for and Barriers to Entry, An Empirical Study in Johor Bahru District, Johor, Malaysia*, University Sains Malaysia, Centre for Policy Research, International Conference on SMEs at New Crossroads, Paper, Penang, 28-30 September.

Hall, C. (1995), *APEC and SME Policy; Suggestions for an Action Agenda*, Australian APEC Study Centre, Issues Paper no 1, Sydney (URL) http:www.arts.monash.edu.au/ausapec/

Hall, C. (1995), *Best Practice Access Policies for SMEs: A Study of Australia, Japan, New Zealand, Peoples' Republic of China, Indonesia, Chinese Taipei and Korea*, Japanese SME International Centre and the Japan Small Business Finance Corporation, Tokyo.

Hall, C. (1998), *APEC SME Indicators: A Feasibility Assessment*, Sydney (on behalf of APEC).

Harper, M. (1984), *Small Business in the Third World*, Cranfield School of Management, IT Publications, London.

Hewison, K. (ed.) (1997), *Political Change in Thailand: Democracy and Participation*, Routledge, London.

Hewison, K. (1989), *Bankers and Bureaucrats: Capital and the Role of the State in Thailand*, Yale University, Monograph Series 34, New Haven.

Higgott, R. and Robison, R. (eds) (1985), *Southeast Asia: Essays in the Political Economy of Structural Change*, Routledge and Kegan Paul, Melbourne.

Holmes, H. and Tangtongtavy, S. (1997), *Working with the Thais: A Guide to Managing in Thailand*, White Lotus, Bangkok, 4th edition.

Ingram, J. (1971), *Economic Change in Thailand: 1850-1970*, Standford University Press, Stanford.

Jackson, K. (ed.) (1999), *Asian Contagion: The Causes and Consequences of a Financial Crisis*, Institute of Southeast Asian Studies, Singapore.

James, K. and Akrasanee, N. (eds) (1988), *Small and Medium Business Improvement in the ASEAN Region*, Institute of Southeast Asian Studies, Singapore, 3 volumes.

Jansen, K. (1990), *Finance, Growth and Stability: Financing Economic Development in Thailand (1960-1986)*, Avebury, Aldershot.

Jomo, K.S. (ed.) (1998), *Tigers in Trouble: Financial Governance, Liberalisation and Crises in East Asia*, Zed Books, London.

Karlsson, C. and others (eds) (1993), *Small Business Dynamics: International, National and Regional Perspectives*, Routledge, London.

Kitahara, A. (1999), *Development Possibility of Rural Small Industry in Central Thailand*, Sains University Malaysia, International Conference on SMEs at New Crossroads, Paper, Penang, 28-30 September.

Klausner, W. (1993), *Reflections on Thai Culture: Collected Writings*, The Siam Society, Bangkok.

Krongkaew, M. (ed.) (1995), *Thailand's Industrialization and its Consequences*, St. Martin's Press, London.

Kunio, Y. (1988), *The Rise of Ersatz Capitalism in South-East Asia*, Oxford University Press, Singapore.

Laothamatas, A. (1992), *Business Associations and the New Political Economy of Thailand: From Bureaucratic Polity to Liberal Corporatism*, Westview Press, Boulder.

Lee, E. (1998), *The Asian Financial Crisis: The Challenge for Social Policy*, International Labour Organization, Geneva.

Leopairote, M. (1999), *Industrial Reform to Enhance Industrial Competitiveness: Implications and Strategies for SME Development*, UNIDO Asia-Pacific Forum, Vision and Challenges for Sustainable Industrial Development, Paper, Bangkok, 23-24 September.

Loveman, G.W. and Piore, M.J. (1992), *The Reemergence of Small Enterprises*, International Labour Organization, Institute of Labour Studies, Geneva.

Low, A. M. and Tan,W.L. (eds) (1996), *Entrepreneurs, Entrepreneurship and Enterprising Culture*, Addison-Wesley, Singapore.

Manarungsan, S. (1989), *Economic Development of Thailand, 1850-1950: Response to the Challenge of the World Economy*, Chulalongkorn University, Institute of Asian Studies, Bangkok.

Masuyama, S. and other authors (eds) (1999), *East Asia's Financial Systems: Evolutions and Crisis*, Institute of Southeast Asian Studies, Singapore.

McVey, R. (ed.) (1992), *Southeast Asian Capitalists*, Cornell University Press, Ithaca.

Milton-Smith, J. (1998), *The Globalization of Japanese SMEs and the Growth of Networking Strategies in Asia*, Euro-Asia Centre, INSEAD, Conference on Asian Foreign Investment in Asia, Paper, Fontainebleau, 6-7 February.

Muscat, R. (1996), *Development Strategy in Thailand: A Study of Economic Growth*, New York, Praeger.

Osmani, S. R. (1995), *Macroeconomic Policy and Small Scale Industry in Developing Asia*, International Labour Organization, New Dehli.

Parnwell, M. (1996), *Uneven Development in Thailand*, Avebury Press, Aldershot.

Penrose, E. (1980), *The Theory of the Growth of the Firm*, Basil Blackwell Publishers, Oxford, 2nd edition.

Phipatseritham, K. and Kunio, Y. (1983), *Business Groups in Thailand*, Institute of Southeast Asian Studies, Singapore.

Phongpaichit, P. and Baker, C. (1996), *Thailand's Boom!* Silkworm Books, Chiang Mai.

Phongpaichit, P. and Baker, C. (1998), *Thailand's Boom and Bust!*, Silkworm Books, Chiang Mai.

Phongpaichit, P. and Igota, S. (1992), *The Informal Sector in Thai Economic Development*, Institute of Developing Economies, Tokyo.

Piore, M. and Sabel, C.F. (1984), *The Second Industrial Divide: Possibilities for Prosperity*, Basic Books, New York.

Piriyarangsan, S. (1983), *Thai Bureaucratic Capitalism: 1932-1960*, Chulalongkorn University, Social Research Institute, Bangkok.

Piriyarangsan, S. (1990), *Political Economy and Industrial Development in Thailand*, Chulalongkorn University, Political Economy Group, Bangkok.

Pongpaichit, P. (1990), *The New Wave of Japanese Investment in ASEAN: Determinants and Prospects*, Institute of Southeast Asian Studies, Singapore.

Pongsapich, A. (ed.) (1994), *Entrepreneurship and Socio-economic Transformation in Thailand and South East Asia*, Chulalongkorn University, Social Research Institute together with French Institute for Scientific Research for Development in Cooperation (ORSTOM), Bangkok.

Preeyanuch, A. (1985), *An Analysis of Factors Affecting the Performance of Small Rural Non-Farm Firms in Thailand*, University of Michigan, Ann Arbor.

Ramamurthy, B. (1996), *The Asian Experience: China, Taiwan, India and Vietnam, A Transaction Costs Approach to Small Industries and Institutional Framework*, International Labour Organization Tripartite Seminar on Macro Policy Environment for Small Scale Industries Development in Africa and Asia, Paper, Nairobi, 26-29 March.

Ratanakomut, S. and other authors (1995), *Manufacturing Industry in Thailand: A Sectoral Analysis*, Institute of Developing Economies, Tokyo.

Rutten, M. and Upadhya, C. (eds) (1997), *Small Business Entrepreneurs in Asia and Europe: Towards a Comparative Perspective*, Sage, New Dehli.

Sahlman, W.A. and Stevenson, H.H. (1992), *The Entrepreneurial Venture*, Harvard Business School, Boston.

Schmitz, H. and Nadvi, K. (1994), *Industrial Clusters in Less Developed Countries: Review of Experience and Research Agenda*, Institute of Development Studies, University of Sussex, Discussion Paper no. 339, Brighton.

Sen, A. (1999), *Beyond the Crisis: Development Strategies in Asia*, Institute of Southeast Asian Studies, Singapore.

Sengenberger, W., Loveman, G.W. and Piore, M.J. (eds) (1990), *The Reemergence of Small Enterprises: Industrial Restructuring in Industrialised Countries*, International Labour Organization, Institute for Labour Studies, Geneva.

Sengenberger, W. and Porter, M. E. (1998), *Clusters and Competition*, Harvard Business School Press, Boston.

Sevilla, R. and Soonthornthada, K. (2000), *SMEs in Thailand: Vision and Reality*, Mahidol University, Institute of Population and Social Research, Draft Paper, Nakhon Pathom.

Siamwalla, A. and Sopchochai, O. (1998), *Responding to the Thai Economic Crisis*, Thailand Development Research Institute, Bangkok.

Siffin, W. (1966), *The Thai Bureaucracy, Institutional Change and Development*, East West Centre Press, Honolulu.

Silcok, T. H. (ed.) (1967), *Thailand: Social and Economic Studies in Development*, Australian National University and Duke University Press, Canberra.

Simachokedee, W. (1999), *SMEs: A Chief Industrial Pillar for the Nation's Recovery*, Prachachon Co. Publishers, Bangkok *(in Thai language)*.

Storey, D. J. (1994), *Understanding the Small Business Sector*, Routledge, London.

Storey, D. J. and other authors (1987), *The Performance of Small Firms*, Croom Helm, London.

Suehiro, A. (1989), *Capital Accumulation in Thailand: 1855-1985*, Tokyo University, Centre for East Asian Cultural Studies, Tokyo.

Tambunan, T. (1999), *The Importance of SMIs for the Rural Poor and the Impact of the Monetary Crisis on the Industries: A Case of Indonesia*, University Sains Malaysia, International Conference of SMEs at New Crossroads, Paper, Penang, 28-30 September.

Tambunlertchai, S. (1981), *Import Substitution and Export Expansion: An Analysis of Industrialization Experience in Thailand*, Thammasat University, Bangkok.

Tambunlertchai, S. and Yamazawa, I. (1981), *Manufactured Exports and Direct Foreign Investment*, Thammasat University, Bangkok.

Thanamai, P. (1985), *Patterns of Industrial Policymaking in Thailand: Japanese Multinationals and Domestic Actors in the Automobile and Electrical Appliances Industries*, University of Wisconsin, Ph.D.

Tomizawa, R. (1998), *Start up and Stay up in Thailand: Stories, Insight and Advice from Enterprising Expats*, Alpha Publishers, Bangkok.

Trulsson, P. (1997), *Entrepreneurial Strategies and Social Change*, Workshop of the European Association of Development Institutes (EADI), Paper, Milan, 19-20 September.

Ueda, Y. (1995), *Local Economy and Entrepreneurship in Thailand*, Kyoto University Press, Kyoto.

Unger, D. (1998), *Building Social Capital in Thailand: Fibers, Finance and Infrastructure*, Cambridge University Press, Cambridge.

Urlacher, L. (1999), *Small Business Entrepreneurship: An Ethics and Human Relations Perspective*, Prentice Hall, New Jersey.

Vichyanond, P. (1994), *Thailand's Financial System: Structure and Liberalization*, Thailand Development Research Institute, Bangkok.

Warr, P. (ed.) (1993), *The Thai Economy in Transition*, Cambridge University Press, Cambridge.

Watcharaphun, P. (1999), *Liquidity Problems of Small Business in Southern Thailand*, University Sains Malaysia, Centre for Policy Research, International Conference on SMEs at the Crossroads, Paper, Penang, 28-30 September.

Whitaker, D.H. (1997), *Small Firms in the Japanese Economy*, Cambridge University Press, Cambridge.
Wiboonchutikula, P. (1994), *Thailand's Industrialization: Past Performance and Future Issues*, Chulalongkorn University, Faculty of Economics, Bangkok.
Wokcik, A. and Yuthavong, Y. (eds) (1997), *Science and Technology in Thailand: Lessons from a Developing Country*, National Science and Technology Development Agency and UNESCO Publishing, Bangkok.
Wonghanchao, W. and Ikemoto, Y. (1988), *Economic Development Policy in Thailand: A Historical Review*, Institute of Developing Economies, Tokyo.
Wyer, P. and Johl, S.K. (1999), *The Implications of the Economic Crisis for SMEs: A Micro Perspective*, University Sains Malaysia, Centre for Policy Research, International Conference on SMEs at the Crossroads, Paper, Penang, 28-30 September.
Yamashita, S. (ed.) (1991), *Transfer of Japanese Technology and Management to the ASEAN Countries*, University of Tokyo Press, Tokyo.

Articles

Abdullah, M.A. (1997), 'Inter-Firm Linkages and the Performance of Urban Small Firms in Malaysia', *Malaysian Management Review*, vol. 30, no. 1, pp. 49-59.
Abu, B. and other authors (1997), 'The Roles of SMEs to Support the Large Industries in the Context of the Malaysian Economy', *Malaysian Management Review*, vol. 32, no. 4, pp. 11-17.
Arghiros, D. (1997), 'Rural Industry and Development in Central Thailand: An Alternative Approach', *The Journal of Entrepreneurship*, vol. 6, no. 1, January-June, pp. 1-18.
Berry, A. and Mazumpar, D. (1991), 'Small-Scale Industry in the Asian-Pacific Region', *Asian-Pacific Economic Literature*, vol. 5, no. 2, pp. 35-67.
Blomstrom, M. and Kokko, A. (1998), 'Multinationals and Spillovers', *Journal of Economic Surveys*, vol. 12, pp. 247-78.
Donckels, R. and Lambrecht, J. (1995), 'Joint Ventures: No Longer a Mysterious World for SMEs from Developed and Developing Countries', *International Small Business Journal*, vol. 13, no 2, January-March, pp. 11-26.
Doner, R. and Ramsay, A. (1997), 'Competitive Clientelism and Economic Governance: The Case of Thailand', in S. Maxfield and B. Schneider (eds), *Business and the State in Developing Countries*, Cornell University Press, Ithaca, pp. 237-76.
Howard, R. (1995), 'Can Small Business Help Countries Compete?', *Harvard Business Review*, November-December, pp. 88-103.
Jennings, P. and Beaver, G. (1997), 'The Performance and Competitive Advantage of Small Firms, A Management Perspective', *International Small Business Journal*, vol.15, no. 2, Issue 58, pp. 63-75.
Karagozolu, N. and Lindell, M. (1998), 'Internationalization of Small and Medium-sized Technology-based Firms: An Exploratory Study', *Journal of Small Business Management*, vol. 36, no. 1, pp. 44-58.

Kawabe, N. (1996), 'Developing Supporting Industries in Thailand and Malaysia: Current Situation and Issues', *APO Productivity Journal* (Asian Productivity Organization), Summer, pp. 99-137.

Kokko, A. (1996), 'Productivity Spillovers from Competition between Local Firms and Foreign Affiliates', *Journal of International Development*, vol. 8, pp. 517-30.

Kooij, E. (van) (1990), 'Industrial Networks in Japan: Technology Transfer to SMEs', *Entrepreneurship and Regional Development*, vol. 2, pp. 279-301.

Kuriyama, N. (1992), 'Japanese Investment and New Technology in Thai Manufacturing and its Employment Implications', *The Review of Business Administration* (Tokyo, Soka University), November, pp. 63-82.

Liedholm, C. and Mead, D. (1998), 'The Dynamics of Macro and Small Enterprises in Developing Countries', *World Development*, vol. 26, no. 1, January, pp. 61-74.

Nagamura, I. (1999), 'Venture Business: Strategic SMEs', *Journal of Business Administration* (Thammasat University, Faculty of Commerce and Accountancy, Bangkok), Special Issue, March 2, pp. 201-16 *(in Thai language)*.

Nooteboom, B. (1993), 'Firm Size Effects on Transaction Costs', *Small Business Economics*, vol. 5, no. 4, pp. 283-95.

Phodhivorakhun, P. (1999), 'Evaluation of Government Policy for SME Promotion in Japan', *Journal of Business Administration* (Thammasat University), Special Issue, March 2, pp. 52-65 *(in Thai language)*.

Phongpaichit, P. (1991), 'Nu, Nit Noi and Thailand's Informal Sector in Rapid Growth' in C. Hongladarom and S. Itoga (eds), *Human Resources Development Strategy: Past, Present and Future*, Institute of Developing Economies, Tokyo.

Phongpaichit, P. (1992), 'Technocrats, Businessmen and Generals: Democracy and Economic Policy-making in Thailand' in A. Macintyre and K. Jayasuria (eds), *The Dynamics of Economic Policy Reform in Southeast Asia and the Southwest Pacific*, Oxford University Press, Kuala Lumpur.

Regnier, P. (1996), 'The Dynamic Asian Economies, Local Systems of SMEs and Internationalization', in OECD, *Networks of Enterprises and Local Development*, OECD Publications, Paris, pp. 225-32.

Regnier, P. (1998), 'Dynamics of Small Enterprise Development, State versus Market in the Asian Newly Industrializing Economies' in P. Cook and other authors (eds) (1998), *Privatization, Enterprise Development and Economic Reform: Experiences of Developing and Transitional Economies*, Edward Elgar, Cheltenham and Northampton, pp. 206-28.

Salazar, M. (1996), 'Problem and Prospects of Micro and Small Industries in the Process of Economic Liberalization in South East Asia', in R. Islam (ed), *Small and Micro Enterprises in a Period of Economic Liberalization: Opportunities and Challenges*, International Labour Organization, New Dehli, pp. 52-116 and 226-35.

Schmitz, H. (1998), 'Fostering Collective Efficiency', *Small Enterprise Development*, vol. 9, no. 1, pp. 1-10.

Sengenberger, W. and Pyke, F. (1991), 'Small Firm Industrial Districts and Local Economic Regeneration', *Labour and Society* (International Labour Organization), vol. 16, no 1, pp.1-16.

SME Group (1998), 'SMEs: The Last Resort for the Thai Economy', *The Master Journal* (Bangkok), August *(in Thai languague)*.

Soonthornsingha, N. (1999), 'Financial System for SMEs', *Journal of Business Administration* (Thammasat University, Bangkok), Special Issue, March 2, pp. 37-51 *(in Thai language)*.

Suehiro, A. (1993), 'Family Business Reassessed: Corporate Structure and Late-Starting Industrialization in Thailand', *The Developing Economies* (Tokyo), vol. 22.

Sungharusamee, S. (1999), 'SMEs: Inspiration to Restore the Thai Economy', *The Interest* (Bangkok), vol. 17, no. 211 and 212, January and February, pp. 109-13 and 52-6 *(in Thai language)*.

Tambunletchai, S. (1999), 'SMEs Promotion and Industrial Spread to the Rural Area in Thailand', *Journal of Business Administration* (Thammasat University, Bangkok), Special Issue, March 2, pp. 91-139 *(in Thai language)*.

Taranapakorn, J. and Paolhaengtong, S. (1999), 'SMEs: Implementation of Thai Economic Restructuring', *Industrial Finance Corporation of Thailand Review*, vol. 18, no. 3, January-March, pp. 14-22 *(in Thai language)*.

Terdsatirasal, N. (1999), 'Role of Government Sector in SMEs Development', *Thailand's Investment Promotion Journal*, vol. 10, no. 2, February, pp. 28-34 *(in Thai language)*.

Tuntithanawatt, S.(1999), 'The Situation of SMEs in Thailand', *Thailand's Investment Promotion Journal*, vol. 10, no 2, February, pp. 18-27 *(in Thai language)*.

Internet Sites

APEC Center for Technological Exchange and Training for SMEs
 http : //www.actetsme.org
ASEAN Supporting Industry Database
 http : //www.asidnet.org
Bangkok Bank Monthly Review
 http : //www.bbl.co.th
Bangkok Post, 1999
 http : //www.bangkokpost.net/99mideco/
 (June 1999 and January 2000) Mid-Year and Year-End Economic Review
Bank of Thailand
 http : //www.bot.go.th
 Summary of Situation and Trend in the Thai Economy, 1999
Board of Investment, Thailand
 http : //www.boi.go.th
Federation of Thai Industries
 http : //www.fti.or.th

Global Information Network for SMEs
  http : //www.gin.sme.ne.jp
International Monetary Fund
  http : //www.imf.org
  (March 18, 1999) Debt and Economic Strategies for Thailand
International Monetary Fund
  http : //www.imf.org/external/np/speeches/1999
International Small Business Congress
  http://www.isbc.or.jp
Ministry of Finance
  http : //www.mof.go.th
Ministry of Industry
  http : //www.Industry.go.th
  Draft of SME Bill, Information on Thai Industry, Industry Directory
Ministry of Industry, Department of Industrial Promotion
  http : //www.dip.go.th
  Action Plan and Measures for SME Promotion
National Economic and Social Development Board of Thailand,
  http : //www.nesdb.go.th (June 11, 1999)
  Thai Economic Crisis and Direction of the 8th Plan Revision
National Science and Technology Development Agency
  http : //www.nstda.or.th
Organization for Economic Co-operation and Development (OECD)
  http : //www.oecd.org
  Best Practice Policies for SMEs (1997 Edition)
SME Financial Advisory Centre
  http://www.sfac.or.th
Thailand Development Research Institute
  http : //www.info.tdri.or.th

Institutions Consulted in Bangkok for Direct Interviews

Asian Development Bank (Bangkok Office)
Association of Thai Small and Medium Entrepreneurs
Department of Industrial Promotion, Ministry of Industry
Faculty of Economics, Chulalongkorn University
Faculty of Economics, Thammasat University
Federation of Thai Industries
Industrial Financial Corporation of Thailand
Institute for SME Development (ISMED), Ministry of Industry
International Labour Organization, Regional Office for Asia and Pacific, East Asia
  Multidisciplinary Advisory Team
Japan External Trade Organization (JETRO)
Japanese International Co-operation Agency (JICA), Department of
  Industrial Promotion, Ministry of Industry

KPMG, Asia Pacific Regional Office
National Economic and Social Development Board
National Science and Technology Development Agency
National Statistics Office
Office of Industrial Economics, Ministry of Industry
Siam Commercial Bank, Research Institute
Small Industry Credit Guarantee Corporation
Small Industry Finance Corporation
Small-Scale Industry Promotion Project (German Development and Technical Cooperation), Department of Industrial Promotion, Ministry of Industry
Swiss-Thai Chamber of Commerce
Thai Chamber of Commerce
Thai Farmers Bank
The Brooker Group
UNICO Industrial Management Consultants (Japan)
World Bank (Bangkok Office)

Index

Agro-food 14, 37, 56, 87, 165
Asian Development Bank (ADB) 2, 76, 80, 82, 98, 150, 158
Association of Thai Small and Medium Entrepreneurs (ATSME) 155
Automotive Industry 21, 27, 37, 41, 44, 56, 64, 66 ,72, 74, 78, 83, 86, 87, 103, 154, 159

Bank of Thailand 30, 34, 46, 58, 70, 81, 92, 94, 95, 97, 157
Bankruptcy 40, 47, 52, 58, 71, 107
Board of Investment (BOI) 36, 64, 65, 66, 83, 86
Business Associations 17, 153

Chart Pattana Party 90
Chavalit (Former Prime Minister) 89
China 13, 67, 103, 152, 159, 162
Clusters 6, 115, 158, 165
Commercial banks 26, 40, 65, 80, 93, 95, 97, 157, 158, 163, 164, 167
Competition, Competitiveness 6-7, 17, 54-5, 72, 77, 93, 109, 114, 160, 162, 164
Components and Parts 21, 52, 55-6, 83, 160
Conglomerates 1, 7, 65, 66, 68, 95, 97, 104, 107
Consumption, Consumers 5, 40-1, 93, 94
Corruption 34, 48, 82, 90, 155
Credit Crunch 39-42, 70, 74, 81, 82, 95, 163, 164

Damri Sukhotanang (DIP Director General) 91
Debt Restructuring, Corporate Debt 2, 47, 57, 76, 78, 95, 155, 162
Department of Industrial Promotion (DIP) 35, 67, 72, 73, 75, 81, 84, 91, 153
Devaluation 2, 6, 40, 44, 86, 93, 108

E-Commerce 79

Education, Dual Education, Higher Education 21, 22, 56, 80, 81, 85, 164, 165
Election, Legislative Election 2, 9, 71, 72, 78, 89, 90, 93, 151, 152
Electrical Industry, Electrical Products 21, 41, 56, 64, 86, 106, 112, 162, 165
Electronics 21, 37, 41, 44-5, 72, 74, 95, 105, 115, 159, 165
Employment and Labour 4, 8, 20, 33, 43-4, 53, 55, 57, 81, 85, 98, 112, 153, 162
Export-Import Bank 30, 76, 82

Family Business 14, 20, 31, 79, 95, 152
Federation of Thai Industries (FTI) 17, 30, 68, 85, 97, 153, 154, 157
Foreign Direct Investment 3, 5, 27, 67, 68, 88, 104, 152, 163, 164

Industrial Finance Corporation of Thailand (IFCT) 30, 47, 68, 76
Innovation 46, 56, 70, 84, 151
Institute for SME Development (ISMED) 73, 74, 85-7
Intermediary Products, Intermediate Goods 41, 55-6, 105, 160
International Labour Organization 44, 98, 153
International Monetary Fund 39, 57, 61, 70, 71, 72, 92, 93, 95, 98, 149

Japan 1, 2, 6, 13-16, 20, 31, 35-7, 39, 41, 44-5, 54-7, 65, 67, 71-3, 76-80, 83-4, 88-9, 93, 98, 103-4, 111, 113, 115, 152, 155, 156
Japanese International Co-operation Agency (JICA) 20, 37, 52

Korea, South Korea 18, 24, 27, 41, 54, 56, 67-9, 86-9, 92, 96, 103-8
Krung Thai Bank 48, 82, 95

180

Malaysia 17, 21, 24, 27, 41, 56, 67, 92, 94, 96, 103-11, 150, 162
Manu Leopairote (Permanent Secretary, MoI) 72, 91
Micro-enterprises 19, 24, 45, 152
Middle Class 8, 18, 68, 89, 151
Ministry of Commerce 18, 30, 47, 91
Ministry of Finance 30, 70, 74, 76, 81, 91, 93-4, 97, 98, 106, 157
Ministry of Industry 2, 4, 22, 24, 30, 46, 48, 63, 66, 67, 69, 72-4, 76, 81, 84, 91, 153-4
Ministry of Labour and Social Welfare 22, 85
Miyazawa Plan 35, 37, 44, 72, 73, 74, 84-5, 88

New Aspiration Party 89, 165
Non-governmental Organizations (NGOs) 153, 156, 157
Non-performing Loans (NPLs) 34, 36, 40-2, 47-9

OECD/OECD Economies 1, 6, 16, 24, 61, 77-8, 81, 103, 152-3, 158-9, 165

Prime Minister Chuan Leekpai 71, 79, 90, 155
Prime Minister's Office 2, 30, 48, 78, 91
Provincial Industrial Offices 66, 67

Re-capitalization 80, 81, 98, 159
Restructuring, Corporate Reform 2, 6, 39-40, 44, 47-8, 57, 64, 69, 76, 77, 81-2, 89, 93-5, 98, 104, 107, 110, 114, 152, 158, 162

Seasonal Workers, Household Workers 32, 44, 152
Siam Commercial Bank 40, 48
Singapore 17, 27, 31, 67, 102, 112, 150, 152, 158, 162
Sino-Thai (Entrepreneurs, Families) 14, 15, 26, 65, 95, 152, 153, 155
Small Industry Credit Guarantee Corporation (SICGC) 30, 76, 77, 82

Small Industry Finance Corporation (SIFC) 30, 67, 69, 76, 77, 82, 83
SME Master Plan 39, 68, 73, 75, 78-81, 85, 88-9, 98, 103, 149, 159
SME Performance, SME Resilience 50-6
SME Promotion Bill 69, 73, 78, 88, 90, 98, 149, 151
Stock Exchange of Thailand 20, 75, 82
Structural Adjustment 37, 69, 149, 162
Subcontracting, Subcontractors 5, 18-19, 26, 46, 55, 68, 72, 79, 97, 103, 105-7, 110, 152, 159, 162, 163, 165
Supachai Panitchpakdi (Deputy Prime Minister) 93
Suwat Liptapanlop, Minister of Industry 30, 72, 90

Taiwan 9, 24, 27, 55, 67, 68, 76, 87, 98, 110, 115, 152, 160, 160, 165
Tarrin Nimmanahaeminda, Minister of Finance 82
Textiles 14, 31, 37, 43, 45, 64, 65, 81, 85
Thaksin Shinawattra 89, 90
Thai Bankers Association (TBA) 97, 153, 154
Thai Chamber of Commerce (TCC) 30, 68, 153-4, 157
Thai Farmers Bank 40, 48, 95, 97
Thai Rak Thai Party 71, 89, 155
Training 46, 53-4, 67, 74, 77, 80-1, 83-5, 155, 164-5
Transnational Corporations (TNCs) 13-14, 16, 64, 83, 86, 114, 159-60, 162, 163-66

USA 18, 27, 46, 72, 78, 111, 152, 160

Value-added Tax 34-6, 53

Western Europe, Europe 9, 14-15, 46, 78, 113, 115, 152
World Bank 2, 18, 35-7, 39, 40, 44, 47-8, 50-2, 57-8, 71, 80, 94, 98
World Trade Organization (WTO) 103, 152, 166